## PARENTS AND EDUCATORS PRAISE
## THE CORE KNOWLEDGE SERIES

"Though I have twenty-five years' teaching experience, this is my first year as a **Core Knowledge** teacher. Now, for the first time in a long time, I am excited about teaching again. As for my students, I seriously believe that many of them would eliminate summer vacation to get on with the business of learning!"
—*Joan Falbey, teacher, Three Oaks Elementary School, Fort Myers, Florida*

"Thank you for writing such wonderful books! My children and I have thoroughly enjoyed them. Your books have been a great source and a guide to us. I have a degree in elementary education and I think this is the best curriculum I have encountered."
—*Barbara de la Aguilera, parent, Miami, Florida*

"For three years, we have been using elements of the **Core Knowledge** program, and I have watched as it invigorated our students. These books should be in every classroom in America."
—*Richard E. Smith, principal, Northside Elementary School, Palestine, Texas*

"Hirsch made it quite clear (in *Cultural Literacy*) that respect for cultural diversity is important but is best achieved when young people have adequate background knowledge of mainstream culture. In order for a truly democratic and economically sound society to be maintained, young people must have access to the best knowledge available so that they can understand the issues, express their viewpoints, and act accordingly."
—*James P. Comer, M.D., professor,*
*Child Study Center, Yale University (in* Parents *magazine)*

# The
# CORE KNOWLEDGE
# Series

## Resource Books for
## Kindergarten Through Grade Six

Bantam Books Trade Paperbacks

New York

## Core Knowledge®

# What Your First Grader Needs to Know

### Fundamentals of a Good First-Grade Education

**(Revised Edition)**

## Edited by E. D. Hirsch, Jr.

2014 Bantam Books Trade Paperback Edition

Published in the United States by Bantam Books, an imprint of Random House, a division of Random House LLC, a Penguin Random House Company, New York.

BANTAM BOOKS and the HOUSE colophon are registered trademarks of Random House LLC.

CORE KNOWLEDGE is a trademark of the Core Knowledge Foundation.

Originally published in hardcover in the United States in 1991. A revised hardcover edition was published in 1997 by Doubleday, an imprint of the Knopf Doubleday Publishing Group, a division of Random House LLC, and subsequently in trade paperback in 1998 by Delta Books, an imprint of Random House, a division of Random House LLC.

Library of Congress Cataloging-in-Publication Data
Hirsch, E. D. (Eric Donald)
What your first grader needs to know (revised and updated) : fundamentals of a good first-grade education / edited by E. D. Hirsch, Jr.
pages  cm
Includes index.
ISBN 978-0-553-39238-8 (paperback) — ISBN 978-0-553-39239-5 (ebook)   1.  First grade (Education)—Curricula—United States.   2.  Curriculum planning—United States.   I. Title.
LB15711st .W53 2014
372.973—dc23
2014004295

Printed in the United States of America on acid-free paper

www.bantamdell.com

2  4  6  8  9  7  5  3  1

Book design by Diane Hobbing

*Editor-in-Chief of the Core Knowledge Series:* E. D. Hirsch, Jr.

*Text Editor:* John Holdren

*Art Editor and Project Manager:* Alice K. Wiggins

*Writers:* Curriculum Concepts, Inc. (Mathematics); Diane Darst (Visual Arts); Matt Davis (History and Geography, Visual Arts); John Holdren (Language and Literature, History and Geography, Music, Mathematics, Science); Susan Tyler Hitchcock (Science, Music); Mary Beth Klee (History and Geography); Robert Pondiscio (Learning to Read); Janet Smith (Music); Linda Bevilacqua (Reading, Writing, and Your First Grader)

*Artists and Photographers:* Catherine Bricker, Leslie Evans, Jonathan Fuqua, Julie Grant, Steve Henry, Hannah Holdren, Sara Holdren, Phillip Jones, Bob Kirchman, Lina Chesak-Liberace, Gail McIntosh, Nic Siler

*Art and Photo Research, Art and Text Permissions:* Emma Earnst, Liza Greene, Martha Clay Sullivan, Jeanne Nicholson Siler, Jamie Talbot

*Research Assistant:* Deborah Hyland

# Acknowledgments

This series has depended on the help, advice, and encouragement of some two thousand people. Some of those singled out here already know the depth of our gratitude; others may be surprised to find themselves thanked publicly for help they gave quietly and freely for the sake of the enterprise alone. To helpers named and unnamed, we are deeply grateful.

*Advisors on Multiculturalism:* Minerva Allen, Barbara Carey, Frank de Varona, Mick Fedullo, Dorothy Fields, Elizabeth Fox-Genovese, Marcia Galli, Dan Garner, Henry Louis Gates, Cheryl Kulas, Joseph C. Miller, Gerry Raining Bird, Connie Rocha, Dorothy Small, Sharon Stewart-Peregoy, Sterling Stuckey, Marlene Walking Bear, Lucille Watahomigie, Ramona Wilson

*Advisors on Elementary Education:* Joseph Adelson, Isabel Beck, Paul Bell, Carl Bereiter, David Bjorklund, Constance Jones, Elizabeth LaFuze, J. P. Lutz, Sandra Scarr, Nancy Stein, Phyllis Wilkin

*Advisors on Technical Subject Matter:* Marilyn Jager Adams, Karima-Diane Alavi, Richard Anderson, Judith Birsh, Cheryl Cannard, Paul Gagnon, David Geary, Andrew Gleason, Blair Jones, Connie Juel, Eric Karell, Morton Keller, Joseph Kett, Mary Beth Klee, Michael Lynch, Sheelagh McGurn, Joseph C. Miller, Jean Osborn, Margaret Redd, Nancy Royal, Mark Rush, Janet Smith, Ralph Smith, Nancy Strother, Nancy Summers, Marlene Thompson, James Trefil, Patricia Wattenmaker, Nancy Wayne, Linda Williams, Lois Williams

*Conferees, March 1990:* Nola Bacci, Joan Baratz-Snowden, Thomasyne Beverley, Thomas Blackton, Angela Burkhalter, Monty Caldwell, Thomas M. Carroll, Laura Chapman, Carol Anne Collins, Lou Corsaro, Henry Cotton, Anne Coughlin, Arletta Dimberg, Debra P. Douglas, Patricia Edwards, Janet Elenbogen, Mick Fedullo, Michele Fomalont, Mamon Gibson, Jean Haines, Barbara Hayes, Stephen Herzog, Helen Kelley, Brenda King, John King, Elizabeth LaFuze, Diana Lam, Nancy Lambert, Doris Langaster, Richard LaPointe, Lloyd Leverton, Madeline Long, Allen Luster, Marcia Mallard, William J. Maloney, Judith Matz, Joseph McGeehan, Janet McLin, Gloria McPhee, John Morabito,

Robert Morrill, Roberta Morse, Karen Nathan, Dawn Nichols, Valeta Paige, Mary Perrin, Joseph Piazza, Jeanne Price, Marilyn Rauth, Judith Raybern, Mary Reese, Richard Rice, Wallace Saval, John Saxon, Jan Schwab, Ted Sharp, Diana Smith, Richard Smith, Trevanian Smith, Carol Stevens, Nancy Summers, Michael Terry, Robert Todd, Elois Veltman, Sharon Walker, Mary Ann Ward, Charles Whiten, Penny Williams, Clarke Worthington, Jane York

*Benefactors:* The Brown Foundation, the Challenge Foundation, Mrs. E. D. Hirsch, Sr., the Walton Family Foundation

Our grateful acknowledgment to these persons does not imply that we have taken their (sometimes conflicting) advice in every case or that each of them endorses all aspects of this project. Responsibility for final decisions must rest with the editors alone. Suggestions for improvements are very welcome, and we wish to thank in advance those who send advice for revising and improving this series.

This book is dedicated to the memory of
Paul Bell, late superintendent of Dade County Public Schools.

"Because he kept the Divine Vision in time of trouble."

(William Blake, *Jerusalem*, II:30)

# A Note to Teachers

We hope you will find this book useful, especially those of you who are teaching in the growing network of Core Knowledge schools. Throughout the book, we have addressed the suggested activities and explanations to "Parents," since you as teachers know your students and will have ideas about how to use the content of this book in relation to the lessons and activities you plan. If you are interested in the ideas of teachers in Core Knowledge schools, please write or call the Core Knowledge Foundation (801 East High St., Charlottesville, VA 22902; 434-977-7550) for information on ordering collections of lessons created and shared by teachers in Core Knowledge schools. Many of these teacher-created lessons are available through the Core Knowledge home page on the Internet at the following address: www.coreknowledge.org.

*Author's earnings from sales of the Core Knowledge series go to the nonprofit Core Knowledge Foundation. E. D. Hirsch, Jr., receives no remuneration for editing the series or any other remuneration from the Core Knowledge Foundation.*

# Contents

## I. Language and Literature

# II. History and Geography

# III. Visual Arts

# IV. Music

# V. Mathematics

# VI. Science

# General Introduction to the Core Knowledge Series

## Schools and Your Child

· · · · · · · · · · · · · · · · · · · · · · · · · · · · · · · · · · · · · · · · · · · · · · · · · · · · · · · · · · ·

If Charles Dickens were alive today and observing the state of American schools, he might be tempted to comment anew that it is the best of times and the worst of times. Seldom has there been more attention and energy aimed at our nation's education system. Unacceptable inequities in achievement between income and ethnic groups, long viewed with alarm, are being addressed with unprecedented urgency and resources. Years of dismay over lackluster performance have created a sense of crisis, even fear, that if we do not set our educational house in order, American competitiveness, our economy, and even our way of life are at risk. The response has been an unprecedented era of educational dynamism and innovation. Seen through this lens, it might seem to be the best of times for American education.

Yet for all our admirable focus, urgency, and investment, we have surprisingly little to show for it. Reading test scores for American seventeen-year-olds, the ultimate report card for our schools, have hardly budged in forty years. That's two generations with no discernible progress. How can this be? We have tried testing every child and holding teachers accountable. We have built charter schools and filled classrooms with computers. We have even made it the law of the land that every child read at grade level, but to no avail. Surely it is the worst of times.

Do not blame teachers. They are among our most committed and generous-spirited citizens. We have not lacked urgency, idealism, or even resources. What we have lacked is a coherent plan for educating all children to proficiency.

The book you hold in your hands exemplifies an essential building block of that coherent plan.

## Why Knowledge Matters in the Era of Google

American public education sprang from the nineteenth-century idea of the common school. We sent our children to learn reading and writing but also a common curriculum of history, geography, math, and other subjects. Such schools also strived to create virtuous, civic-minded citizens for the new nation. As America matured and became more diverse, the concept of a common curriculum gradually melted away. Today we have all but abandoned the notion that there is a body of knowledge that every child should learn in school, and the broad mission of education is to maximize each individual's potential. But there is good reason to believe that the idea of common schooling is even more relevant and effective today than ever before.

Ask yourself: Would I rather have my child go to school to gain knowledge of history, science, art, and music? Or should schools emphasize skills such as critical thinking and problem solving? The answer should ideally be both. Knowledge and skills are not two different things; they are two sides of the same coin. Thinking skills are what psychologists call "domain specific." In plain English, this means that you cannot think critically about a subject you know little about. If we want our children to be broadly competent readers, thinkers, and problem solvers, they must have a rich, broad store of background knowledge to call upon, enabling them to flex those mental muscles.

Unfortunately, too many of our schools have lost touch with this critical insight. It is commonly believed to be a fool's errand to think we can teach children all they need to know—far better simply to spark in children a lifelong love of learning. Indeed, many well-intentioned educators believe that the in-depth study of a few topics, practice with a variety of "thinking skills," and access to the Internet are all anyone needs today. Why clutter our minds with facts and trivia when you can just Google them? Today's classroom and curriculum, it is commonly argued, should be built around "twenty-first-century skills" such as media literacy and working cooperatively to solve "authentic" problems. These are the skills that will ensure a lifetime of learning, productivity, and engaged citizenship. The rest is mere trivia. Right?

On its surface, the idea that skills are more important than knowledge has a basic, commonsense appeal. Why should your child learn about the American Revolution, the parts of an atom, or who painted the *Mona Lisa*? What child hasn't asked, "Why do we need to know this?" Unfortunately, this benign, even obvious-sounding idea contains a great paradox: It takes knowledge to gain knowledge. Those who repudiate a coherent, knowledge-rich curriculum on the grounds that you can always look things up have failed to learn an important lesson from cognitive science: De-emphasizing factual knowledge actually prevents children from looking things up effectively. When you have just a little bit of information about a subject, you cannot readily evaluate the importance of new knowledge. When you know nothing, you're flying blind, like reading a book whose words you don't know. Thus, emphasizing procedural skill at the expense of factual knowledge hinders children from learning to learn. Yes, the Internet has placed a wealth of information at our fingertips. But to be able to use that information—to absorb it, to add to our knowledge—we must already possess a storehouse of knowledge. That is the paradox disclosed by cognitive research.

## Common Knowledge, Not "One Size Fits All"

All children are different. Similar to the idea that skills are more important than knowledge, there is a warm, intuitive appeal to the idea that we should tailor schooling to allow every child to find what most excites and engages him and let those interests drive his "child-centered" education. But, again, this ignores some fundamental facts about how we learn.

Language and vocabulary—like critical thinking and problem solving—also depend a great deal on a broad base of shared knowledge. When a sportscaster describes a surprising performance by an underdog basketball team as "a Cinderella story," or when a writer compares an ill-fated couple to Romeo and Juliet, it is assumed that the audience will know and understand the reference. So much of our language is dependent on a shared body of knowledge. Yes, you must know the words. But you must also understand the context in order to understand and be understood. The word "shot," for example, means something different in a doctor's office, on a basketball court, or when a repairman says your dishwasher is beyond fixing. Fluency depends on context, and context is largely a function of shared background knowledge.

Yet it remains all too easy to deride a knowledge-rich curriculum as "mere facts" and "rote learning." The idea that all children should be taught a common body of knowledge to enable them to read, communicate, and work cooperatively with others does sound old-fashioned, but the overwhelming evidence argues that this is precisely the case. Learning builds on learning: Children (and adults) gain new knowledge only by augmenting what they already know. It is essential to establish solid foundations of knowledge in the early grades, when children are most receptive, because for the vast majority of children, academic deficiencies from the first six grades can permanently impair the success of later learning. Poor performance of American students in middle and high school can be traced to shortcomings inherited from elementary schools that have not imparted to children the knowledge and skills they need for further learning.

All of the highest-achieving and most egalitarian elementary school systems in the world (such as those in Sweden, France, and Japan) teach their children a specific core of knowledge in each of the first six grades, thus enabling all children to enter each new grade with a secure foundation for further learning. U.S. schools, with their high student mobility rates, would especially benefit from a carefully sequenced core curriculum in the elementary and middle school years.

## Commonly Shared Knowledge Makes Schooling More Effective

We know that the one-on-one tutorial is the most effective form of schooling, in part because a parent or teacher can provide tailor-made instruction for the individual child. But in a non-tutorial situation—in, for example, a typical classroom with twenty-five or more students—the instructor cannot effectively impart new knowledge to all the students unless each one shares the background knowledge upon which the lesson is being built.

Consider this scenario. In third grade, Ms. Franklin is about to begin a unit on early explorers—Columbus, Magellan, and others. In her class, she has some students who were in Mr. Washington's second-grade class last year and some students who were in Ms. Johnson's second-grade class. She also has a few students who have moved in from other towns. As Ms. Franklin begins the unit on explorers, she asks the children to look at a globe and use their fingers to trace a route across the Atlantic Ocean from Europe to North America. The students who had Mr. Washington look blankly at her: They didn't learn that last year. The students who had Ms. Johnson, however, eagerly point to the proper places on the globe, while two of the students who came from other towns pipe up and say, "Columbus and Magellan again? We did that last year."

When all the students in a class share the relevant background knowledge, a classroom can begin to approach the effectiveness of a tutorial. Even when some children in a class do not have elements of the knowledge they were supposed to acquire in previous grades, the existence of a specifically defined core makes it possible for the teacher or parent to identify and fill the gaps, giving all students a chance to fulfill their potential in later grades.

## Commonly Shared Knowledge Makes Schooling Fairer and More Democratic

When all the children who enter a grade can be assumed to share some of the same building blocks of knowledge, and when the teacher knows exactly what those building blocks are, then all the students are empowered to learn. In our current system, children from disadvantaged backgrounds too often suffer from unmerited low expectations that translate into watered-down curricula. But if we specify the core of knowledge that all children should share, then we can guarantee equal access to that knowledge and compensate for the academic advantages some students are offered at home. In a Core Knowledge school, all children enjoy the benefits of important, challenging knowledge that will provide the foundation for successful later learning.

## Commonly Shared Knowledge Helps Create Cooperation and Solidarity in Our Schools and Nation

Diversity is a hallmark and strength of our nation. American classrooms are usually made up of students from a variety of cultural backgrounds, and those different cultures should be honored by all students. At the same time, education should create a school-based culture that is common and welcoming to all because it includes knowledge of many cultures and gives all students, no matter what their background, a common foundation for understanding our cultural diversity.

## Commonly Shared Knowledge Creates the Conditions That Make Higher-Order Thinking Possible

"We don't just read about science. We do science," a teacher in New York City recently wrote. One of the greatest misconceptions in contemporary education is the idea that in order to best prepare students for college and careers, we should train them to "think like an expert." In other words, we should help them understand and practice what scientists, historians, and other highly skilled professionals do. But it is clear from cognitive science that in order to think like an expert, you must know what the expert knows. Unfortunately, there are no shortcuts to expertise. Deep knowledge and practice are essential. Yet our schools try to teach children to engage in learning by doing, under the assumption that skills trump knowledge. They do not. You cannot have one without the other.

All of our most cherished goals for education—reading with understanding, critical thinking, and problem solving—are what psychologists call domain-specific skills. Simply put, there is no such thing as an all-purpose critical thinker or problem solver. Such skills are a function of your background knowledge.

## What Knowledge Needs to Be Taught?

One of the primary objections to a content-rich vision of education is that it offends our democratic sensibilities. The title of this book—*What Your First Grader Needs to Know*—can easily be viewed as presumptuous: "Who are you to say what knowledge matters? Why do you get to decide what goes in my child's curriculum and what gets left out?" Deciding what we want our children to know can be a politically and emotionally charged minefield. No grade-by-grade sequence of knowledge or course of study will satisfy everyone. But it is educationally reckless to ignore what we know about the importance of a broad knowledge base. The effort may be difficult, but we are duty-bound to try.

The content in this and other volumes in the Core Knowledge series is based on the *Core Knowledge Sequence*, a document of specific grade-by-grade content guidelines in history, geography, mathematics, science, language arts, and fine arts. As the core of a school's curriculum, it offers a solid, coherent foundation of learning while allowing flexibility to meet local needs. The entire sequence, from preschool to eighth grade, can be downloaded for free at the Core Knowledge Foundation's website (www.coreknowledge.org/download-the-sequence).

The Core Knowledge Foundation invested a considerable amount of time, energy, and resources in an attempt to find a consensus on the most enabling knowledge—the content that would most enable all children to read, write, listen, and speak with understanding.

Shortly after the establishment of the Core Knowledge Foundation in 1987, we analyzed the many reports issued by state departments of education and by professional organizations—such as the National Council of Teachers of Mathematics and the American Association for the Advancement of Science—that recommend general outcomes for elementary and secondary education. We also tabulated the knowledge and skills, through grade six, specified in the successful educational systems of several other countries, including France, Japan, Sweden, and West Germany.

In addition, we formed an advisory board on multiculturalism, which proposed a specific knowledge of diverse cultural traditions that all American children should share as part of their school-based common culture. We sent the resulting materials to three independent groups of teachers, scholars, and scientists across the country, asking them to create a master list of the knowledge children should have by the end of grade six. About one hundred fifty education professionals (including college professors, scientists, and administrators) were involved in this initial step.

These items were amalgamated into a master plan, and further groups of teachers and specialists were asked to agree on a grade-by-grade sequence of the items. That sequence was then sent to some one hundred educators and specialists, who participated in a national conference to hammer out a working agreement on an appropriate core of knowledge for the first six grades; kindergarten, grades seven and eight, and preschool were subsequently added to the *Core Knowledge Sequence*.

This important meeting took place in March 1990. The conferees were elementary school teachers, curriculum specialists, scientists, science writers, officers of national organizations, representatives of ethnic groups, district superintendents, and school principals from across the country. A total of twenty-four working groups decided on revisions to the *Core Knowledge Sequence*. The resulting provisional sequence was further fine-tuned during a year of implementation at a pioneering school, Three Oaks Elementary, in Lee County, Florida.

In only a few years, many more schools—urban and rural, rich and poor, public and private—joined in the effort to teach Core Knowledge. Based largely on suggestions from these schools, the *Core Knowledge Sequence* was revised in 1995; separate guidelines were added for kindergarten, and a few topics in other grades were added, omitted, or moved from one grade to another, in order to create an even more coherent sequence for learning. Because the *Sequence* is intended to be a living document, it has been—and will continue to be—periodically updated and revised. In general, however, there is more stability than change in the *Sequence*.

The purpose of the *Core Knowledge Sequence* is not to impose a canon. It is an attempt to *report* on a canon—to identify the most valuable, empowering knowledge across subject areas and to create a plan for imparting it from the first days of school.

## Knowledge Still Matters

This book, as well as the work of the Core Knowledge Foundation and the efforts of Core Knowledge teachers in hundreds of schools nationwide, swims strongly against the anti-knowledge tide of mediocrity that threatens to drag down our schools, our children, and ultimately our nation.

A broad, rich store of background knowledge is not merely nice to have. Knowledge is the essential raw material of thinking. Cognitive scientist Daniel Willingham observes, "Knowledge is not only cumulative, it grows exponentially. Those with a rich base of factual knowledge find it easier to learn more—the rich get richer. In addition, factual knowledge enhances cognitive processes such as problem solving and reasoning. The richer the knowledge base, the more smoothly and effectively these cognitive processes—the very ones that teachers target—operate. So, the more knowledge students accumulate, the smarter they become."

If all of our children are to be fully educated and participate equally in civic life, then we must provide each of them with the shared body of knowledge that makes literacy and communication possible. This concept, so central to the new Common Core State Standards adopted by more than forty states and to the Core Knowledge Foundation's goal of equity and excellence in education, manifests itself in the *Core Knowledge Sequence*—and in these popular grade-by-grade books. It is a pleasure to introduce this latest refinement of them to a new generation of readers.

*E. D. Hirsch, Jr.*
*Charlottesville, Virginia*

# I
# Language and
# Literature

# Learning to Read

Literate adults are constantly interacting with text in one form or another. Think about the reading and writing you do on any given day. Perhaps you start the morning with a glance at a newspaper or headlines on your tablet. You might hastily scribble a note for your daughter's lunch bag. Billboards and road signs compete for your attention as you drive around town. At work there are memos, reports, and email to read and write. Your child's knapsack carries home forms to fill out and announcements from his school or teacher. There are recipes to be read, bills to be paid, and account statements to be examined. When time allows, perhaps you end the day with a novel, a magazine, or Facebook posts from friends and family.

Each of these activities and countless others involve reading and writing. But we rarely think about our ability to write or make sense of printed words. It feels like something we do without thinking about it at all. In reality, our ability to make sense of the printed word is one of our greatest intellectual achievements. Most of us learn to speak and listen naturally, without formal instruction. But reading and writing are different. There's nothing at all natural about acquiring these abilities.

## Reading Is Not a Skill

Most of us think learning to read is like learning to ride a bike. It's a skill we acquire as children and never lose. Moreover, riding a bike is also a transferable skill. Once you learn how, you can safely ride almost any bike. Surely it's the same with reading: Some of us may read faster or slower than others, but reading is reading is reading. Once you learn how to read, you can read anything, right?

Unfortunately, it's not that simple. Your ability to translate written symbols into sounds—what reading experts call decoding—is a transferable skill. This explains why you can "read" nonsense words, even if you've never seen them before, such as those found in the famous Lewis Carroll poem "Jabberwocky."

> 'Twas brillig, and the slithy toves
> Did gyre and gimble in the wabe:
> All mimsy were the borogoves,
> And the mome raths outgrabe.

Few of us would disagree on how to pronounce words such as "brillig" and "mimsy," even though they don't exist. But there's more to reading than simply decoding the words on a page. Reading is about comprehension—your ability to make meaning of written words. If we can't make sense of the words on the page, we really cannot be said to be "reading." Unlike decoding, reading comprehension is not a transferable skill at all. It's the result of years and years of vocabulary growth and of building up a store of knowledge about the world, which helps you make sense of what you read. Reading about a subject that you know little about can be awkward and disorienting. For example, in his book *The Making of Americans*, Core Knowledge founder E. D. Hirsch describes reading this account of a cricket match in a British newspaper:

> *Thus, as the final day dawned and a near capacity crowd lustily cheered every run Australia mustered, much depended on Ponting and the new wizard of Oz, Mike Hussey, the two overnight batsmen. But this duo perished either side of lunch—the latter a little unfortunate to be adjudged leg-before—and with Andrew Symonds, too, being shown the dreaded finger off an inside edge, the inevitable beckoned, bar the pyrotechnics of Michael Clarke and the ninth wicket.*

You probably know nearly all the words in this passage, but it's nearly impossible to understand what the writer is trying to say. Even common words such as "lunch" and "overnight" suddenly seem awkward and strange. Knowing that this is an account of a cricket match played by a team from Australia doesn't help. Your lack of knowledge about how the game is played keeps you from understanding what the words mean. This might strike you as an extreme example, but think of how it feels when you try to make sense of directions for installing an operating system on your computer or struggle to understand a product warranty. Your rate of reading slows. You read and reread, struggling to understand.

Why is this so hard? Isn't reading like riding a bike?

Your ability to make sense of what you read depends heavily on your prior knowledge—the stuff you already know. "Prior knowledge is vital to comprehension, because writers omit information," notes University of Virginia cognitive scientist Daniel Willingham. Suppose you read, "He just got a new puppy. His landlord is angry." According to Willingham, you easily understand the logical connection between those sentences because you have prior knowledge of puppies (they aren't housebroken), carpets (urine stains them), and landlords (they are protective of their property). But what if you didn't know those things? You would be confused, and comprehension would break down.

In short, it's deeply misleading to think of reading as a "skill" at all. Reading is really a two-part process. The first part is decoding, which is a skill. The second part is comprehension, which depends almost entirely on vocabulary and background knowledge—you need to know all the words. But, critically, you also need to know the things to which those words refer. And comprehension is most certainly not a skill. It's the product of years and years of language growth and knowledge acquisition. The work of acquiring that knowledge begins in earnest the day your child sets foot in kindergarten.

## The Knowledge Connection

When we use this lens, it becomes clear that "knowing stuff" is critical to reading comprehension. Broad general knowledge is not merely nice to have. It's essential if our children are to read widely with understanding. When children struggle with comprehension, it is usually not because they cannot "read." More often, it's because they lack the vocabulary and background knowledge to understand what the writer is trying to say.

The Core Knowledge approach to reading is built on this essential understanding: Broad general reading ability correlates with broad general knowledge. If we want our children to become literate adults, they first must be explicitly taught to decode writing at a very early age. But their education must also furnish the broad, rich knowledge that educated Americans take for granted and assume others have as well. With a broad base of background knowledge, children will more easily become fully literate and read fluently and with comprehension.

# First Grade and Your Child

Most of us do not take on the task of teaching our children how to read and write. We send our children off to school and encourage them to work hard and pay attention, and we assume their teachers are caring and competent. But you would not be holding this book in your hands if you were not deeply concerned about your child's education. Thus, it's useful to know what a good first-grade language arts program should look like. It's worth paying careful attention, since the early days of formal education are critical to the goal of helping your child become a proficient reader.

## Listening and Learning

We tend to think of the three R's—reading, writing, and arithmetic—as the foundations of a good, skills-based early childhood education. But to build this foundation, a good first-grade classroom should probably be equally focused on the two L's—listening and learning.

Think of the way language develops. Oral language development (speaking and listening) precedes written language development (reading and writing). Nearly all children learn to listen and speak long before they can read and write. Science confirms what we know from common sense: Children must be able to understand words before they can produce and use them independently—

attention paid to listening and speaking will provide a solid foundation for later reading and writing.

Listening comprehension also develops faster than reading comprehension and remains more advanced for far longer than you might expect: Your child's ability to independently comprehend material on the printed page probably won't catch up to his or her ability to listen and understand the same material read out loud until the end of middle school. Our brains can do only so much at one time. When a child is learning to read, a significant amount of mental energy is devoted to decoding and reading with fluency. When she listens to text read out loud, attention is freed up to focus on the material itself. Thus, a good first-grade classroom is one in which children are given lots of opportunities to be exposed to rich language by being read aloud to often.

Most first-grade teachers read to their students. They know that small children love a good story. But the wisest teachers understand the importance of building vocabulary and background knowledge. They read nonfiction picture books and take advantage of a child's curiosity to begin establishing background knowledge of the world—knowledge that is critical to mature reading comprehension.

Read-alouds—both fiction and nonfiction—yield another important benefit: The language of books is richer and more formal than spoken English. By listening to stories or nonfiction selections read aloud, children can experience the complexities of written language without expending cognitive energy on decoding.

Helping young children develop the ability to listen to and understand written texts read aloud must be an integral part of any literacy initiative. A good first-grade teacher takes advantage of not just the natural benefits of listening and learning but also the nuanced benefits provided when read-alouds are done in a coherent, systematic fashion. To achieve this, careful consideration should first be given to the selection of text read aloud, to ensure that the vocabulary and syntax presented are rich and complex. Furthermore, to make efficient use of instructional time, read-alouds must create a broad knowledge base while simultaneously boosting listening comprehension and language skills. To do this, the selection of read-alouds within a given grade level and across grade levels should not be random but rather should be guided by a coherent, sequenced approach to building knowledge.

# Common Core State Standards and Your Child

One of the most important changes in U.S. schools in the past few decades has been the creation of Common Core State Standards in English Language Arts and Math. By 2013, the standards describing what every child should know and be able to do had been adopted by forty-five states. State tests to determine if children were meeting standards became a dominant feature of schooling in the era of the No Child Left Behind Act, which was passed in 2001. But fifty different states meant fifty different sets of standards and assessments, making it difficult to know whether children were truly proficient at reading and math or whether states were just lowering the bar to create the illusion of student achievement.

By establishing a single set of standards and common assessments, the Common Core State Standards were designed to ensure clarity and consistency across the country. In many early elementary school classrooms, the new standards may mean dramatic changes in teaching and learning. Here are a few of the changes you should expect to see in your child's classroom and how you can support high-level learning at home.

## A Balance of Fiction and Nonfiction

For more than twenty-five years, the Core Knowledge movement has been built on the understanding that a rich, knowledge-based curriculum isn't merely "nice to have" but essential. A well-rounded curriculum is fundamental to reading comprehension, vocabulary development, and language proficiency. Common Core State Standards (CCSS) reflect this understanding. Indeed, some have described CCSS as "adding nonfiction to the curriculum," but what it really does is restores art, music, history, and literature to the curriculum.

The same idea of domain-specific reading—that knowing a little bit (or, sometimes, a lot) about the subject you are studying is important in order to understand what you read about it—is also true about creativity, critical thinking, and problem solving. Indeed, nearly all of our most cherished goals for schooling are knowledge dependent. The more general knowledge you possess, the more fluid your thinking skills are. Yet how many times have we heard it said that schools are going to get away from teaching "mere facts" and focus on skills such as critical thinking, creativity, and problem solving? Unfortunately, it doesn't work that way. Common Core State Standards rescue knowledge from those who would trivialize it or who simply don't understand its fundamental role in human cognition.

Common Core State Standards call for an even balance between fiction and nonfiction in the early grades. Elementary classrooms will always rely heavily on stories, poems, and imagination, but a child's sense of wonder and awe is just as easily captured by animals, castles, and flying machines. To your child, those are fun things to learn about, play with, and talk about. To a teacher, they build background knowledge. Both engagement and knowledge are essential ingredients, encouraging children to learn, explore, and grow. As a parent, you should be seeing your child exposed to a broad range of subjects in school. And you can support that at home by reading with your child on a wide variety of subjects—not just stories and fables—and encouraging his or her interest in real-world topics.

## Explore the World Through Reading and Listening

Many teachers try to encourage young children to be independent readers by helping them to find books that are the right level for them to read on their own. There's nothing wrong with that; however, that shouldn't be the only opportunity that your child has to interact with printed text in school, or even the most important one. Research tells us that children are able to understand text at a much higher level of sophistication when it's read out loud. Indeed, a child's ability to comprehend text read independently generally doesn't catch up to his ability to understand text read out loud until about the eighth grade.

In the early grades, read-alouds are a valuable way to help children interact with written text well above their ability to read independently. Most teachers understand this, but the Common Core encourages teachers to use read-alouds not just for fictional stories and poems but to build background knowledge and language skills across subject areas. If schools wait for a child to develop mature reading comprehension and read independently about nonfiction topics of interest, they're wasting valuable time that could be spent establishing background knowledge and exposing children to rich language and content that will pay dividends for the rest of their reading lives. Under the Common Core State Standards, early childhood teachers are expected to devote significant time during language arts to reading aloud on a wide range of nonfiction topics, not only stories and poems.

One of the primary architects of the new standards put it eloquently: Common Core "restores elementary school teachers to their rightful place as guides to the world." As parents, you can support this in the same way—open your children's eyes to the world around them. And through books, videos, visits to museums, and travel where possible, expose them to the wonders of the world.

## A Focus on Evidence

Common Core Standards require students to pay greater attention to evidence in reading, writing, speaking, and listening. To meet standards, children are more likely to be asked not just to offer an opinion about a book or story but also to back up that opinion with facts and details from the story. This may sound like a heavy lift for very young children, but it needn't be. When discussing readings with your children, ask probing questions. When discussing the story "Tom

Thumb," ask your child how Tom outsmarted the characters he met along the way. What makes Tom such a clever trickster? Questions that require your child to give examples from a story or text will prepare her for more complex reading and writing tasks later on.

Similarly, Common Core State Standards require that children spend less time writing "responses" to what they read and more time making coherent arguments in writing backed by evidence. It is far more common for children and parents to read together at home than to write. But to the degree that your child enjoys writing independently, encourage her not only to write stories but to create her own "books" that use real-life details and afford the opportunity for her to show what she knows about a topic.

## Academic Vocabulary

The Common Core standards call on schools and teachers to help develop "academic vocabulary" in children. This merely means that certain words in our language tend to be subject-specific. You are unlikely to encounter the words "invertebrate" and "exoskeleton" unless you're reading about animals and insects, for example. Children love learning and saying "big words," and you should encourage them to do so. But academic vocabulary is more than just technical jargon. Learning about a subject encourages general vocabulary growth. We learn new words not by memorizing lists of words but by encountering them in everyday speech and reading. Academic vocabulary supports this general language and vocabulary growth. When a child is learning about ancient Egypt, for example, he may learn that "annual flooding in the Nile Delta was predictable enough for the Egyptians to plan agriculture around it." Your child's teacher may want him to know the academic vocabulary terms "agriculture" and "delta." But knowing those terms also allows children to make sense of the unfamiliar words such as "annual" and "predictable," which they will encounter again and again. In this way, academic vocabulary and general word growth support each other seamlessly.

Vocabulary is a slow-growing plant. We learn new words in context. Thus, the surest way to grow your child's vocabulary is to expose her to the richness of language in reading and speech. Do not be shy about using as much sophisticated vocabulary as possible when speaking and reading to your child.

## Coherence

The Common Core asks not just for more nonfiction but also for a knowledge-rich curriculum in English language arts. Yes, there's a difference. Perhaps the gravest disservice done to children in recent memory is the misguided attempt to teach and test reading comprehension not only as a skill but as a transferable skill—a set of tips and "reading strategies" that can be applied to virtually any text, regardless of subject matter. "The mistaken idea that reading is a skill," Daniel Willingham has said, "may be the single biggest factor holding back reading achievement in the country. Students will not meet standards that way. The knowledge base problem must be solved." CCSS aims to solve it with a curriculum "intentionally and coherently structured to develop rich content knowledge within and across grades." You can support this at home by identifying your child's interests and encouraging her to learn more and more about those things. Again, the benefit is not just learning about an interesting subject; knowing a lot about a subject is a sure way to grow language proficiency. By some estimates, vocabulary growth occurs four times faster when students are familiar with the knowledge domain in which they encounter a new word. Thus, the knowledge-rich classroom or home is also a language-rich classroom or home.

Perhaps the most important thing to understand is that standards are not curriculum. The Common Core State Standards note that "by reading texts in history/social studies, science, and other disciplines, students build a foundation of knowledge in these fields that will also give them the background to be better readers in all content areas. Students can only gain this foundation when the curriculum is intentionally and coherently structured to develop rich content knowledge within and across grades." This is the fundamental insight upon which the

Core Knowledge movement was built decades ago. Note that Common Core is silent on which texts and what knowledge is important. Decisions on the content of your child's education will largely be made at the state and local levels. But understanding that broad, rich, coherent knowledge is the key to vocabulary growth and language ability will allow you to be a watchful, effective advocate for your child and to work with her school and teachers to ensure the knowledge- and language-rich education she deserves.

# Building Literacy at Home

You don't need to be an early childhood literacy expert to help your son or daughter become a strong reader and writer. A few basic ideas and activities pursued diligently will pay big dividends and set your child on the road to full literacy.

## Read to Your First Grader

Read to your child daily.

Without question, the single most important and helpful thing you can do is to set aside twenty minutes or more regularly, daily if possible, to read aloud to your child.

Remember that your child's ability to follow and enjoy a story when read aloud far surpasses her ability to read independently. Plus, studies confirm that the language of children's books is richer and more complex than the spoken language of even college graduates. Thus, reading aloud to your child is an unparalleled opportunity to expose him to sophisticated language, vocabulary, and background knowledge. As you read, stop and talk about the story with your child to engage her in the story and check for understanding. Make inferences, predictions, and connections ("What do you think is going to happen next?" "This reminds me of the time when we . . ."), and encourage your child to do the same. And while small children love to hear familiar stories over and over, use your reading time to expand your child's horizons and knowledge through non-fiction picture books as well as fictional stories.

## Talk to Your Child

Engage your child in conversation and ask lots of questions. A home that's rich in spoken words confers a tremendous boost to a child's language development. In a landmark study published in 1995, researchers Betty Hart and Todd R. Risley found that the number of words children heard in their homes from birth to age four accurately predicted how many words they understood and how fast they could learn new words in kindergarten. In some cases, the differences amounted to tens of millions of words heard before a child even set foot in a classroom for the first time.

"With few exceptions, the more parents talked to their children, the faster the children's vocabularies were growing and the higher the children's IQ test scores at age three and later," the researchers observed. Indeed, early language competence still predicted comprehension for children five years later, in the third grade. The preschoolers who had heard more words at home between birth and age four, and subsequently learned more words orally, became better readers.

The richest, most productive use of parent talk is back-and-forth conversation with your child. Don't just talk at your child; engage her in conversation and ask questions. Provide as many opportunities as possible for children to listen to and speak adult language, and don't feel compelled to simplify your vocabulary. Longer and more complex conversations with sophisticated words are a good way to expose your child to rich language.

## Limit TV Time

Comparison studies of language complexity show that the language used on television is far less rich and complex than the language used in children's books and the typical conversation of college-educated parents. In addition, television distracts children from play and interaction with others. Most parents understand that television, like candy, is something that children may love but should have limited access to. The American Academy of Pediatrics has warned that screen time has no educational value at all for children under age two. Very young children learn more efficiently through interactions with people and things, not screens. For older children, TV can afford opportunities for learning and building knowledge, but it's no substitute for more enriching activities and contributes less to language growth than reading and speaking.

## Choose Activities That Build Background Knowledge

Every activity you do with your child, in the home or outside, is an opportunity to amass background knowledge, vocabulary, and language skill. Trips to the park, the zoo, and a children's museum are an opportunity to expose your child to new things and ideas. Even a trip to the grocery store can be a way to engage your child, teaching the names of fruits and vegetables and where they come from. ("What do milk, cheese, and yogurt have in common?" "How come bananas don't grow where we live?" "How do you think those peaches got inside this can?")

Watching educational TV shows about animals or faraway places is a way to expand your child's awareness of other cultures and lands. Talking about what you see and do together builds language skill and vocabulary. If your child shows an interest in a particular topic, visit your local library. It will encourage your child's curiosity and teach her that books are a great way to learn more about interesting things.

## Be a Reader, Raise a Reader

A large and comprehensive study across twenty-seven countries found that growing up in a home where there are lots of books, compared to a "bookless" home, has as great an effect on the level of education a child will attain as having parents who are barely literate, compared to having college-educated parents—about 3.2 years of advantage, on average. It may seem strange to suggest that merely having books in the home is enough to give kids an advantage, but the presence of books sends an unmistakable signal to children about what their parents value. When a child sees a parent reading on his or her own, it reinforces the idea that reading is an important and valuable use of time. Take every opportunity not just to read with your child but also to demonstrate by example the importance of literacy in your own life.

# A Few Rules for Writing

First graders should practice using the following rules, though they should not be expected to use them with 100 percent accuracy in all their writings. As part of their practice and review, children should sometimes be asked in school to apply what they have learned by proofreading and correcting selected samples of their written work.

- **Capital letters:** Use a capital letter at the beginning of a sentence and at the beginning of names, such as: Abraham Lincoln was born in Kentucky. When you refer to yourself, capitalize "I."
- **End punctuation:** When you write a sentence, use a punctuation mark to show where the sentence stops.

Use a period to end most sentences:    **.**

If you're asking a question, use a question mark:    **?**

To show excitement, use an exclamation point:    **!**

- **Contractions:** We sometimes combine two words into one short word called a contraction. To show that letters have been left out in a contraction, use the punctuation mark called an apostrophe. For example:

$$\text{I am} = \text{I'm} \qquad \text{do not} = \text{don't} \qquad \text{it is} = \text{it's}$$

- **Making words plural:** Plural means more than one. Singular means just one. You can put an "s" at the end of many words and change them from singular to plural. For example:

| Singular | Plural |
| --- | --- |
| leg | legs |
| horse | horses |
| book | books |

# Want to Learn More?

The Core Knowledge Foundation website (www.coreknowledge.org) offers a wide variety of information and resources for parents and professional educators. The *Core Knowledge Sequence* is designed to provide schools with a framework for a coherent, cumulative, and content-specific curriculum. In Core Knowledge schools, teaching and learning are more effective, as teachers help students build upon prior knowledge and make more efficient progress from one year to the next. All students enjoy more equal educational opportunities as they are motivated by consistently challenging content. And all children are prepared to become members of the wider national community, respectful of diversity while strengthened by the shared knowledge that helps unite us on common ground.

To learn more, visit the Core Knowledge Reading Room on our website (www.coreknowledge.org/reading-room).

You can also find the following articles and video online:

"Building Knowledge: The Case for Bringing Content into the Language Arts Block and for a Knowledge-Rich Curriculum Core for All Children"
By E. D. Hirsch, Jr.
*American Educator,* Spring 2006
www.aft.org/newspubs/periodicals/ae/spring2006/hirsch.cfm

"How Knowledge Helps: It Speeds and Strengthens Reading Comprehension, Learning—and Thinking"

By Daniel T. Willingham

*American Educator,* Spring 2006

www.aft.org/newspubs/periodicals/ae/spring2006/willingham.cfm

"Teaching Content Is Teaching Reading"

By Daniel T. Willingham

www.youtube.com/watch?v=RiP-ijdxqEc

"The Early Catastrophe: The 30 Million Word Gap by Age 3"

By Betty Hart and Todd R. Risley

*American Educator,* Spring 2003

www.aft.org/newspubs/periodicals/ae/spring2003/hart.cfm

# Literature

## Introduction

There is one simple practice that can make a world of difference for your first grader. Read aloud to your child often, daily if possible. Reading aloud opens the doors to a world of meaning that most children are curious to explore but in first grade are only beginning to enter on their own. In reading aloud, you can offer your child a rich and varied selection of literature, including poetry, fiction, and nonfiction.

For your first grader, we offer a selection of poetry, including some traditional rhymes, Mother Goose favorites, and familiar tongue twisters. We also include some poems by favorite modern and contemporary writers. All of these selections should be considered a starting point. We encourage you to read many more poems with your child, to delight in the play of language, and to occasionally help your child memorize a personal favorite.

The stories presented here are written in language more complex than most first graders will be able to read on their own, though they can readily be understood and enjoyed when the words are read aloud with expression and talked about with an adult. These stories are meant to complement, not replace, the stories with controlled vocabularies and syntax that children should be given as part of their instruction in learning to read. (See "Learning to Read," page 3.)

In this book, we present many familiar and traditional tales that have stood the test of time. Some of the selections from other lands may not be familiar to

American readers, but by including them here we hope to make them so. Among the stories, you will find favorite folktales from many lands and cultures. We have paired two stories—"Issun Boshi: One-Inch Boy" and "Tom Thumb"—to help children see that people in different countries tell similar stories. We've also included some classics of modern literature, such as *The Tale of Peter Rabbit* and a selection from *The House at Pooh Corner*.

Some of the stories in this first-grade volume build upon the selection of fairy tales by the Brothers Grimm, and others build on stories presented in *What Your Kindergartner Needs to Know*. For children, such fairy tales can delight and instruct and provide ways of dealing with darker human emotions like jealousy, greed, and fear. As G. K. Chesterton observed, fairy tales "are not responsible for producing in children fear, or any of the shapes of fear. . . . The baby has known the dragon intimately ever since he had an imagination. What the fairy tale provides for him is a St. George to kill the dragon." And as the celebrated writer of children's tales Wanda Gag wrote in 1937, "A fairy story is not just a fluffy puff of nothing . . . nor is it merely a tenuous bit of make believe. . . . Its roots are real and solid, reaching far back into man's past . . . and into the lives and customs of many peoples and countries." Whatever the geographical origins of the traditional tales we tell here—Africa, Japan, Europe, America, etc.—the stories have universal messages and lasting appeal across cultures and generations.

Consider this selection of stories a starting point for further exploration. Beyond stories and poems, you can share appropriate works of nonfiction with your child. Many first graders enjoy, for example, illustrated books that explain what things are and how they work, books about animals and how they live, and biographies of famous people.

Your local library has a treasury of good books, and you might want to consult the lists of recommended works in such guides as:

*Books That Build Character* by William Kilpatrick et al. (Simon & Schuster/ Touchstone, 1994)
*Books to Build On: A Grade-by-Grade Resource Guide for Parents and Teachers* edited by John Holdren and E. D. Hirsch, Jr. (Delta, 1996)

*The New Read-Aloud Handbook* by Jim Trelease (Penguin Books, 1995)

*The New York Times Parent's Guide to the Best Books for Children* by Eden Ross Lipson (Times Books, revised and updated 1991)

## Read-Aloud Activities

Try to set aside a regular time for reading aloud, a time free from other obligations or distractions (including the television, which must be off). When you read aloud, don't feel embarrassed about hamming it up a bit. Be expressive; try giving different characters different voices.

If your child is not used to hearing stories read aloud, you may want to begin by reading some poems or some of the shorter selections in this book. If your child starts to squirm as you read longer stories, take a break from reading and get your child involved: Have him look at a picture, or ask him some questions, or ask him to tell you what he thinks about what has happened so far, or have him draw a picture to go with the part of the story you've read.

When you read aloud, most of the time your child will be involved in the simple pleasure of listening. At other times, you can involve your child in some additional activities to encourage comprehension and interest. Remember, these activities are not tests. Use them with a gentle touch: Relax; have fun together.

- Let your child look through the book before you read it. Let him skim the pages and look at the pictures.
- Direct your child's attention to the book's title page. Point to the author's name and read it as written—for example, "Written by Peggy Parrish." If the book is illustrated, also read the illustrator's name—for example, "Illustrated by Jerry Pinkney." Discuss what the words "author" and "illustrator" mean. As you read more and more books, talk with your child about her favorite authors or illustrators. Look in the library for more works by your child's favorite authors and illustrators.
- Sometimes let your child pick the books for reading aloud. If your child has picked a book or books from the library, she may soon learn the lesson that "you can't tell a book by its cover." If you begin a book that she has

chosen and she expresses dislike or lack of interest, don't force her to finish hearing it. Just put the book aside with the understanding that "maybe we'll like this better later."

- As you read, sometimes run your finger below the words as you say them. This will help confirm your child's sense of the left-to-right direction of print. In rereading a selection, you can direct your child's attention to individual words as you say them aloud. You can also ask your child to try to read occasional words and phrases, especially ones that he is likely to have some success with.

- After reading a story, discuss the sequence of events. "Can you tell me what happened first?" "What did he do next?" You can draw three or four simple pictures representing scenes in the story, then ask your child to arrange the pictures in the proper sequence as she retells the story.

- After reading a poem or a story or a segment of a longer book, help your child recall details by asking questions. Keep in mind the five W's: Who? What? When? Where? Why? For example, after reading "The Boy at the Dike," ask, "Where did Peter live?" "Whom did Peter go to visit?" "Why did he go there?" "What happened on the way home?" "Why couldn't he leave the dike?" "When did somebody find him?" (Maintain a playful, conversational tone; this is not a test!)

- In talking about stories, occasionally use words that are common in the discussion of literature, such as "character," "hero," and "heroine." For example, you might ask, "Who is your favorite character in *The House at Pooh Corner?*" Not all stories have heroes or heroines, but you can bring up the terms when appropriate; you might ask, "Isn't it surprising that the hero of 'Issun Boshi' is no bigger than your thumb (at least for most of the story)?" Or, "That was a brave thing for Gretel to do. She's a real heroine, isn't she?"

- Engage your child in a discussion of the story by asking questions that go beyond recall of details and take her into interpretation. For example, after reading "The Crowded, Noisy House," ask, "Why do you think the story has that title? What do you think it means?"

- Help your child memorize a favorite poem.
- Act out a story or scenes from a story. Your child doesn't need to memorize a set script; she can use her own language to express a character's thoughts. A few simple props can help: paper bags for masks, old shirts for costumes, a broomstick for a horse—all can be transformed by your child's active imagination.

## Poetry and Rhymes

### Little Sally Walker

Little Sally Walker
Sitting in the saucer
Rise, Sally, rise
Wipe your weepy eyes.
Put your hands on your hips
And make your backbone slip.
Oh, shake it to the east
Oh, shake it to the west
Oh, shake it to the one
    that you love best

### The Queen of Hearts

The Queen of Hearts
She made some tarts,
    All on a summer's day.
The **Knave** of Hearts
He stole the tarts,
    And took them clean away.

The King of Hearts
Called for the tarts,
    And beat the Knave full sore.
The Knave of Hearts
Brought back the tarts,
    And vowed he'd steal no more.

> **New Word**
> A **knave** is a boy servant.

## If Wishes Were Horses

If wishes were horses, beggars would ride.
If turnips were watches, I would wear one by my side,
And if "ifs" and "ands" were pots and pans,
There'd be no work for tinkers!

## Three Wise Men of Gotham

Three wise men of Gotham
Went to sea in a bowl;
If the bowl had been stronger
My song had been longer.

## Solomon Grundy

Solomon Grundy,
Born on a Monday,
Christened on Tuesday,
Married on Wednesday,
Took ill on Thursday,
Worse on Friday,
Died on Saturday,
Buried on Sunday:
This is the end
Of Solomon Grundy.

## Thirty Days Hath September

Thirty days hath September
April, June, and November
All the rest have thirty-one,
But February has twenty-eight alone,
Except in leap year, that's the time
When February's days are twenty-nine.

## Tongue Twisters

Peter Piper picked a peck of pickled peppers;
A peck of pickled peppers Peter Piper picked.
If Peter Piper picked a peck of pickled peppers,
Where's the peck of pickled peppers Peter Piper picked?

Moses supposes his toeses are roses,
But Moses supposes erroneously;
For nobody's toeses are posies of roses,
As Moses supposes his toeses to be.

How much wood would a woodchuck chuck
If a woodchuck could chuck wood?
He would chuck as much wood as a woodchuck could chuck
If a woodchuck would chuck wood.

Swan swam over the sea;
Swim, swan, swim.
Swan swam back again;
Well swum, swan.

She sells seashells by the seashore.

# Riddle Rhymes

(For answers, turn this page upside down.)

Higher than a house, higher than a tree,
Oh, whatever can it be?
(a star)

A hill full, a hole full
Yet you cannot catch a bowl full.
(mist or smoke)

Thirty white horses upon a red hill,
Now they tramp, now they champ,
now they stand still.
(teeth)

Riddle me, riddle me, what is that
Over the head, and under the hat?
(hair)

## More Poems for First Grade

. . . . . . . . . . . . . . . . . . . . . . . . . . . . . . . . . . . . . . . . . . . . . . . . . . . .

### The Pasture
by Robert Frost

I'm going out to clean the pasture spring;
I'll only stop to rake the leaves away
(And wait to watch the water clear, I may):
I shan't be gone long.—You come too.

I'm going out to fetch the little calf
That's standing by the mother. It's so young,
It totters when she licks it with her tongue.
I shan't be gone long.—You come too.

### Hope
by Langston Hughes

Sometimes when I'm lonely,
Don't know why,
Keep thinkin' I won't be lonely
By and by.

## A Good Play

by Robert Louis Stevenson

We built a ship upon the stairs
All made of the back-bedroom chairs,
And filled it full of sofa pillows
To go a-sailing on the billows.

We took a saw and several nails,
And water in the nursery pails;
And Tom said, "Let us also take
An apple and a slice of cake";
Which was enough for Tom and me
To go a-sailing on, till tea.

We sailed along for days and days,
And had the very best of plays;
But Tom fell out and hurt his knee,
So there was no one left but me.

## The Swing

by Robert Louis Stevenson

How do you like to go up in a swing,
　　Up in the air so blue?
Oh, I do think it the pleasantest thing
　　Ever a child can do!

Up in the air and over the wall,
　　Till I can see so wide,
Rivers and trees and cattle and all
　　Over the countryside—

Till I look down on the garden green,
　　Down on the roof so brown—
Up in the air I go flying again,
　　Up in the air and down!

# The Frog

by Hilaire Belloc

Be kind and tender to the Frog,
    And do not call him names,
As "Slimy skin," or "Polly-wog,"
    Or likewise "Ugly James,"
Or "Gape-a-grin," or "Toad-gone-wrong,"
    Or "Billy Bandy-knees":
The Frog is justly sensitive
    To epithets like these.
No animal will more repay
    A treatment kind and fair;
At least so lonely people say
Who keep a frog (and, by the way,
    They are extremely rare).

## The Owl and the Pussy-Cat
by Edward Lear

The Owl and the Pussy-cat went to sea
    In a beautiful pea-green boat,

They took some honey, and plenty of money,
    Wrapped up in a five-pound note.

The Owl looked up to the stars above,
    And sang to a small guitar,

        "O lovely Pussy! O Pussy, my love,
            What a beautiful Pussy you are,

            You are,

            You are!

        What a beautiful Pussy you are!"

        Pussy said to the Owl, "You elegant fowl!
            How charmingly sweet you sing!

        O let us be married! too long we have tarried:
            But what shall we do for a ring?"

        They sailed away, for a year and a day,
            To the land where the Bong-tree grows

        And there in a wood a Piggy-wig stood
            With a ring at the end of his nose,

            His nose,

            His nose,

        With a ring at the end of his nose.

"Dear Pig, are you willing to sell for one shilling
    Your ring?" Said the Piggy, "I will."

So they took it away, and were married next day
    By the Turkey who lives on the hill.

They dined on mince, and slices of quince,
    Which they ate with a runcible spoon;

And hand in hand, on the edge of the sand,
    They danced by the light of the moon,

        The moon,

        The moon,

They danced by the light of the moon.

## The Purple Cow
### by Gelett Burgess

I never saw a Purple Cow,
I never hope to see one;
But I can tell you, anyhow,
I'd rather see than be one.

**Make a Connection**
Learn about various animal habitats on pages 378–93 in the "Science" chapter.

## I Know All the Sounds That the Animals Make
### by Jack Prelutsky

I know all the sounds that the animals make,
and make them all day from the moment I wake,
I roar like a mouse and I purr like a moose,
I hoot like a duck and I moo like a goose.

I squeak like a cat and I quack like a frog,
I oink like a bear and I honk like a hog,
I croak like a cow and I bark like a bee,
no wonder the animals marvel at me.

## My Shadow

by Robert Louis Stevenson

I have a little shadow that goes in and out with me,
And what can be the use of him is more than I can see.
He is very, very like me from the heels up to the head;
And I see him jump before me, when I jump into my bed.

The funniest thing about him is the way he likes to grow—
Not at all like proper children, which is always very slow;
For he sometimes shoots up taller like an india-rubber ball,
And he sometimes gets so little that there's none of him at all.

He hasn't got a notion of how children ought to play,
And can only make a fool of me in every sort of way.
He stays so close beside me, he's a coward you can see;
I'd think shame to stick to nursie as that shadow sticks to me!

One morning, very early, before the sun was up,
I rose and found the shining dew on every buttercup;
But my lazy little shadow, like an arrant sleepy-head,
Had stayed at home behind me and was fast asleep in bed.

**Do It Yourself**

Do you have a streetlamp in your neighborhood? You can play with your shadow! If not, set up a lamp or find a place with lots of light to play with your shadow.

## Rope Rhyme

by Eloise Greenfield

Get set, ready now, jump right in
Bounce and kick and giggle and spin
Listen to the rope when it hits the ground
Listen to that clappedy-slappedy sound
Jump right up when it tells you to
Come back down, whenever you do
Count to a hundred, count by ten
Start to count all over again
That's what jumping is all about
Get set, ready now,
    jump
        right
            out!

**Make a Connection**

Practice counting by tens. See page 339 in the "Mathematics" chapter.

## Table Manners

by Gelett Burgess

The Goops they lick their fingers,
And the Goops they lick their knives;

They spill their broth on the tablecloth—
Oh, they lead disgusting lives!

The Goops they talk while eating,
And loud and fast they chew;

And that is why I'm glad that I
Am not a Goop—are you?

## Sing a Song of People
### by Lois Lenski

Sing a song of people
    Walking fast or slow;
People in the city,
    Up and down they go.

People on the sidewalk,
People on the bus;
People passing, passing,
In back and front of us.
People on the subway
Underneath the ground;
People riding taxis
Round and round and round.

People with their hats on,
Going in the doors;
People with umbrellas
When it rains and pours.

People in tall buildings
And in stores below;
Riding elevators
Up and down they go.

People walking singly,
People in a crowd;
People saying nothing,
People talking loud.
People laughing, smiling,
Grumpy people too;
People who just hurry
And never look at you!

Sing a song of people
    Who like to come and go;
Sing of city people
    You see but never know!

## Washington

by Nancy Byrd Turner

He played by the river when he was young.
He raced with rabbits along the hills,
He fished for minnows, and climbed and swung,
And hooted back at the whippoorwills.
Strong and slender and tall he grew—
And then, one morning, the bugles blew.

Over the hills the summons came,
Over the river's shining rim.
He said that the bugles called his name,
He knew that his country needed him,
And he answered, "Coming!" and marched away
For many a night and many a day.

Perhaps when the marches were hot and long
He'd think of the river flowing by
Or, camping under the winter sky,
Would hear the whippoorwill's far-off song.
Boy or soldier, in peace or strife,
He loved America all his life!

## Wynken, Blynken, and Nod

by Eugene Field

Wynken, Blynken, and Nod one night
    Sailed off in a wooden shoe,—
Sailed on a river of crystal light
    Into a sea of dew.
"Where are you going, and what do you wish?"
    The old moon asked the three.
    "We have come to fish for the herring-fish
    That live in this beautiful sea;
    Nets of silver and gold have we,"
        Said Wynken,
        Blynken,
        And Nod.


The old moon laughed and sang a song,
    As they rocked in the wooden shoe;
And the wind that sped them all night long
    Ruffled the waves of dew;
The little stars were the herring-fish
    That lived in that beautiful sea.
    "Now cast your nets wherever you wish,—
    Never afraid are we!"
    So cried the stars to the fishermen three,
        Wynken,
        Blynken,
        And Nod.

All night long their nets they threw
        To the stars in the twinkling foam,—
Then down from the skies came the wooden shoe,
        Bringing the fishermen home:
'Twas all so pretty a sail, it seemed
        As if it could not be;
And some folk thought 'twas a dream they'd dreamed
        Of sailing that beautiful sea;
But I shall name you the fishermen three:
            Wynken,
            Blynken,
            And Nod.


Wynken and Blynken are two little eyes,
        And Nod is a little head,
And the wooden shoe that sailed the skies
        Is a wee one's trundle-bed;
So shut your eyes while mother sings
        Of wonderful sights that be,
And you shall see the beautiful things
        As you rock in the misty sea
Where the old shoe rocked the fishermen three:—
            Wynken,
            Blynken,
            And Nod.

## Thanksgiving Day

by Lydia Maria Child

Over the river, and through the
    wood,
To grandfather's house we go;
The horse knows the way
To carry the sleigh
Through the white and drifted
    snow.

Over the river, and through the
    wood—
Oh, how the wind does blow!
It stings the toes
And bites the nose
As over the ground we go.

Over the river, and through the
    wood,
To have a first-rate play.
Hear the bells ring
"Ting-a-ling-ding,"
Hurrah for Thanksgiving Day!

Over the river, and through the
    wood,
Trot fast, my dapple-gray!
Spring over the ground,
Like a hunting-hound!
For this is Thanksgiving Day.

Over the river, and through the
    wood,
And straight through the barn-yard
    gate.
We seem to go
Extremely slow,—
It is so hard to wait!

Over the river and through the
    wood—
Now grandmother's cap I spy!
Hurrah for the fun!
Is the pudding done?
Hurrah for the pumpkin-pie!

## Aesop's Fables

A fable is a special kind of story that teaches a lesson. People have been telling some fables over and over for hundreds of years. It is said that many of these fables were told by a man named Aesop [EE-sop], who lived in Greece a very, very long time ago.

Aesop knew bad behavior when he saw it, and he wanted people to be better. But he knew that we don't like to be told when we're bad. That is why many of his fables have animals in them. The animals sometimes talk and act like people. In fact, the animals behave just as well and just as badly as people do. That's because, even when a fable is about animals, it is really about people. Through these stories about animals, Aesop teaches us how we should act as people.

At the end of the fable, Aesop often tells us a lesson we should learn. The lesson is called the moral of the story.

Here are six of Aesop's fables, most with animals in them. The moral of the story is stated at the end of each fable. As you read the fables, try saying what you think the lesson might be before you read the moral.

## The Boy Who Cried Wolf

There was once a young shepherd boy who **tended** his sheep at the foot of a mountain near a dark forest. It was lonely for him watching the sheep all day. No one was near, except for three farmers he could sometimes see working in the fields in the valley below.

**New Word**

Does your child know what **tended** means? "Tended" means took care of or protected.

One day the boy thought of a plan by which he could get a little company and have some fun. He ran down toward the valley, crying, "Wolf! Wolf!"

The men ran to meet him, and after they found out there was no wolf after all, one man remained to talk with the boy awhile.

The boy enjoyed the company so much that a few days later he tried the same trick again, and again the men ran to help him.

A few days later, a real wolf came from the forest and began to steal the sheep. The boy ran toward the valley, and more loudly than ever he cried, "Wolf! Wolf!"

But the men, who had been fooled twice before, thought that he was tricking them again. No one came to help the boy. And so the wolf had a very good meal.

**Moral:** If you often lie, people won't believe you even when you are telling the truth.

## The Fox and the Grapes

One hot summer day, a fox was strolling along when he noticed a bunch of juicy grapes, just turning ripe, hanging on a vine high above. "Mmm, that's just the thing to take care of my thirst," said the fox. He trotted back a few steps, then ran forward and jumped, but he missed the grapes. He turned around and tried again. "One, two, three, go," he said, and he leaped with all his might. But again he missed the grapes.

Again and again he tried, but at last he gave up. And he walked away with his nose in the air, saying, "I didn't want those old grapes anyway. I'm sure they are sour."

**Moral:** When people cannot get what they want, they sometimes tell themselves that what they want is no good anyway.

### Sour Grapes

"Sour grapes" has become a common saying. People say, "It's just sour grapes," to refer to griping or unkind remarks someone makes about something he or she can't have. For example:

Malik turned to his teacher, Mr. Rodriguez, and asked, "Why did Mark say our class play isn't going to be any good?"

"Oh, that's just sour grapes," said Mr. Rodriguez. "Mark wanted to be the star, but he's playing a smaller part. But once he sees how much fun it is, he'll change his mind."

## The Dog in the Manger

There was once a dog who liked to nap on hot days in the cool barn. He liked to sleep in the manger, the long wooden box where hay was put for the farm animals to eat.

One hot day after a long afternoon pulling the plow, the oxen returned to the barn, hungry for their dinner. But the dog was lying in the manger on the hay.

"Excuse me," said a tired ox, "would you please move so that I can eat my hay?"

The dog, angry at being awakened from his nap, growled and barked at the ox.

"Please," said the ox, "I've had a hard day and I'm very hungry."

But the dog, who of course did not eat hay, only barked and snapped at the ox and refused to **budge**. At last the poor ox had to give up and went away tired and hungry.

**Moral:** Don't be mean and stingy when you have no need of things yourself. Don't be a dog in the manger.

**New Word**

Ask your child what **budge** means. "Budge" means to move just a little bit.

## The Maid and the Milk Pail

Peggy, the milkmaid, was going to market. There she planned to sell the fresh sweet milk in the pail that she had learned to carry balanced on her head.

As she went along, she began thinking about what she would do with the money she would get for the milk. "I'll buy some chickens from Farmer Brown," she said, "and they will lay eggs each morning. When those eggs hatch, I'll have more chickens. Then I'll sell some of the chickens and some of the eggs, and that will get me enough money to buy the blue dress I've wanted, and some blue ribbon to match. Oh, I'll look so lovely that all the boys will want to dance with me at the fair, and all the girls will be jealous. But I don't care; I'll just toss my head at them, like this!"

She tossed back her head. The pail flew off, and the milk spilled all over the road. So Peggy had to return home and tell her mother what had happened. "Ah, my child," said her mother, "don't count your chickens before they're hatched."

**Moral:** Don't count your chickens before they're hatched. Have you heard this saying before? It means: Do not count on getting everything you want or having everything turn out exactly as you plan, because you may be disappointed.

### The Wolf in Sheep's Clothing

Night after night a wolf prowled around a flock of sheep looking for one to eat, but the shepherd and his dogs always chased him away. But one day the wolf found the skin of a sheep that had been thrown aside. He pulled the skin carefully over him so that none of his fur showed under the white fleece. Then he strolled among the flock. A lamb, thinking that the wolf was its mother, followed him into the woods—and there the wolf made a meal of the lamb!

So for many days the wolf was able to get a sheep whenever he pleased. But one day the shepherd decided to cook lamb for his own dinner. He chose the biggest, fattest sheep he could find and killed him on the spot. Guess who it was—the wolf!

**Two morals:** (1) Beware of a wolf in sheep's clothing: Things are not always what they appear to be. (2) If you pretend to be what you are not, you might get caught.

## A Wolf in Sheep's Clothing

People sometimes use the phrase "a wolf in sheep's clothing" to describe someone who appears to be harmless or friendly but who is really dangerous or untrustworthy. For example:

"I can't believe Ronnie took my idea for his art poster. He said he just wanted to know what I was working on, so I told him, but then he did it himself. What a wolf in sheep's clothing!"

## The Goose That Laid the Golden Eggs

Once a farmer went to the nest of his goose and found there an egg, all yellow and shiny. When he picked it up, it was heavy as a rock. He was about to throw it away because he thought that someone was playing a trick on him. But on second thought, he took it home, and there he discovered to his delight that it was an egg of pure gold!

He sold the egg for a handsome sum of money. Every morning the goose laid another golden egg, and the farmer soon became rich by selling eggs.

As he grew rich, he grew greedy. "Why should I have to wait to get only one egg a day?" he thought. "I will cut open the goose and take all the eggs out of her at once."

And so he killed the goose and cut her open, only to find—nothing.

**Moral:** He who wants more often loses all. When you want something, be patient. If you are greedy, you might lose what you already have.

## Stories

## All Stories Are Anansi's

*(A tale from West Africa)*

**PARENTS:** Anansi [ah-NAHN-see], the spider, is a popular figure in the folklore of parts of West Africa. Like Brer Rabbit in America (see later, page 62), Anansi is a "trickster" figure—clever, cunning, sometimes mischievous—who uses his wits to make up for what he lacks in size and strength. This story tells how Anansi became the "owner" of all stories.

Long ago, there were no stories on Earth. In those days all stories belonged to the sky god, Nyame, who kept them in a box beneath his throne.

Because they had no stories to share, the people of the Earth did not have much to do. They just sat around their campfires and whistled. Anansi the spider could see that the people were restless and bored. He decided he would bring them something that would help them pass the time.

Anansi stretched his eight legs and wove a wonderful web that reached all the way to the sky. He climbed up the web until he arrived at the throne of the sky god, Nyame, the keeper of all stories.

"Nyame," Anansi said, "great, wise god of the sky. I would like to take the stories to the people who live on the Earth. Will you let me have the great box where you keep the stories?"

"I will give you the stories," said Nyame, in a booming voice. "But the price is high. You must bring me three things: Onini [oh-NEE-nee], the great python who can swallow a goat; Osebo [oh-SAY-boe], the mighty leopard, whose teeth are as sharp as spears; and Mmoboro [mmoh-BOH-roh], the hornet whose sting burns like a needle of fire."

"I will pay the price," said Anansi.

Anansi made his way back down the web to Earth. He went to speak with his wife, Aso. Together, they came up with a plan to capture Onini, the great python who could swallow a goat.

The next morning Anansi walked into the forest, waving a big branch. As he walked, he spoke to himself. "She's wrong," he said, pretending to be very upset. "I know she is. He is much, much longer than this branch."

As Anansi drew near the watering hole, a large snake rose up. It was Onini, the great python who could swallow a goat.

"What are you muttering about, Anansi?" asked Onini. "You are disturbing my nap."

"I have been quarreling with my wife," said Anansi. "She says that you are shorter than this branch. But I say you are longer. She will not listen to me, and I do not see how I can prove to her that I am right."

"That is easy," said Onini. "Lay your branch on the ground and I will lie next to it. Then you shall see that I am longer."

The great snake slithered over and lay next to Anansi's branch.

"It looks like you may be longer," said Anansi. "But I can't tell for sure because you are not quite straightened out. Could I straighten you out a bit?"

"Certainly," said Onini.

"Let me fasten your tail at this end," said Anansi as he worked. "That way I can really straighten you out. And let me fasten you here, by your head, as well." Before the python realized what Anansi was up to, Anansi had spun a web around Onini and tied him to the branch.

"Now you are caught!" said Anansi.

With that, Anansi carried Onini the python to Nyame.

"That is one thing," said Nyame. "Two things remain."

Anansi went back to Earth and began to think about how he might catch Osebo, the mighty leopard with teeth as sharp as spears. Anansi dug a pit on the path Osebo used to get to the watering hole. He laid branches across the pit and covered the branches with sticks, leaves, and dirt. When Anansi was satisfied that the hole was well hidden, he scurried home and went to sleep.

When Osebo came out to hunt during the night, he fell right into Anansi's trap. Anansi found him down in the pit the next morning.

"Osebo," said Anansi, "what are you doing down in that pit?"

"You fool!" said Osebo. "Can't you see that I have fallen into a trap? You must help me get out."

"I will see what I can do," said Anansi.

Anansi found a large willow tree and bent the top of the tree over the pit. He spun two silky cords and used them to fasten the tree. Then he spun another silky cord. He attached one end of this third cord to the top of the tree and let the other end dangle down into the pit.

"Tie this cord to your tail," said Anansi. "Then I will lift you up."

Osebo tied the cord to his tail.

Then Anansi cut the two cords that were holding the tree down. The tree sprang back to its original position, carrying Osebo with it. Osebo dangled from the tree.

"Now you are caught!" said Anansi.

Anansi wove a web around Osebo the leopard and carried him to Nyame.

The sky god was impressed. "That is two things," he said. "Only one thing remains."

Anansi went back to Earth to catch Mmoboro, the hornet whose sting burned like a needle of fire. He cut a gourd from a vine and hollowed out the inside. Then he filled the gourd with water and went to the nest where Mmoboro the hornet made his home.

Anansi poured some of the water in the gourd over his own head. Then he dumped the rest of the water on the hornet's nest. Mmoboro the hornet came out, buzzing angrily. He saw Anansi standing nearby, holding a leaf over his head.

"Oh, my!" said Anansi. "The rainy season seems to have come early this year, and it looks like you have no shelter from the rain. Would you like to take shelter in my gourd until the rain goes away?"

"Thank you, Anansi," said Mmoboro the hornet, as he flew into the gourd.

"You're welcome!" said Anansi, as he closed up the opening in the gourd with a leaf and wove a web to hold the leaf in place.

"Now you are caught!" said Anansi.

Anansi carried Mmoboro the hornet to Nyame.

Nyame was very impressed. "That is the last thing!" he proclaimed. "You have succeeded, Anansi, where many before you have failed. You have paid the price."

Then Nyame called out, in a voice like thunder: "Listen to me! Anansi has paid the price for the stories of the sky god, and I do hereby give the stories to him. From this day forward, all of the stories belong to Anansi. Whenever someone tells one of these stories, he or she must acknowledge that it is Anansi's tale."

Anansi took the box of stories back to Earth and shared them with the people. The people were grateful for the stories and told them to their children, and to their children's children, who told them to their children, and so on. Even to this day, these stories are known as "spider stories."

Check your library for more stories about Anansi, such as:

*Anansi and the Moss-Covered Rock* and *Anansi Goes Fishing* retold by Eric A. Kimmel (Holiday House, 1988 and 1992)

*Anansi Finds a Fool* by Verna Aardema (Dial Books for Young Readers, 1992)

## The Boy at the Dike

Many years ago, there lived a boy who did a brave deed. His name was Peter, and he lived in Holland, a country by the sea.

In Holland, the sea presses in on the land so much that the people built big walls of earth and stone to hold back the waters. Every little child in Holland was taught that these big walls, called dikes, must be watched at every moment. No water must be allowed to come through the dikes. Even a hole no larger than your little finger was a very dangerous thing.

One afternoon in the early fall, when Peter was seven years old, his mother called to him. "Come, Peter," she said. "I want you to go across the dike and take these cakes to your friend the blind man. If you go quickly, you will be home again before dark."

Peter was happy to go, because his friend the blind man lived alone and was always glad to have a visitor. When he got to the blind man's home, Peter stayed awhile to tell him of his walk along the dike. He told about the bright sun and the flowers and the ships far out at sea. Then Peter remembered that his mother wanted him to return home before dark. So he said goodbye and set out for home.

As he walked along, he noticed how the water beat against the side of the dike. There had been much rain, and the water was higher than before. Peter remembered how his father always spoke of the "angry waters."

"I suppose Father thinks they are angry," thought Peter, "because we have been keeping them out for so long. Well, I am glad these dikes are so strong. If they gave way, what would become of us? All these fields would be covered with water. Then what would happen to the flowers, and the animals, and the people?"

Suddenly Peter noticed that the sun was setting. Darkness was settling on the land. "Mother will be watching for me," he said. "I must hurry." But just then he heard a noise. It was the sound of trickling water! He stopped, looked down, and saw a small hole in the dike, through which a tiny stream was flowing.

A leak in the dike! Peter understood the danger at once. If water ran through a little hole, it would soon make a larger one; then the waters could break through and the land would be flooded!

Peter saw what he must do. He climbed down the side of the dike and thrust his finger in the tiny hole. The water stopped!

"The angry waters will stay back now," said Peter. "I can keep them back with my finger. Holland will not be drowned while I am here."

But then he thought, "How long can I stay here?" Already it was dark and cold. Peter called out, "Help! Is anyone there? Help!" But no one heard him. No one came to help.

It grew darker and colder still. Peter's arm began to grow stiff and numb. "Will no one come?" he thought. Then he shouted again for help. And when no one came, he cried out, "Mother! Mother!"

Many times since sunset, his mother had looked out at the dike and expected to see her little boy. She was worried, but then she thought that perhaps Peter was spending the night with his blind friend, as he had done before. "Well," she thought, "when he gets home in the morning, I will have to scold him for staying away from home without permission."

Poor Peter! He would rather have been home than anywhere else in the world, but he could not move from the dike. He tried to whistle to keep himself company, but he couldn't because his teeth chattered with cold. He thought of his brother and sister in their warm beds, and of his father and mother. "I must not let them be drowned," he thought. "I must stay here until someone comes."

The moon and stars looked down on the shivering child. His head was bent and his eyes were closed, but he was not asleep. Now and then he rubbed the hand that was holding back the angry waters.

Morning came. A man walking along the dike heard a sound, something like a groan. He bent down and saw the child below. He called out, "What's the matter, boy? Are you hurt? Why are you sitting there?"

In a voice faint and weak, the boy said, "I am keeping the water from coming in. Please, tell them to come quickly!"

The man ran to get help. People came with shovels to fix the dike, and they carried Peter, the little hero, home to his parents.

'Tis many a year since then; but still,
When the sea roars like a flood,
The children are taught what a child can do
Who is brave and true and good.
For all the mothers and fathers
Take their children by the hand
And tell them of brave little Peter
Whose courage saved the land.

## Brer Rabbit Gets Brer Fox's Dinner

**PARENTS:** The Brer Rabbit stories are African American folktales that were collected and retold in the late nineteenth century by the American writer Joel Chandler Harris. Harris told the tales in the voice of a character he called Uncle Remus, an old African American man who speaks to a young boy on a Southern plantation. The tales reflect the vernacular of the time, and so use words like "ain't." They are rich in humor and come alive when read aloud.

One day Brer Rabbit had nothing much to do, so he went over to see what Brer Fox was up to. When he got to Brer Fox's house, he saw Brer Fox up on the roof, nailing down shingles. Brer Fox was hammering and banging as fast as he could.

Brer Rabbit saw something else, too. It was Brer Fox's dinner pail. The food in the pail smelled good. In fact, it smelled so good that Brer Rabbit started thinking of ways he might get it out of the pail, where it was doing him no good at all, and into his belly, where he reckoned it would do him a whole lot of good.

"Brer Fox!" Brer Rabbit shouted. "How you doin' today?"

"Busy!" said Brer Fox. "Ain't got time to be **flappin' gums** with you."

"Whatchya doin' up there?"

"Puttin' on a new roof before winter comes."

"Need any help?"

"I do, but where am I going to get it?"

"I'm a powerful man with a hammer, Brer Fox. Let me come up and help you."

Brer Rabbit snatched off his coat and scampered up the ladder. Soon he was nailing down roof tiles as fast as could be, as if winter were right on the outskirts of town. *Bang, bang, bang!* And all the time he was nailing, he was thinking of ways he might get his paws on Brer Fox's dinner. He nailed and nailed, and thought and thought, until he was nailing right next to Brer Fox's big, puffy tail.

Brer Rabbit kept on nailing. So did Brer Fox. Then all of a sudden Brer Fox

> ### Talk and Think
> What do you think "**flappin' gums**" means? How are your gums flapping when you talk?

dropped his hammer and hollered, "Ouch! Brer Rabbit, you done nailed my tail!"

Brer Rabbit looked innocently at Brer Fox and said, "What's that I done? Nailed your tail? That can't be. You must be joking." By this time, Brer Fox was furious. He hollered and shouted and jumped up and down on the roof. "Un-nail my tail, Brer Rabbit!" he yelled. "Un-nail my tail!"

Brer Rabbit hurried down the ladder. On his way down, he said, "I feel mighty bad that I nailed your tail, Brer Fox. Yes, I feel just awful. I ain't never nailed a tail to a roof before. I can't remember when I did something that made me feel so bad."

Brer Rabbit, he kept on muttering to himself while he went down the ladder.

Brer Fox, he went on hollering and screaming up on the roof.

Soon Brer Rabbit was safely back down on the ground. He was still muttering to himself. "Making a mistake like that is upsetting to me," he said, shaking his head. "In fact, it's so upsetting that it makes me hungry."

Brer Rabbit made his way over and opened Brer Fox's dinner pail. It was

chock-full of molasses and biscuits and corn. Brer Rabbit helped himself, dug in and gobbled up every morsel, or crumb, that was inside. When he finished the last bite, he wiped his mouth, burped loudly once or twice, and set off on his merry way.

As he hopped off, he muttered again, "I can't remember when I've felt as bad as I do. I just feel awful that I nailed Brer Fox's nice long tail to the roof!"

## The Frog Prince

*(A tale from the Brothers Grimm, retold by Wanda Gag)*

In the olden days when wishing was still of some use, there lived a King. He had several beautiful daughters, but the youngest was so fair that even the sun, who sees so many wonders, could not help marveling every time he looked into her face.

Near the King's palace lay a large dark forest, and there, under an old linden tree, was a well. When the day was very warm, the little Princess would go off into this forest and sit at the rim of the cool well. There she would play with her golden ball, tossing it up and catching it deftly in her little hands. This was her favorite game and she never tired of it.

Now it happened one day that, as the Princess tossed her golden ball into the air, it did not fall into her uplifted hands as usual. Instead, it fell to the ground, rolled to the rim of the well and into the water. *Plunk, splash!* The golden ball was gone.

The well was deep and the Princess knew it. She felt sure she would never see her beautiful ball again, so she cried and cried and could not stop.

"What is the matter, little Princess?" said a voice behind her. "You are crying so that even a hard stone would have pity on you."

The little girl looked around and there she saw a frog. He was in the well and was stretching his fat ugly head out of the water.

"Oh, it's you—you old water-splasher!" said the girl. "I'm crying over my golden ball. It has fallen into the well."

"Oh, as to that," said the frog, "I can bring your ball back to you. But what will you give me if I do?"

"Whatever you wish, dear old frog," said the Princess. "I'll give you my dresses, my beads, and all my jewelry—even the golden crown on my head."

The frog answered: "Your dresses, your beads, and all your jewelry, even the golden crown on your head—I don't want them. But if you can find it in your heart to like me and take me for your playfellow, if you will let me sit beside you at the table, eat from your little golden plate, and drink from your little golden cup, and if you are willing to let me sleep in your own little bed besides: If you promise me all this, little Princess, then I will gladly go down to the bottom of the well and bring back your golden ball."

"Oh, yes," said the Princess, "I'll promise anything you say if you'll only bring back my golden ball to me." But to herself she thought: "What is the silly frog chattering about? He can only live in the water and croak with the other frogs; he could never be a playmate to a human being."

As soon as the frog had heard her promise, he disappeared into the well. Down, down, down, he sank, but he soon came up again, holding the golden ball in his mouth. He dropped it on the grass at the feet of the Princess, who was wild with joy when she saw her favorite plaything once more. She picked up the ball and skipped away with it, thinking no more about the little creature who had returned it to her.

"Wait! Wait!" cried the frog. "Take me with you; I can't run as fast as you."

But what good did it do him to scream his "quark! quark!" after her as loud as he could? She wouldn't listen to him but hurried home, where she soon forgot the poor frog, who now had to go back into his well again.

The next evening, the Princess was eating her dinner at the royal table when—*plitch plotch, plitch plotch*—something came climbing up the stairs. When it reached the door, it knocked at the door and cried:

*Youngest daughter of the King,*
*Open the door for me!*

The Princess rose from the table and ran to see who was calling her—when she opened the door, there sat the frog, wet and green and cold! Quickly she slammed the door and sat down at the table again, her heart beating loud and fast. The King could see well enough that she was frightened and worried, and he said, "My child, what are you afraid of? Is there a giant out there who wants to carry you away?"

"Oh, no," said the Princess. "It's not a giant but a horrid old frog!"

"And what does he want of you?" asked the King.

"Oh, dear father, as I was playing under the linden tree by the well, my golden ball fell into the water. And because I cried so hard, the frog brought it back to me; and because he insisted so much, I promised him that he could be my playmate. But I never, never thought that he would ever leave his well. Now he is out there and wants to come in and eat from my plate and drink from my cup and sleep in my little bed. But I couldn't bear that, Papa; he's so wet and ugly and his eyes bulge out!"

While the Princess was talking, the frog knocked at the door once more and said:

*Youngest daughter of the King,*
*Open the door for me.*
*Mind your words at the old well spring;*
*Open the door for me!*

At that the King said, "If we make promises, daughter, we must keep them; so you had better go and open the door."

The Princess still did not want to do it but she had to obey. When she opened the door, the frog hopped in and followed her until she reached her chair. Then he sat there and said, "Lift me up beside you."

She hesitated—the frog was so cold and clammy—but her father looked at her sternly and said, "You must keep your promise."

After the frog was on her chair, he wanted to be put on the table. When he was there, he said, "Now shove your plate a little closer, so we can eat together like real playmates."

The Princess shuddered, but she had to do it. The frog enjoyed the meal and ate heartily, but the poor girl could not swallow a single bite. At last the frog said, "Now I've eaten enough and I feel tired. Carry me to your room so I can go to sleep."

The Princess began to cry. It had been hard enough to touch the cold fat frog, and worse still to have him eat out of her plate, but to have him beside her in her little bed was more than she could bear.

"I want to go to bed," repeated the frog. "Take me there and tuck me in."

The Princess shuddered again and looked at her father, but he only said, "He helped you in your trouble. Is it fair to **scorn** him now?"

> **New Word**
> **Scorn** means to disrespect or treat someone or something badly.

There was nothing for her to do but to pick up the creature—she did it with two fingers—and to carry him up into her room, where she dropped him in a corner on the floor, hoping he would be satisfied. But after she had gone to bed, she heard something she didn't like. *Ploppety plop! Ploppety plop!*

It was the frog hopping across the floor, and when he reached her bed he said, "I'm tired and the floor is too hard. I have as much right as you to sleep in a good soft bed. Lift me up or I will tell your father."

At this the Princess was bitterly angry, but she picked him up and put him at the foot-end of her bed. There he stayed all night, but when the dark was graying into daylight, the frog jumped down from the bed, out of the door, and away, she knew not where.

The next night it was the same. The frog came back, knocked at the door, and said:

*Youngest daughter of the King,*
    *Open the door for me.*
*Mind your words at the old well spring;*
    *Open the door for me!*

There was nothing for her to do but let him in. Again he ate out of her golden plate, sipped out of her golden cup, and again he slept at the foot-end of her bed. In the morning he went away as before.

The third night he came again. This time he was not content to sleep at her feet.

"I want to sleep under your pillow," he said. "I think I'd like it better there."

The girl thought she would never be able to sleep with a horrid, damp, goggle-eyed frog under her pillow. She began to weep softly to herself and couldn't stop until at last she cried herself to sleep.

When the night was over and the morning sunlight burst in at the window, the frog crept out from under her pillow and hopped off the bed. But as soon as his feet touched the floor, something happened to him. In that moment he was no longer a cold, fat, goggle-eyed frog but a young Prince with handsome friendly eyes!

"You see," he said, "I wasn't what I seemed to be! A wicked old woman bewitched me. No one but you could break the spell, little Princess, and I waited and waited at the well for you to help me."

The Princess was speechless with surprise but her eyes sparkled.

"And will you let me be your playmate now?" said the Prince, laughing. "Mind your words at the old well spring!"

At this the Princess laughed too, and they both ran out to play with the golden ball.

For years they were the best of friends and the happiest of playmates, and it is not hard to guess, I'm sure, that when they were grown up they were married and lived happily ever after.

> **Make a Connection**
> Do you think the princess is following the advice in the poem "The Frog" on page 35?

## Hansel and Gretel

*(A tale from the Brothers Grimm)*

Once upon a time, near a deep, dark forest, there lived a poor woodcutter with his wife and two children. The boy was named Hansel, and the girl was named Gretel. The family never had very much to eat, and now, when times were hard

and people around the land were starving, the poor woodcutter could not get enough food to feed even his family. As he lay in bed one night, tossing and turning with worry, he turned to his wife and said, "What is going to happen to us? How can we feed our poor children when we haven't got enough for ourselves?"

"Listen to me," said his wife, who was not the children's real mother. She was their stepmother, and she did not care for the children. "Early tomorrow morning," the coldhearted woman said, "we'll take the children deep into the woods. We'll make a fire and give each of them a piece of bread. Then we'll leave them and go about our work. They will never find the way home, and we will be rid of them."

"No!" said the man. "I cannot do that. I cannot leave my children alone in the woods, where the wild animals would swallow them up."

"Then you are a fool," snapped the woman. "You might as well get four coffins ready, for we shall all starve." Then she nagged the poor man, and scolded him, and kept at him until at last he agreed. "But I feel so sorry for the poor children," he said quietly.

The two children were so hungry that they had not been able to sleep, and so they heard everything their stepmother said to their father. Gretel cried, but Hansel whispered, "Don't worry, I will think of something." And when the parents had gone to sleep, Hansel got up, put on his little coat, and sneaked outside. The moon was shining brightly, and the white pebbles that lay in front of the house glittered like silver coins. Hansel stooped and gathered as many pebbles as he could find. Then he tiptoed back to bed and said to Gretel, "Go to sleep, little sister."

At daybreak the woman came and woke the two children. "Get up, you lazybones! We're going to the forest to get some wood." She gave them each a piece of bread and said, "That's for dinner, and you must not eat it before then, because it's all you're going to get."

Gretel carried both pieces of bread in her apron, for Hansel's pockets were full of pebbles. They all started out on their way to the forest. As they walked, Hansel kept turning and looking back at the house, again and again. His father said, "Hansel, what are you looking at? You must watch where you're going."

"Oh," said Hansel, "I'm just looking at my little white kitten, who is sitting on the roof of the house to say goodbye."

The wife said, "You little fool, that's not your kitten. That's just the sun shining on the chimney. Now, come along!"

But Hansel stayed a few steps behind and kept turning, and each time he turned, he dropped a pebble from his pocket to mark the way.

When they were deep in the forest, the father said, "Gather some firewood, children. I'll start a fire so you won't get cold." Hansel and Gretel gathered a little mountain of twigs and sticks, and when the fire was burning, the wife said, "Stay by the fire, you two. We have to go and cut wood. When we're finished, we'll come back to get you." So Hansel and Gretel sat by the fire. After a time, they ate their bread. And after a longer time, they got so tired that they closed their eyes and fell asleep. When they woke, it was dark, and they were all alone. Gretel began to cry, but Hansel comforted her. "Wait a little until the moon rises," he said.

And when the full moon had risen, Hansel took his little sister by the hand and followed the pebbles, which glittered like silver coins and showed them the way. They walked on through the night, and at last, at the break of day, they came to their father's house. They knocked on the door, and when the woman opened it, she was shocked. But she only said, "You naughty children, why did you stay so long in the forest? We thought you were never coming home again." But their father was glad, for it had broken his heart to leave them alone.

Not very long afterward, times were again hard, and there was little food to be eaten. Again the children heard their stepmother say to their father one night in bed, "There's nothing left but half a loaf of bread. After that, we're done for! We must get rid of the children. This time we'll take them so deep in the forest that they'll never find their way back."

"But, wife," said the man, with a heavy heart, "it would be better to share our last bite with the children." But the wife would not listen to him. And, after all, once you've said yes, it's hard to say no. So she kept at him until once again he gave in to her and agreed with her plan.

When the parents were asleep, Hansel got up to collect pebbles. But he couldn't get out—the woman had locked the door! He got back in bed and tried to think of a different plan.

Early the next morning the woman pulled the children out of bed. She gave them a piece of bread, even smaller than before. As they walked into the wood, Hansel broke up the bread in his pocket and often stopped to throw a crumb on the ground.

"Hansel," said his father, "what do you keep stopping and looking back for?"

"I'm looking at my little pigeon that's sitting on the roof and wants to say goodbye to me," answered Hansel.

"Little fool," said the wife, "that's no pigeon. It's only the sun shining on the chimney." So they walked on, and Hansel dropped bread crumbs all along the way.

The woman led the children deep into the forest where they had never been before in all their lives. Again they gathered sticks for a fire, and the woman said, "Sit there, children, and when you are tired, go to sleep. We're going to cut wood, and when we're finished, we'll come get you."

Later, when it was noon, Gretel shared her small piece of bread with Hansel, since he had left his in crumbs along the road. Then they fell asleep, and as evening came, no one came to get them. When they woke, it was dark and they were alone. When the moon rose, they started for home, but they could not find the bread crumbs, for the birds had eaten them up. "Come, Gretel," said Hansel, "I know we can find our way." But they didn't find it. They went on all night, and the next day from morning until evening, but they could not find their way out of the forest. They were terribly hungry, for they had nothing to eat but a few berries. And when they were so tired that they could drag themselves no farther, they lay down under a tree and fell asleep.

It was now the third morning since they had left their father's house. They started on again, always looking for the way home but instead only getting deeper into the forest. Unless help came soon, they would surely die of hunger.

About noon they saw a pretty snow-white bird sitting on a branch and singing so beautifully that they stopped to listen. Then the bird spread its wings and flew before them, as though to say, "Follow me!" And so the children followed the bird until they came to a little house. The bird flew up and perched on the roof. And then the children saw that the walls of the house were made of gingerbread, and the roof was made of cake, and the windows of clear sugar candy.

"Let's eat!" cried Hansel. Hansel reached up and broke off a piece of the roof, while Gretel chewed on a wall.

Suddenly they heard a thin, screechy voice call out from inside the house:

*"Nibble, nibble, like a mouse,*
*Who is nibbling at my house?"*

The children answered,

*"It's only the air heaving a sigh.*
*It's only the wind passing by."*

And they were so hungry that they went on eating. But then the door opened, and a very old woman came out, leaning on a crutch. Hansel and Gretel were so frightened that they dropped the food from their hands. But the old woman just nodded her head and said, "My dear little children, what has brought you here? Come inside and stay with me. I'll take good care of you."

So she took them by the hand and led them into her little house. There they found a wonderful meal of hot pancakes, with honey, nuts, apples, and cold milk. After that, the old woman showed them two little white beds, and Hansel and Gretel lay down and wondered if they were in heaven.

Now, the old woman seemed kind, but in fact she was a wicked witch. She had built her house just to trap little children, and once she had them, she would cook them and eat them! She had bad eyes and could not see well, but she could smell as well as any animal, and earlier in the day she had sniffed Hansel and Gretel coming near.

The next morning, before the children were awake, the witch got up and looked at their rosy cheeks. "Mmm, what a fine meal I will have," she cackled. Then she dragged Hansel out of bed and locked him in a cage outside. Then she went back and shook Gretel awake and shouted, "Get up, lazybones! Fetch water, and cook something nice for your brother. Feed him well, for once he's nice and fat, I will eat him!"

Gretel screamed and cried, but it was no use. She had to do what the wicked witch said. Day after day she cooked pots full of rich food for Hansel, while she herself ate nothing but crumbs. Every morning the wicked witch would creep to the cage and say, "Hansel, stick out your finger so I can tell if you are fat enough to cook." But clever Hansel held out a little bone, and the old woman, who had bad eyes, couldn't tell that it wasn't Hansel's finger. She wondered why he wasn't getting any fatter. And when four weeks had passed and Hansel seemed as thin as ever, she lost patience. "Hurry up and get some water," she snarled at Gretel. "Be he fat or thin, I'm going to cook him and eat him."

The tears ran down poor Gretel's cheeks as she fetched water and lit the fire. "First we will bake," said the old woman. "I've heated the oven, and the dough is ready." Then she pushed poor Gretel toward the oven, where the flames were burning brightly. "Stick your head in," the witch said to Gretel, "and tell me if it's hot enough for us to bake the bread." But Gretel knew what the witch had in mind: She knew that the witch meant to shut her in the oven, and bake her, and eat her! So Gretel said, "I don't know how to do it. Where do I look in? Could you show me how?"

"You stupid goose!" cried the old woman. "There's a big opening, don't you see? Why, I could fit in myself!" And she stuck her head in the oven. Then Gretel rushed up and, with all her might, pushed the witch into the oven. She shut the iron door and locked it tight. Gretel did not stay to hear the witch's howls and shrieks. She ran right to Hansel and let him out of the cage.

"Come, Hansel, we are free!" she cried. "The old witch is dead!" Hansel sprang out and hugged Gretel, and the children danced for joy. Then, since they had nothing to fear, they went back inside the witch's house. There they found chests full of pearls and precious jewels. "These are better than pebbles!" laughed Hansel as he filled his pockets, while Gretel filled her apron.

"Now, away we go," said Hansel. Then he said quietly, "If only we can find our way out of the witch's wood."

When they had walked for a few hours, they came to a wide lake. "There's no bridge, and no stepping-stones," said Hansel. "We can't get across."

"And there's no boat either," said Gretel. "But look," she said. "Here comes a duck. I will ask her for help." So she called out,

*"Duck, duck, here we stand,*
*Hansel and Gretel on the land.*
*Stepping-stones and bridge we lack,*
*Carry us over on your nice soft back."*

And, lo and behold, the duck came over. Hansel got on her back and told Gretel to sit behind him. "No," said Gretel, "that would be too hard on the duck. Let us go across one at a time."

And so that is how they did it. When they were on the other side, they walked on for a little while and soon found a path. The forest began to look more and more familiar. At last, in the distance, they saw their father's house. They began to run as fast as they could. They burst through the door and cried out, "Father! We're home!" Then they threw themselves upon him.

Since he had left the children in the wood, the man had been worried sick. And as for his mean wife—well, she had died. Now he hugged his children as though he would never let them go. As he squeezed Gretel to him, the pearls and jewels fell from her apron. Then Hansel reached into his pockets and pulled out handful after handful of treasure.

They were together again, their troubles were over, and they lived in perfect happiness for a long, long time.

## In Which Tigger Comes to the Forest and Has Breakfast

*(A selection from* The House at Pooh Corner *by A. A. Milne)*

**PARENTS:** If your children have not yet met the bear named Winnie-the-Pooh and his friends in the Hundred Acre Wood, you might first want to read to them from the book called *Winnie-the-Pooh* by A. A. Milne (a chapter from which is included in *What Your Kindergartner Needs to Know*).

Winnie-the-Pooh woke up suddenly in the middle of the night and listened. Then he got out of bed, and lit his candle, and stumped across the room to see if anybody was trying to get into his honey-cupboard, and they weren't, so he stumped back again, blew out his candle, and got into bed. Then he heard the noise again.

"Is that you, Piglet?" he said.

But it wasn't.

"Come in, Christopher Robin," he said.

But Christopher Robin didn't.

"Tell me about it tomorrow, Eeyore," said Pooh sleepily.

But the noise went on.

"*Worraworraworraworraworra,*" said Whatever-it-was, and Pooh found that he wasn't asleep after all.

"What can it be?" he thought. "There are lots of noises in the Forest, but this is a different one. It isn't a growl, and it isn't a purr, and it isn't a bark, and it isn't a noise-you-make-before-beginning-a-piece-of-poetry, but it's a noise of some kind, made by a strange animal. And he's making it outside my door. So I shall get up and ask him not to do it."

He got out of bed and opened his front door.

"Hallo!" said Pooh, in case there was anything outside.

"Hallo!" said Whatever-it-was.

"Oh!" said Pooh. "Hallo!"

"Hallo!"

"Oh, there you are!" said Pooh. "Hallo!"

"Hallo!" said the Strange Animal, wondering how long this was going on.

Pooh was just going to say "Hallo!" for the fourth time when he thought that he wouldn't, so he said: "Who is it?" instead.

"Me," said a voice.

"Oh!" said Pooh. "Well, come here."

So Whatever-it-was came here, and in the light of the candle he and Pooh looked at each other.

"I'm Pooh," said Pooh.

"I'm Tigger," said Tigger.

"Oh!" said Pooh, for he had never seen an animal like this before. "Does Christopher Robin know about you?"

"Of course he does," said Tigger.

"Well," said Pooh, "it's the middle of the night, which is a good time for going to sleep. And tomorrow morning we'll have some honey for breakfast. Do Tiggers like honey?"

"They like everything," said Tigger cheerfully.

"Then if they like going to sleep on the floor, I'll go back to bed," said Pooh, "and we'll do things in the morning. Good night." And he got back into bed and went fast asleep.

When he awoke in the morning, the first thing he saw was Tigger, sitting in front of the glass and looking at himself.

"Hallo!" said Pooh.

"Hallo!" said Tigger. "I've found somebody just like me. I thought I was the only one of them."

Pooh got out of bed, and began to explain what a looking-glass was, but just as he was getting to the interesting part, Tigger said:

"Excuse me a moment, but there's something climbing up your table," and with one loud *Worraworraworraworraworra* he jumped at the end of the tablecloth, pulled it to the ground, wrapped himself up in it three times, rolled to the other end of the room, and, after a terrible struggle, got his head into the daylight again, and said cheerfully: "Have I won?"

"That's my tablecloth," said Pooh, as he began to unwind Tigger.

"I wondered what it was," said Tigger.

"It goes on the table and you put things on it."

"Then why did it try to bite me when I wasn't looking?"

"I don't *think* it did," said Pooh.

"It tried," said Tigger, "but I was too quick for it."

Pooh put the cloth back on the table, and he put a large honey-pot on the cloth, and they sat down to breakfast. And as soon as they sat down, Tigger took a large mouthful of honey . . . and he looked up at the ceiling with his head on one side, and made exploring noises with his tongue and considering noises, and *what-have-we-got-here* noises . . . and then he said in a very decided voice:

"Tiggers don't like honey."

"Oh!" said Pooh, and tried to make it sound Sad and Regretful. "I thought they liked everything."

"Everything except honey," said Tigger.

Pooh felt rather pleased about this, and said that, as soon as he had finished his own breakfast, he would take Tigger round to Piglet's house, and Tigger could try some of Piglet's haycorns.

"Thank you, Pooh," said Tigger, "because haycorns is really what Tiggers like best."

So after breakfast they went round to see Piglet, and Pooh explained as they went that Piglet was a Very Small Animal who didn't like bouncing, and asked Tigger not to be too Bouncy just at first. And Tigger, who had been hiding behind trees and jumping out on Pooh's shadow when it wasn't looking, said that Tiggers were only bouncy before breakfast, and that as soon as they had had a few haycorns they became Quiet and Refined. So by and by they knocked at the door of Piglet's house.

"Hallo, Pooh," said Piglet.

"Hallo, Piglet. This is Tigger."

"Oh, is it?" said Piglet, and he edged round to the other side of the table. "I thought Tiggers were smaller than that."

"Not the big ones," said Tigger.

"They like haycorns," said Pooh, "so that's what we've come for, because poor Tigger hasn't had any breakfast yet."

Piglet pushed the bowl of haycorns towards Tigger, and said: "Help yourself," and then he got close up to Pooh and felt much braver, and said, "So you're Tigger? Well, well!" in a careless sort of voice. But Tigger said nothing because his mouth was full of haycorns. . . .

After a long munching noise he said:

"Ee-eers o I a-ors."

And when Pooh and Piglet said "What?" he said "Skoos ee," and went outside for a moment.

When he came back he said firmly:

"Tiggers don't like haycorns."

"But you said they liked everything except honey," said Pooh.

"Everything except honey and haycorns," explained Tigger.

When he heard this Pooh said, "Oh, I see!" and Piglet, who was rather glad that Tiggers didn't like haycorns, said, "What about thistles?"

"Thistles," said Tigger, "is what Tiggers like best."

"Then let's go along and see Eeyore," said Piglet.

So the three of them went; and after they had walked and walked and walked, they came to the part of the Forest where Eeyore was.

"Hallo, Eeyore!" said Pooh. "This is Tigger."

"What is?" said Eeyore.

"This," explained Pooh and Piglet together, and Tigger smiled his happiest smile and said nothing.

Eeyore walked all round Tigger one way, and then turned and walked all round him the other way.

"What did you say it was?" he asked.

"Tigger."

"Ah!" said Eeyore.

"He's just come," explained Piglet.

"Ah!" said Eeyore again.

He thought for a long time and then said:

"When is he going?"

Pooh explained to Eeyore that Tigger was a great friend of Christopher Robin's, who had come to stay in the Forest, and Piglet explained to Tigger that he mustn't mind what Eeyore said because he was *always* gloomy; and Eeyore explained to Piglet that, on the contrary, he was feeling particularly cheerful this morning; and Tigger explained to anybody who was listening that he hadn't had any breakfast yet.

"I knew there was something," said Pooh. "Tiggers always eat thistles, so that was why we came to see you, Eeyore."

"Don't mention it, Pooh."

"Oh, Eeyore, I didn't quite mean that I didn't want to see you—"

"Quite—quite. But your new stripy friend—naturally, he wants his breakfast. What did you say his name was?"

"Tigger."

"Then come this way, Tigger."

Eeyore led the way to the most thistly-looking patch of thistles that ever was, and waved a hoof at it.

"A little patch I was keeping for my birthday," he said; "but, after all, what are birthdays? Here today and gone tomorrow. Help yourself, Tigger."

Tigger thanked him and looked a little anxiously at Pooh.

"Are these really thistles?" he whispered.

"Yes," said Pooh.

"What Tiggers like best?"

"That's right," said Pooh.

"I see," said Tigger.

So he took a large mouthful, and he gave a large crunch.

"*Ow!*" said Tigger.

He sat down and put his paw in his mouth.

"What's the matter?" asked Pooh.

"*Hot!*" mumbled Tigger.

"Your friend," said Eeyore, "appears to have bitten on a bee."

Pooh's friend stopped shaking his head to get the prickles out, and explained that Tiggers didn't like thistles.

"Then why bend a perfectly good one?" asked Eeyore.

"But you said," began Pooh—"you *said* that Tiggers liked everything except honey and haycorns."

"*And* thistles," said Tigger, who was now running round in circles with his tongue hanging out.

Pooh looked at him sadly.

"What are we going to do?" he asked Piglet.

Piglet knew the answer to that, and he said at once that they must go and see Christopher Robin.

"You'll find him with Kanga," said Eeyore. He came close to Pooh, and said in a loud whisper:

"*Could* you ask your friend to do his exercises somewhere else? I shall be having lunch directly, and don't want it bounced on just before I begin. A trifling matter, and fussy of me, but we all have our little ways."

Pooh nodded solemnly and called to Tigger.

"Come along and we'll go and see Kanga. She's sure to have lots of breakfast for you."

Tigger finished his last circle and came up to Pooh and Piglet.

"Hot!" he explained with a large and friendly smile. "Come on!" and he rushed off.

Pooh and Piglet walked slowly after him. And as they walked Piglet said nothing, because he couldn't think of anything, and Pooh said nothing, because he was thinking of a poem. And when he had thought of it he began:

*What shall we do about poor little Tigger?*
*If he never eats nothing he'll never get bigger.*
*He doesn't like honey and haycorns and thistles*
*Because of the taste and because of the bristles.*
*And all the good things which an animal likes*
*Have the wrong sort of swallow or too many spikes.*

"He's quite big enough anyhow," said Piglet.

"He isn't *really* very big."

"Well, he *seems* so."

Pooh was thoughtful when he heard this, and then he murmured to himself:

*But whatever his weight in pounds, shillings, and ounces,*
*He always seems bigger because of his bounces.*

"And that's the whole poem," he said. "Do you like it, Piglet?"

"All except the shillings," said Piglet. "I don't think they ought to be there."

"They wanted to come in after the pounds," explained Pooh, "so I let them. It is the best way to write poetry, letting things come."

"Oh, I didn't know," said Piglet.

Tigger had been bouncing in front of them all this time, turning round every now and then to ask, "Is this the way?"—and now at last they came in sight of Kanga's house, and there was Christopher Robin. Tigger rushed up to him.

"Oh, there you are, Tigger!" said Christopher Robin. "I knew you'd be somewhere."

"I've been finding things in the Forest," said Tigger importantly. "I've found a pooh and a piglet and an eeyore, but I can't find any breakfast."

Pooh and Piglet came up and hugged Christopher Robin, and explained what had been happening.

"Don't *you* know what Tiggers like?" asked Pooh.

"I expect if I thought very hard I should," said Christopher Robin, "but I thought Tigger knew."

"I do," said Tigger. "Everything there is in the world except honey and hay-corns and—what were those hot things called?"

"Thistles."

"Yes, and those."

"Oh, well then, Kanga can give you some breakfast."

So they went into Kanga's house, and when Roo had said "Hallo, Pooh" and "Hallo, Piglet" once, and "Hallo, Tigger" twice, because he had never said it before and it sounded funny, they told Kanga what they wanted, and Kanga said very kindly, "Well, look in my cupboard, Tigger dear, and see what you'd like." Because she knew at once that, however big Tigger seemed to be, he wanted as much kindness as Roo.

"Shall I look, too?" said Pooh, who was beginning to feel a little eleven o'clockish. And he found a small tin of condensed milk, and something seemed to tell him that Tiggers didn't like this, so he took it into a corner by itself, and went with it to see that nobody interrupted it.

But the more Tigger put his nose into this and his paw into that, the more things he found which Tiggers didn't like. And when he found everything in the cupboard, and couldn't eat any of it, he said to Kanga, "What happens now?"

But Kanga and Christopher Robin and Piglet were all standing round Roo, watching him have his Extract of Malt. And Roo was saying, "Must I?" and Kanga was saying, "Now, Roo dear, you remember what you promised."

"What is it?" whispered Tigger to Piglet.

"His Strengthening Medicine," said Piglet. "He hates it."

So Tigger came closer, and he leant over the back of Roo's chair, and suddenly he put out his tongue, and took one large golollop, and, with a sudden jump of surprise, Kanga said, "Oh!" and then clutched at the spoon again just as it was disappearing, and pulled it safely back out of Tigger's mouth. But the Extract of Malt had gone.

"Tigger *dear*!" said Kanga.

"He's taken my medicine, he's taken my medicine, he's taken my medicine!" sang Roo happily, thinking it was a tremendous joke.

Then Tigger looked up at the ceiling, and closed his eyes, and his tongue went round and round his chops, in case he had left any outside, and a peaceful smile came over his face as he said, "So *that's* what Tiggers like!"

Which explains why he always lived at Kanga's house afterwards, and had Extract of Malt for breakfast, dinner, and tea. And sometimes, when Kanga thought he wanted strengthening, he had a spoonful or two of Roo's breakfast after meals as medicine.

"But *I* think," said Piglet to Pooh, "that he's been strengthened quite enough."

## Issun Boshi: One-Inch Boy

**PARENTS:** "Issun Boshi" [IH-soon BOH-she] is a folktale from Japan. If you have access to a world map or globe, help your child locate Japan. Like the next story in this book, "Tom Thumb," this story is about the adventures of a very little person.

Long ago in a village in Japan, there lived an old man and his wife. More than anything else in the world, they wanted to have a child. They hoped and they wished. They went to the temple and prayed to the gods. "May we be blessed with a child," they said, "even if he is no larger than our thumbs."

Eventually their prayers were answered. In nine months' time, a fine baby boy was born to the old couple. The child was lovely but very small. They called him Issun Boshi, which means "One-Inch Boy," for he was no taller than his father's thumb.

Issun Boshi grew up to be strong, smart, and helpful. However, he never grew any bigger. When he was twelve he went to his parents and said, "Father and Mother, please give me your permission to go to the capital city, for I wish to see the world, learn about life, and make a name for myself."

His parents were worried. They were scared to think of all the bad things that could happen to Issun Boshi in such a large city. However, they knew their boy was smart and strong, so in the end they agreed to let him go. They made him a tiny spear out of a sewing needle. They also gave him a rice bowl for a boat and some chopsticks for oars.

Issun Boshi floated down the river in his rice bowl. When the waters were rough, he used the chopsticks to help keep his balance. He used his sword to catch fish. In a few days he arrived in the city of Kyoto. "My, what a busy place this is!" he thought. "So many people crammed into so little space!" Issun Boshi made his way through the streets, dodging feet and cart wheels. He kept walking until he came to a beautiful house, the largest in the city. Near the entrance to this house sat a pair of wooden shoes. They belonged to the owner of the house, who was the wealthiest lord in the city.

The door of the great house opened. The owner of the house stepped out and slipped his feet into the wooden shoes. Issun Boshi called out, "Hello! Hello there!" The man looked around and, seeing no one, began to walk away. But

Issun Boshi called out, "Down here! I'm down here, near your shoes! Please be careful or you might step on me." The man leaned down and squinted until he caught sight of Issun Boshi. Issun Boshi bowed and politely introduced himself. "My name," he said, "is Issun Boshi. I have just arrived in the city, and I would like to work for you."

The lord picked Issun Boshi up and held him in the palm of his hand. In a friendly voice he asked, "But what can a little fellow like you do?"

Issun Boshi saw that a fly was buzzing around and bothering the lord. He reached for his sewing-needle spear. Then, *zing*! He impaled the fly on his spear.

"You are quite an impressive little fellow!" laughed the lord. "Come! I will hire you to work in my house."

And so, tiny Issun Boshi went to work for the noble lord in his big, beautiful house. He made friends with everyone there, especially the princess, the lord's lovely daughter. It seemed that Issun Boshi was always at her side, helping her in whatever way he could. He would hold down the paper when she wrote a letter and ride on her shoulder when she went for a walk in the beautiful gardens behind the house. In time, the princess came to feel a strong affection for her little helper.

In the spring, Issun Boshi traveled with the princess and her companions to the cherry blossom festival. On their way home, they heard strange grunting noises in the woods. They could see nothing in the shadows, then, suddenly, a huge monster leaped into their path.

Everyone screamed and ran—everyone except Issun Boshi and the princess.

"Who are you?" cried Issun Boshi. "And what do you want?"

"I am an oni [OH-nee]," growled the monster.

Issun Boshi knew all about the oni. They were demonic monsters, and the Japanese people were very afraid of them.

But Issun Boshi was not afraid. He stepped forward and shouted, "Get out of the way, you demon! I am here to guard the princess. Step back!"

"Ha! We'll see about that!" growled the oni. Then he snatched up Issun Boshi, popped him into his mouth, and—*gulp*—swallowed him whole. Down, down Issun Boshi slid until he landed—*plop*—in the oni's stomach.

"You should be more careful about what you eat," shouted Issun Boshi. Then he pulled out his sewing-needle sword and began to jab it into the side of the oni's stomach.

"Ow! Ooh! Agh!" shouted the oni. Then he gave a loud burp, and out popped Issun Boshi! The oni ran away, burping as he ran.

Issun Boshi went to check on the princess. She was bending down and picking something up from the ground. "Look!" she called out. "The oni was so scared that he dropped this magic hammer. If you make a wish on it, it will come true."

Issun Boshi bowed to the princess and said, "My lady, I would ask that you make a wish."

"No, Issun Boshi," said the princess. "You have served me bravely, and your bravery has won you this prize. Make a wish!"

Issun Boshi took the hammer and said, "I already have my greatest wish, which is to serve you. But if I could have another wish, I would wish to be as tall as other people."

Then he gave the hammer to the princess, who made a silent wish on it herself. Then and there, Issun Boshi began to grow taller. He grew and grew—and the princess soon found herself looking up at a handsome young man, several inches taller than her.

That night the princess told her father how brave Issun Boshi had been, and how he had risked his life to save her. The noble lord was so happy that he gave Issun Boshi permission to marry the princess. And so, you see, the princess's wish came true, too.

Issun Boshi's brave deeds were celebrated throughout the land. He and the princess lived happily together, along with Issun Boshi's proud and happy parents, whom Issun Boshi had brought to the lord's house to be part of his new family.

# Tom Thumb

**PARENTS:** People in many lands tell different stories about the little fellow called Tom Thumb. This version is from Germany, as collected by the Brothers Grimm. You might find it interesting to read this story to your child along with the previous story, a folktale from Japan called "Issun Boshi" (One-Inch Boy). At the end of this story, you'll find suggestions for reading other similar stories from different lands.

There was once a poor farmer who used to sit and poke at the fire while his wife sat at her spinning wheel. Night after night the man would let out a big sigh and say, "How sad it is that we have no children. Our house is so quiet, while other people's houses are so noisy and cheerful."

"Yes, it's true," said the wife. "If only we had a child. Why, I would be happy to have one no bigger than my thumb."

Some time after this, she had a little boy, who was strong and healthy in every way—and he was no bigger than a thumb. The man and woman said, "Small as he is, we will love him dearly." They named him Tom Thumb. And as Tom grew up, he proved to be a very clever lad.

One day, as Tom's father was getting ready to go to the forest to cut wood, he said, "I wish there was someone to bring the horse and cart to meet me."

"I'll do it!" said Tom.

"But how can you?" his father laughed. "You're much too small even to hold the reins."

"Never mind that, Father," said Tom. "Ask Mother to harness the horse, then I'll sit in the horse's ear and tell him which way to go." And so his mother harnessed the horse and put Tom in the horse's ear. Tom called out, "Giddy-up." The horse started walking.

Now it happened that as the horse and cart turned a corner, two strange men were walking by, and one of them heard Tom calling out directions to the horse.

"Look," he said to his friend, "there goes a wagon, and the driver is calling to his horse, but the driver is nowhere to be seen!"

"Let's follow and see where it goes," said his friend.

So they followed the horse and wagon to the place where Tom's father was chopping wood. When Tom Thumb caught sight of his father, he cried out, "Whoa, boy! Look, Father, here I am with the wagon. Now, help me down, please."

Tom's father lifted his son down out of the horse's ear and set him on a stump. When the two strangers saw this, one of them turned to the other and whispered, "Look here, that little fellow could make us rich! Let's take him to town and charge people money to see him." So they went up to Tom's father and said, "See here, how about selling the little man to us? We'll pay you well, and we'll take good care of him."

But Tom's father said, "No! He is the apple of my eye, and I would not part with him for all the money in the world."

Tom, however, crept up the folds of his father's coat to his shoulder, then whispered in his ear, "Go ahead, Father, sell me to them for a lot of money. Let them take me, and I'll be back in no time."

"But, Tom—" his father began.

"Trust me, Father," Tom broke in. "I'll take care of everything."

So his father sold Tom for a great deal of money. Off went Tom, riding on the brim of one man's hat. As evening fell, Tom asked to be put down, but the man refused. Tom insisted loudly, "I need to get down, now!" So the man set him down by the roadside. And as soon as he did, Tom scooted away and slipped into a mouse hole, crying out, "So long, my good fellows, have a good trip without me!" The men got down on their hands and knees and put their noses to the ground and poked sticks into mouse holes, but they never found Tom. So, angry and penniless, they made their way home.

When the men were gone, Tom came out of the mouse hole. He found an empty snail shell and said, "This looks like a safe place to spend the night." But just as he settled down to rest, he heard two men walking by. One said to the other, in a rough whispering voice, "Yes, the rich parson won't be back until to-morrow morning, so now is the time to rob his house. But how can we do it?"

Tom sprang out of his shell and shouted, "I can tell you!"

"Who was that?" asked one of the frightened robbers. "Come out and show yourself," he said.

"Take me with you and I'll help you," said Tom.

"Who's talking? Where are you?" asked the robbers.

"Down here!" cried Tom.

The robbers looked down, and there they saw Tom, waving and calling to them. One robber lifted him up and said, "Well, little elf, how are you going to help us rob the parson?"

"It will be easy," said Tom. "The parson keeps his money behind iron bars, right? I can slip between the bars and hand out to you as much money as you want."

"Hee-hee, that's a fine idea, little elf," said the robbers, and they snickered all the way to the parson's house. Then they fell quiet and whispered to Tom, "Speak softly, y'hear? We don't want to wake up anyone and get caught!"

"Of course!" said Tom. He sneaked into the parson's room, then slipped between the bars where the money was kept. Then he called out to the robbers, in just as big and loud a voice as he could manage, "HOW MUCH DO YOU WANT? DO YOU WANT IT ALL?"

"Shh, quiet!" hissed the robbers. "You'll wake the dead, you noisy little elf. We can hear you fine. Just start handing out the money."

But Tom pretended not to hear them, and once again he shouted, "WHAT'S

THAT YOU SAY? YOU WANT TO TAKE ALL THE MONEY? I'LL GIVE YOU EVERYTHING, JUST HOLD OUT YOUR HANDS."

Tom's shouts were loud enough to wake the cook and the maid, who jumped out of bed and came running to see what was the matter. When the cook and the maid burst through the door, the robbers ran as though wild animals were after them. The maid went to get a light, but by the time she came back with it, Tom Thumb had slipped away to the barn.

Tom found a nice place to sleep in a big pile of hay. He settled down to rest but—poor Tom!—his troubles had just begun. Early the next morning the maid came to the barn and pitched a large bundle of hay to the cow for breakfast. And who should be in the middle of that bundle of hay but Tom! The cow ate up the hay and Tom with it. He was lucky not to be crushed between her teeth. After she chewed awhile, she swallowed, and down went Tom to the cow's stomach.

"Goodness me," he said, "somebody forgot to put any windows in this house. It would be nice to have a candle, not to mention some fresh air!" Suddenly, *whump!*, something heavy fell on Tom's head. It was a lump of wet, sticky, chewed hay! The cow was eating again, and the more she ate, the more wet, sticky hay fell on Tom. He was almost squashed when he thought to call out, as loud as he could, "That's enough! No more hay! I'm quite full, thank you! I don't need any more food now!"

The maid happened to be milking the cow at this time, and when she heard the voice come out of the cow, she let out a scream and fell backward off her milking stool, knocking over the bucket of milk. She ran to the parson and said, "Oh, good sir, the cow—the cow has spoken!"

"What? Don't be silly," said the parson. He went to the barn to see for himself what was happening, and the maid walked fearfully behind him.

The parson looked at the cow and said, "So, this is the talking cow? Well, I don't hear anything." But just at that moment Tom shouted, "Thanks for the hay, but I'm quite full now. Perhaps I'll have dessert later!"

The parson jumped back. "Surely this animal is bewitched!" he cried. And so he ordered that the unlucky cow be made into steaks and ground beef. When the cow was cut up, the stomach, with Tom in it, was thrown onto a garbage heap. Tom struggled to get out, and he had just managed to poke out his head when, *zing*, a hungry wolf snapped up the stomach in his teeth and ran off with it.

As the wolf ran, Tom bounced along and thought, "Well, some days are better than others." Then he said to the wolf, "Mr. Wolf, why do you want to eat this nasty old cow stomach? I can tell you where to find some delicious treats."

"And where might that be?" growled the wolf.

"In a house near the forest," said Tom. "There you'll find sausages, ham, beef, cakes, as much as you can possibly eat." So the wolf, his mouth watering, went where Tom told him. And where do you think Tom was taking him? Back to his mother and father's house!

When they got there, the wolf ate until he was stuffed. That's when Tom called out to his parents, "Help! Help! There's a big bad wolf in here! Help!"

Tom's father came running with a big stick. He whacked the wolf and sent him howling into the woods. "Good work, Father," said Tom.

His father looked down and cried out, "Tom, where have you been? I've been so worried about you! Mother, come quick, our Tom is back!"

"Well," said Tom, "I've been in a mouse hole, and a snail's shell, and a cow's stomach. And I think that from now on I would rather stay with you!"

"Oh, my little Tom," said his father, "I never should have sold you, and I never will again!"

For Tom, there were plenty of hugs and kisses, and lots of food and drink, and even some new clothes, for, as you may well imagine, his old ones had been spoiled by his adventures.

> **Talk and Think**
> You may want to talk with your child about how stories from different lands can be alike in many ways. After reading "Issun Boshi" and "Tom Thumb," you might begin by asking your child if she noticed some ways the two stories are alike.

**PARENTS:** For similar stories from different lands, check your library for titles such as:

*The Egyptian Cinderella* and *The Korean Cinderella* by Shirley Climo, illustrated by Ruth Heller (HarperCollins, 1989 and 1993).

*Lon Po Po: A Red Riding Hood Story from China* by Ed Young (Philomel Books, 1989; also available from Scholastic).

*Mufaro's Beautiful Daughters: An African Tale* by John Steptoe (Lothrop, Lee & Shepard, 1987). A "Cinderella" story from Africa.

*Sootface: An Ojibwa Cinderella Story* by Robert D. San Souci (Doubleday Books for Young Readers, 1994).

*Thumbelina* by Amy Ehrlich (Penguin/Puffin, 1979). A Hans Christian Andersen story, here beautifully illustrated by Susan Jeffers.

*Tom Thumb* by Richard Jesse Watson (Harcourt Brace, 1989). A "Tom Thumb" story from England, different from the Tom Thumb character in this book.

## The Crowded, Noisy House

Once there was a poor Jewish man who went to speak with his rabbi.

"Rabbi," the man said, "you must help me. My life is terrible. I live with my wife, our five children, and my mother-in-law. There is only one room for all eight of us. The children, they cry and fight. My wife, she screams a lot. My mother-in-law, she **kvetches** about everything. It is crowded and noisy and horrible, I tell you. Honestly, Rabbi, I don't think it could be any worse!"

**New Word**

Do you know what "kvetches" means? It means to grumble and complain all the time.

The rabbi rubbed his chin thoughtfully for a few moments. Then he spoke. "My son," he said, "if you will promise to do as I tell you, your life will get better. Will you promise?"

"Yes, yes!" said the man. "I promise."

"Tell me," said the rabbi, "do you own any animals?"

"Yes," said the man, "I have a goat—"

"Good!" said the rabbi. "Go home and take the goat into your house. Let it eat and sleep with you for a few days."

The man was stunned. Take the goat into the house? The rabbi's advice sounded like a crazy idea. But everyone knew the rabbi was a wise man, and so the poor man agreed to do what he said. He went home and led the goat into his house.

**Make a Connection**

Read more about rabbis and the Jewish religion on pages 183–88.

Two days later, the man went back to the rabbi.

"Oy vey!" he said. "I did as you said. I brought my goat into the house, and now things are even worse than before. The children, they cry and fight. My wife, she screams a lot. My mother-in-law, she *kvetches* about everything. The goat, she butts us with her head and knocks the dishes off the shelves. Help me, Rabbi. I don't think it could be any worse!"

The rabbi sat quietly for a moment. Then he asked the man, "Do you have any other animals?"

"Yes," said the man. "I have a cow—"

"Good!" said the rabbi. "Go home and take the cow into your house. Let it eat and sleep with you for a few days."

Again, the man did as he was told. He went home and led the cow into his house.

Two days later, the man went back to see the rabbi.

"Oy vey!" he moaned. "I did as you said. I brought the cow into the house, and things are even worse than before. The children, they cry and fight. My wife, she screams a lot. My mother-in-law, she *kvetches* about everything. The goat, she butts us with her head and knocks the dishes off the shelves. The cow, she eats our clothing. The house is like a barn! We can't sleep for all of the bleating and moo- ing! Help me, Rabbi. I don't think it could be any worse!"

The rabbi was silent for a few moments. Then he asked, "Do you have any other animals?"

"Well," said the man, "I have a goose."

"Perfect!" said the rabbi. "Go home and take the goose into your house. Let it eat and sleep with you."

Two days later, the man went back to the rabbi.

"Oy vey!" he groaned. "Things are worse than ever! The children, they cry and fight. My wife, she screams a lot. My mother-in-law, she *kvetches* about everything. The goat, she butts us with her head and knocks the dishes off the shelves. The cow, she eats our clothing. The goose, he honks and poops all over the floor. I tell you, Rabbi, it is wrong for a man to eat and sleep with animals. I don't think it could be any worse!"

"My son," said the rabbi in a gentle voice, "you are right. Go home and take the animals out of your house. You will find the answer."

The next day the man came running to the rabbi.

"Rabbi!" he cried, his face beaming. "You have made life sweet for me. Now that all the animals are outside, the house is so quiet, so roomy, and so clean! How wonderful!"

## Jack and the Beanstalk

Once upon a time there was a poor widow who had an only son named Jack and a cow named Milky-white. All they had to live on was the milk the cow gave every morning, which they carried to the market and sold. But one morning Milky-white gave no milk.

"Oh, Jack," said the poor widow, wringing her hands, "we have nothing to eat and no money. We must sell poor Milky-white."

"Cheer up, Mother," said Jack. "It's market day today. I'll sell Milky-white, then we'll be better off, you'll see."

So Jack took the cow and started down the road. He had not gone far when he met a strange-looking old man. The old man said, "Good morning, Jack."

"Good morning to you," said Jack, and wondered how the old man knew his name.

"Well, Jack, where are you off to?" said the man.

"I'm going to market to sell our cow here."

"Oh, yes, you look like just the sort of fellow to sell a cow," said the man. "Now, I wonder," he asked Jack, "do you know how many beans make five?"

Jack thought this was a strange question, but he answered anyway. "Two beans in each hand, and one bean in your mouth—that makes five."

"Right you are!" said the old man. And then, pulling something out of his pocket, he said, "And here they are." He held out five very strange-looking beans. "Now, because you're such a smart fellow," he said to Jack, "I will trade you these beans for your cow."

"Well, now," said Jack, "that would be a nice trade for you!"

"Ah, but you don't know what kind of beans these are," said the man. "If you plant them tonight, then by morning they'll grow right up to the sky."

"Really?" said Jack, who was beginning to get interested.

"Yes," said the man. "And if it doesn't turn out to be true, then you can have your cow back."

"All right, then," said Jack. He gave the man the cow, and took the beans, and went home.

"Jack, are you back already?" said his mother. "I see you've sold Milky-white. How much did you get for her?"

"Mother, you'll never guess," said Jack.

"Oh, you good boy!" said his mother. "Did you get five? Or ten? Maybe even—no, it can't be—twenty?"

"I told you you couldn't guess!" said Jack. Then, reaching into his pocket, he said, "See here, Mother. I got five . . . beans. You plant them and overnight they—"

"What!" cried his mother. "Beans! You gave away my Milky-white for beans? How could you be such a fool? Off to bed with you, and no supper. And as for your precious beans, here they go, out the window!"

So Jack went to his little attic room, where he flopped down and finally fell asleep.

When he woke up, the room looked funny. The sun was shining into part of it, but all the rest was dark and shady. He jumped up and went to the window. And what do you think he saw? Why, the beans his mother had thrown out the

window had landed in the garden, and overnight they had sprung up into a big beanstalk, which went up and up and up till it reached the sky. So the old man had been telling the truth!

The beanstalk grew up close to Jack's window. All he had to do was step out onto it and then start climbing it, like a ladder. So Jack climbed, and he climbed and he climbed and he climbed and he climbed and he climbed till at last he reached the sky. And when he got there, he saw a long straight road. He followed the road until he came to a great big tall house, and on the doorstep there was a great big tall woman.

"Good morning, ma'am," said Jack, quite politely. "Could you be so kind as to give me some breakfast?"

"Oh, so you want breakfast?" said the great big tall woman. "Well, you'll be breakfast if you don't get out of here. My husband is a **fierce** giant, and there's nothing he likes better than a nice cooked boy on buttered toast. You'd better get going, for he'll be coming soon."

"Oh, please, ma'am," said Jack, "I haven't eaten since yesterday, really and truly."

Well, the giant's wife wasn't so bad after all. So she took Jack into the kitchen and gave him a chunk of bread and cheese and a jug of milk. But Jack hadn't half finished these when—*thump! thump! thump!*—the whole house began to tremble with the noise of someone's coming—someone big!

"Goodness gracious, it's my old man!" said the giant's wife. "What on earth shall I do? Quick, jump in here!" And Jack jumped into the oven just as the giant came in.

He was a big one, to be sure. He had three cows tied to his belt. He threw them down on the table and said rudely to his wife, "Here, woman, cook me a couple of these for breakfast. But wait—what's this I smell?

> **New Word**
> Fierce means mean or violent.

*"Fee-fi-fo-fum*
*I smell the blood of an Englishman.*
*Be he alive or be he dead*
*I'll grind his bones to make my bread!"*

"Now, dear," said his wife, "it's nothing but the leftover smell of that little boy you had for dinner yesterday. Run along and wash up, and by the time you come back, I'll have breakfast ready."

So the giant went off, and Jack was about to jump out of the oven when the woman whispered, "Wait till he's asleep. He always has a nap after breakfast."

The giant gulped down his breakfast. Then he went to a big chest and took out two big bags. He sat down, and from the bags he took out piles of gold coins. He began counting them, very slowly—"One . . . two . . . uh, three . . . um, ah, four . . ."—then his head began to nod, and then he began to snore, so that the whole house shook.

Jack crept out of the oven, tiptoed past the giant, grabbed one of the bags of gold (which he could barely lift), and ran lickety-split back to the beanstalk. He threw down the bag of gold, which fell—*plump!*—into his mother's garden, then climbed down till at last he reached the ground.

"Well, Mother?" he said. "Wasn't I right about the beans? They really are magic!"

For a while Jack and his mother bought what they needed, and a little more, with the bag of gold. But at last the bag was empty, so Jack made up his mind to try his luck again at the top of the beanstalk. He climbed and he climbed and he climbed, and once again, sure enough, there was the great big tall woman standing on the doorstep. And once again he asked for something to eat.

"Go away, boy," said the woman, "or else my man will eat you up for breakfast. But, say—aren't you the youngster who came here once before? Do you know, on that very day my man lost one of his bags of gold?"

"Did he, now," said Jack. "How very strange! Maybe I could help you find it, but I'm so hungry that first I must have something to eat."

So the great big tall woman gave him something to eat. But he had hardly taken a bite when—*thump! thump! thump!*—they heard the giant's footsteps. Once again the wife hid Jack in the oven.

And all happened as it had before. In came the giant, bellowing, "Fee-fi-fo-fum!" Then, after gulping down three broiled oxen for breakfast, the giant said, "Wife, bring me my hen and my golden harp!"

The wife brought them. The giant looked at the hen and barked, "Lay!" And the hen laid an egg, all of gold. Then the giant looked at the golden harp and said, "Sing!" And the golden harp sang beautifully. And it went on singing until the giant fell asleep and started snoring like thunder.

Jack sneaked out of the oven and crept like a mouse on his hands and knees. Then he crawled up the table, grabbed the hen and golden harp, and dashed toward the door. But the hen began to cluck, and the harp called out, "Master! Master!" The giant woke up just in time to see Jack running away with his treasures.

Jack ran as fast as he could, and the giant came bounding after him and would have caught him, only Jack had a head start. When he got to the beanstalk, he climbed down as fast as he could. The giant reached the beanstalk and stopped short—he didn't like the idea of climbing down such a ladder. But, like it or not, the giant swung himself down on the beanstalk, which shook with his weight.

By this time, Jack had climbed down and run home. "Mother!" he cried. "Give me an axe, and hurry!" His mother came rushing out with an axe in her hand. She ran with Jack to the beanstalk, then she screamed with fright as she saw the giant's legs poking down through the clouds.

Jack swung the axe and gave a chop at the beanstalk. The giant felt the beanstalk shake, and he stopped to see what was the matter. Jack gave another chop, and another, and another, and the beanstalk began to topple over. Then the giant fell down and broke his crown, and the beanstalk came tumbling after.

From then on, Jack and his mother had all the money and music they wanted, for the hen gave them golden eggs, and the harp sang for them all day long. And so they lived happily ever after.

## The Knee-High Man

*(An African American folktale retold by Julius Lester)*

Once upon a time there was a knee-high man. He was no taller than a person's knees. Because he was so short, he was very unhappy. He wanted to be big like everybody else.

One day he decided to ask the biggest animal he could find how he could get big. So he went to see Mr. Horse. "Mr. Horse, how can I get big like you?"

Mr. Horse said, "Well, eat a whole lot of corn. Then run around a lot. After a while you'll be as big as me."

The knee-high man did just that. He ate so much corn that his stomach hurt. Then he ran and ran and ran until his legs hurt. But he didn't get any bigger. So he decided that Mr. Horse had told him something wrong. He decided to go ask Mr. Bull.

"Mr. Bull? How can I get big like you?"

Mr. Bull said, "Eat a whole lot of grass. Then bellow and bellow as loud as you can. The first thing you know, you'll be as big as me."

So the knee-high man ate a whole field of grass. That made his stomach hurt. He bellowed and bellowed and bellowed all day and all night. That made his throat hurt. But he didn't get any bigger. So he decided that Mr. Bull was all wrong too.

Now he didn't know anyone else to ask. One night he heard Mr. Hoot Owl hooting, and he remembered that Mr. Owl knew everything. "Mr. Owl? How can I get big like Mr. Horse and Mr. Bull?"

"What do you want to be big for?" Mr. Hoot Owl asked.

"I want to be big so that when I get into a fight, I can whip everybody," the knee-high man said.

Mr. Hoot Owl hooted. "Anybody ever try to pick a fight with you?"

The knee-high man thought a minute. "Well, now that you mention it, nobody ever did try to start a fight with me."

Mr. Owl said, "Well, you don't have any reason to fight. Therefore, you don't have any reason to be bigger than you are."

"But, Mr. Owl," the knee-high man said, "I want to be big so I can see far into the distance."

Mr. Hoot Owl hooted. "If you climb a tall tree, you can see into the distance from the top."

The knee-high man was quiet for a minute. "Well, I hadn't thought of that."

Mr. Hoot Owl hooted again. "And that's what's wrong, Mr. Knee-High Man. You hadn't done any thinking at all. I'm smaller than you, and you don't see me worrying about being big. Mr. Knee-High Man, you wanted something that you didn't need."

# The Little Half-Chick (Medio Pollito)

*(A Hispanic folktale)*

Once there was a hen who had a large brood of little chicks. They were all fine, plump little birds, except the youngest. He was quite unlike his brothers and sisters. He looked as if he had been cut in half. All of his brothers and sisters had two wings and two legs and two eyes, but he had only one wing, one leg, and one eye. And he had only half a head and half a beak. His mother shook her head sadly as she looked at him. "Poor thing!" she said. "He is only a half-chick."

The mother hen called her youngest chick Medio Pollito [MEH-dee-o poh-YEE-toh], which is Spanish for "half-chick." She thought that he would never be able to take care of himself. She decided that she would have to keep him at home and look after him.

But Medio Pollito had a different idea. He turned out to be a very stubborn and independent little chick. Even though his brothers and sisters did just what they were told to do, Medio Pollito did not. When his mother called for him to come back to the chicken house, he hid in the cornfield. Sometimes he pretended that he could not hear her (because, of course, he had only one ear). The older he became, the more willful he became. He would not listen to his mother and he was often rude to his brothers and sisters, even though they were always extra nice to him.

One day Medio Pollito strutted up to his mother and made an announcement: "I am tired of life in this dull barnyard. I am going to Madrid to dine with the king."

"Madrid!" exclaimed his mother. "Why, that is a long journey, even for a grown-up. You aren't old enough to go to Madrid yet. Wait a bit. When you are a little older, I will take you to see the city."

But Medio Pollito had made up his mind. He would not listen to his mother, or to his brothers and sisters, all of whom pleaded with him to stay. "I am going to Madrid to dine with the king," he declared. "And when I get there I will make my fortune and live in a big house. Perhaps I will even invite the rest of you to pay me a short visit sometime." With that, he turned and hopped off on his one leg.

His mother ran after him and called out, "Be sure to be kind to everyone you meet!" But Medio Pollito did not listen. He was in a hurry and, as usual, was thinking only of himself.

Medio Pollito hopped on until he came to a little stream of water that was almost choked with weeds. "Oh, Medio Pollito," the stream called out, "please help me by pulling some of these weeds so I can flow freely!"

"Help you?" exclaimed Medio Pollito, tossing his head and shaking the few feathers in his tail. "Do you think I have time to waste on that sort of thing? Help yourself, and don't bother busy travelers like me. I am off to Madrid to dine with the king." And away he hopped.

A little later Medio Pollito came to a fire that some campers had left burning in the woods. "Oh, Medio Pollito," the fire said, "please toss some sticks on me so I won't burn out!"

"Poo!" said Medio Pollito. "Do you think I have time to waste on that sort of thing? I am off to Madrid to dine with the king." And away he hopped.

The next morning, as he was nearing Madrid, Medio Pollito came upon a large chestnut tree in which the wind had gotten tangled up. "Oh, Medio Pollito," said the wind, "won't you climb up here and help me get myself untangled?"

"It's your own fault for going so high up there," said Medio Pollito. "And besides, I don't have time to waste on that sort of thing. I am off to Madrid to dine with the king." And away he hopped.

When he entered the city, Medio Pollito saw the royal palace shining in the sun. He was so excited to meet the king, he hopped right into the courtyard without a moment's hesitation. The king's cook spotted him and called out, "Glory be to God! This little bird will make a dainty appetizer for the king!" The cook grabbed Medio Pollito by his neck and took him back to the kitchen. He put a pot of water on the stove and tossed Medio Pollito into the pot. Then he slammed a heavy lid on top.

Medio Pollito was very wet. "Oh, water," he cried, "don't soak me like this!" But the water replied, "You would not help me when I was a little stream choked with weeds, so why should I help you now?"

Then the fire on the stove began to heat the water. Medio Pollito felt very hot.

"Oh, fire," he cried, "don't cook me like this!" But the fire replied, "You would not help me when I was about to burn out, so why should I help you now?"

The fire got hotter and hotter. The heat was so unbearable that Medio Pollito grew more and more desperate to escape. Just then, the cook raised the lid of the pot to see if the soup was ready.

"What's this?" said the cook. "I have overcooked the chicken. He is all blackened and burnt to a crisp. I can't serve this to the king!"

The cook grabbed Medio Pollito and threw him out the kitchen window. With a gust, the wind caught him and carried him away so fast he could hardly breathe.

"Oh, wind," Medio Pollito cried, "don't push me around that way. Please, set me down!" But the wind replied, "You would not help me when I was caught in the tree, so why should I help you now?" And with that the wind lifted Medio Pollito up in the air to the top of the tallest church in town and left him stuck on top of the steeple.

And that is where you can find Medio Pollito, to this very day. If you go to Madrid and look for the tallest church in town, you will see a black weather vane in the shape of half a chicken, turning in the wind. That is Medio Pollito, the chick who would not help others. Now he helps everyone by showing them which way the wind is blowing.

**Take a Look**
How does the weather vane in the picture help you to see which way the wind is blowing?

## The Pied Piper of Hamelin

Rats! Everywhere in the little town of Hamelin, there were rats, rats, and more rats. There were so many that no amount of traps could catch them, and no amount of poison could kill them. They fought the dogs and chased the cats. They made nests in the people's hats. They ate the food right off the tables. They ran up and down the streets in broad daylight, flicking their tails and twitching their whiskers. And they made such a squeaking and shrieking that you could not hear yourself speak, or get a wink of good sleep.

In the middle of Hamelin at the Town Hall, a crowd had gathered. The people were shaking their fists and shouting, "Mr. Mayor! Mr. Mayor! You must get rid of these rats, or we will get rid of you!"

"What do you expect me to do?" asked the mayor. He sat his big round body down in a big wooden chair. "I've racked my brain again and again, but all in vain." Then, giving his head a rap, he cried, "Oh for a trap, a trap, a trap!"

Just then at the door came a gentle tap. "It's a rat!" cried the mayor.

"Rats don't knock," said a townsman.

"Oh, yes, of course," said the mayor. Then, trying to sound brave, he called out, "Come in!" And in came the strangest-looking person you've ever seen.

He was tall and thin, with sharp blue eyes, each like a pin. His long coat, half of yellow and half of red, stretched from his heel to his head. From underneath a floppy hat flowed his hair, long and white, and in his hand he carried a silver pipe.

"Who are you?" asked the mayor.

And the strange-looking figure answered, "People call me the Pied Piper. On my pipe I play music that charms all things under the sun—all creatures that creep, or swim, or fly, or run. Whenever I play, they follow me, wherever I go. I can charm the birds of the air. I can charm the fishes of the sea. I can charm the wild beasts that live in the forests."

"And rats?" said the mayor. "What about rats? Can you charm them?"

"That I can," said the Pied Piper. "I can charm every last rat from your town. Give me a thousand gold pieces and I will set to it."

"A thousand?" said the mayor. "Why, you may have fifty thousand if you can do it!" And the townspeople cried, "Yes, yes, we will gladly give him fifty thousand. Just get rid of the rats!"

"As you wish," said the stranger. Then, with a strange smile, he stepped out into the street and put the pipe to his lips. And he had hardly played three notes when, from every direction, rats came running, tumbling, tripping, hurrying, scurrying.

*Great rats, small rats, lean rats, brawny rats,*
*Brown rats, black rats, gray rats, tawny rats,*
*Grave old plodders, gay young friskers,*
    *Fathers, mothers, uncles, cousins,*
*Cocking tails, and prickling whiskers,*
    *Families by tens and dozens,*
*Brothers, sisters, husbands, wives—*
*Followed the Piper for their lives.*
*From street to street he piped advancing,*
*And step by step they followed dancing.*

The Pied Piper walked slowly down the street, playing his merry tune. And when he came to the river, the rats jumped in and were carried under and away by the rushing water.

The townspeople hurrayed and hurrahed and rang the bells till they rocked the steeples. But they fell quiet as the Pied Piper returned. He walked up to the

mayor and said, "The rats are gone. It is time to pay the Piper. I will take my thousand gold pieces and go."

But the mayor hemmed and hawed and harrumphed and said that, really, he didn't see why the Piper should be paid so much for what was such an easy job. After all, what had he done but walk down the street and play on a pipe? And, really, wouldn't the Piper think it fair to be paid, say, about ten gold pieces, yes, ten, didn't that seem about right for so easy a job?

And as the mayor spoke, the townspeople nodded and began to whisper among themselves that, indeed, this funny-looking man hardly deserved a thousand gold pieces just for playing a silly pipe—why, the very idea!

"You promised to pay me a thousand," said the Piper. "You even offered me fifty thousand. Come now, I have no time to waste. I must be on my way. It's a thousand we've agreed on, and a thousand you must pay."

The mayor put ten gold pieces on the table and said with a huff, "Take it or leave it. Now, fellow, be off with you."

Once more the Pied Piper stepped into the street. Once more he began to play. And after only a few notes, there was a rustling, and a bustling, and a sound of small feet pattering, and little tongues chattering. Out came the children, all the children of Hamelin town, tripping and skipping and running merrily after the music with shouting and laughter.

The townspeople could not speak. They could not move. They stood as though they had been changed to blocks of wood. They could not shout or utter a cry as they watched the children skipping by.

As the children danced merrily behind him, the Pied Piper played his tune. And the tune seemed to make a promise, a promise of a joyous land where the sun was shining and birds were singing, and children played in fields in which flowers bloomed brighter than rainbows. And on they danced, as the Piper led them far from town, until they came to a mountainside. And there, in the rock, a door opened wide. The Piper walked in, and the children followed. And when all were in to the very last, the door in the mountainside shut fast.

The townspeople searched high and low, up and down. But they never again saw the Pied Piper or the children of Hamelin town.

## Pinocchio

### Pinocchio Runs Away

There was once a poor woodcarver named Geppetto [jeh-PET-toe]. One day, Geppetto picked out an unusual block of wood and said, "I will carve a fine puppet out of this, one that can dance and jump when I pull the strings." And he thought that perhaps he could travel with the puppet and put on shows and earn a living.

"What shall I name my puppet?" thought Geppetto. "I know—Pinocchio. That sounds like a lucky name!" And so he started carving. First he worked on the head. He carved the eyes, and to his surprise, the eyes opened and stared at him! Then he carved the nose. Geppetto jumped back: The nose was growing longer and longer! "Stop, nose, stop!" Geppetto cried. Finally it stopped growing, but, oh, it was long! Geppetto next worked on the mouth. As soon as he finished the mouth, the puppet began to laugh, and it kept on laughing. "Stop laughing, you!" said Geppetto. The puppet stopped laughing—but it stuck out its tongue!

"Pinocchio!" said Geppetto. "You're not even finished and already you're a bad boy!"

Geppetto kept carving, and he finished the legs and feet. But as soon as he did, the puppet raised a foot and kicked him in the nose!

"Come, you mischief-maker," said Geppetto. "Let us see if you can use those legs." He put Pinocchio on the ground and held him up. At first Pinocchio's legs were so stiff that he could not walk. Geppetto showed him how to put one foot in front of another, and Pinocchio began to walk by himself. Then he began to run around the room. When he saw that the door was open, he jumped out and ran away!

Pinocchio ran through the village until he came to the fields and meadows. He leaped over brambles and bushes and across brooks and ponds. He heard the *chirp-chirp-chirping* sound of a cricket. Suddenly the cricket began to talk. "Pinocchio, listen to me," said the cricket. "Bad boys who run away and disobey their parents will never be happy."

"You silly cricket," said Pinocchio. "If I go back home, I know what will happen: I'll have to go to school, and whether I want to or not, I'll have to study. But it's much more fun to chase butterflies, and climb trees, and do just as I please."

"Then you are a silly wooden-head!" said the cricket. "If that's the way you spend your time, you'll grow up to be a big donkey, and everyone will make fun of you."

Pinocchio was angry. He picked up something heavy and threw it—and there was no more talking or chirping from the cricket.

As Pinocchio walked away, he felt a new feeling, a strange emptiness inside him. Along with the emptiness came a loud growling sound. "Why, I'm hungry," the puppet said. "I'm hungry as a wolf."

He ran back to the village. It was dark. The shops were closed, and all the doors and windows were shut tight. "Oh, I'm so terribly hungry," he cried. He walked up to a house and rang the bell, again and again. "That's sure to wake someone up," he thought. And he was right. A window opened upstairs and a sleepy man stuck out his head. In an angry voice he said, "What do you want at this time of night?"

"I'm a poor hungry boy," Pinocchio said. "Please feed me."

"Wait a minute, I'll be right back," said the man.

The puppet looked up at the window and imagined the wonderful treats that the man might be bringing. Then—*splash!*—Pinocchio was hit in the face by a shower of ice-cold water!

"Maybe that cricket was right after all," Pinocchio grumbled. He found his way back to Geppetto's cottage. The old man was very glad to see him. "You must promise not to run away again," he said. "You must go to school, like a good boy."

"Yes, Father, I'll be good," said Pinocchio.

*Pinocchio at the Puppet Show*

The next morning Geppetto, who was very poor, sold his only coat in order to buy Pinocchio an A-B-C book. With his new book in hand, Pinocchio started for school.

"I will be a good boy," he said. But he had not gone very far when he saw a sign for a puppet show. "I can go to school any old day," he thought, "but I must see that show today!" So he sold his book for the price of a ticket and went to see the show.

The theater was full of people laughing loudly at the puppets on the stage. Then a most unexpected thing happened: The puppets onstage cried out, "Look, it's Pinocchio, our fellow puppet! Pinocchio, come up here!" Pinocchio began leaping over people's heads to get to the stage. Well, you never saw anything like it or heard such a great clattering, as the puppets knocked their wooden arms and legs together in their rush to hug Pinocchio.

The people in the audience were angry that the play had stopped. "The play! We want the play!" they shouted.

Suddenly the puppet master came out. He was a fierce-looking man, with a long black beard, sharp yellow teeth, and eyes like glowing red coals. "What's this? You don't belong here!" he roared as he grabbed Pinocchio. "So," he said, "you're made of wood. Then I will use you for firewood."

**Talk and Think**

Do you remember what "fierce" means? See page 102. How are the giant in "Jack and the Beanstalk" and the puppet master alike?

"No, please don't," pleaded Pinocchio. "Please spare me. My poor old father will miss me so much. Just this morning he sent me off to school, and he bought me an A-B-C book with the money he got from selling his only coat. It was an old coat, too, full of patches."

The puppet master looked fierce, but he wasn't all bad. With a loud sniff he said to Pinocchio, "I feel sorry for your poor father. Go back to him, and give him these five gold pieces to buy a new coat."

*The Fox and the Cat*

Pinocchio thanked the puppet master a thousand times and started on his way home. But he had not gone far when he met a fox who seemed to be lame and a cat who seemed to be blind.

"Good morning, Pinocchio," said the fox.

"How do you know my name?" asked the puppet.

"I know your father," said the sly fox. "I saw him yesterday morning, standing in the doorway of his house wearing only a tattered shirt. He was cold and shivering."

"But he will be warm soon!" said Pinocchio. Then, holding out the five gold coins, he said, "See, I'm rich! I'm going to buy my father a fine new coat."

When he saw the gold pieces, the fox, who was supposed to be lame, jumped up, and the cat, who was supposed to be blind, stared with wide-open eyes that looked like two green lamps. But all this happened so quickly that Pinocchio didn't notice.

"My, my," said the fox, "so much money. And what exactly do you plan to do with it?"

"I'll buy Father a coat and myself a new A-B-C book," said Pinocchio.

"An A-B-C book?" asked the fox in a doubtful voice.

"Yes," said Pinocchio. "I'm going to school to study."

"Study!" exclaimed the fox. "Do you know what happens when you study? I tried to study once, and now look at me—I am lame!"

"I also tried to study once," said the cat, "and now look at me—I am blind."

"You don't need to study or work," said the fox. "Just listen to me, my boy. How would you like to see those five gold coins turn into ten? Or twenty? Or a hundred? Or even a thousand?"

"Really?" said the puppet. "How?"

"Why, it's very easy," laughed the fox. "Do you know the place called the Field of Wonders? You just go there and dig a little hole in the ground. Then you cover the hole with a little dirt, water it, and go away. During the night your gold pieces will sprout and grow. And in the morning you'll find a tree loaded with gold pieces!"

"Oh, how wonderful!" cried Pinocchio. "How can I ever thank you? Oh, I know. When I have picked all the gold pieces, I will give you a hundred of them."

But the fox cried out, as though he were surprised and embarrassed, "A present! For us! No, really, we simply could not accept. Our greatest pleasure is to bring happiness and wealth to others."

"Oh, yes," said the cat, "helping other people is all the reward we ask."

"Come on, then!" exclaimed Pinocchio. "Let's go to the Field of Wonders!"

"Certainly," said the fox. "But shall we stop for dinner on the way? I believe that one of your gold coins should be enough to feed us all."

*The Return of the Cricket, and the Field of Wonders*

At dinner the fox and cat stuffed themselves as though they were eating a meal to last a lifetime. Pinocchio was not very hungry, so he stepped outside to think about all the money he would soon have. He heard a small voice calling his name.

"Who is calling me?" asked Pinocchio.

"I am the spirit of the talking cricket," said the voice.

"What do you want?" asked the puppet.

"I want to give you a few words of advice," said the voice. "Return home and give the four gold pieces you have left to your father. Do not listen to those who promise to make you rich overnight. Either they are fools or they will make a fool out of you. Listen to me, Pinocchio, and go home."

"No," said the puppet. "I'm going to do what I want."

"It is very late," said the voice.

"I'm going to do what I want."

"The night is dark."

"I'm going to do what I want."

"There are dangers ahead."

"I'm going to do what I want."

"Remember that children who insist on doing what they want will be sorry for it, sooner or later."

"I've heard all that before," said the stubborn puppet.

Just then the fox and cat came out and joined him again. Together they walked on to the Field of Wonders. As they walked, Pinocchio kept thinking to himself, "I wonder how much gold the tree will grow? What if it's a thousand pieces? Or maybe two thousand? Or even five thousand? Oh, I will have a grand palace, and a thousand toys, and a kitchen filled with candy and cakes!"

They came at last to a large field. No one was in sight. "Here we are, my young friend," said the fox. "Now dig a hole and put your gold pieces in it."

Pinocchio dug a hole, placed the four remaining gold pieces in it, and carefully covered them with dirt. Then he went to a nearby well and filled his shoe with water, which he brought back and sprinkled on the ground where he had planted the coins.

"Is there anything else?" he asked the fox.

"Nothing else at all," said the fox. "Now you simply have to leave this place for about twenty minutes. And when you return, you will find a tree covered with money."

"Thank you, thank you, a thousand times thank you," said Pinocchio as he jumped up and down for joy.

The fox and the cat went one way, and Pinocchio went another. He counted the minutes, one by one. When he thought it was time, he ran back to the Field of Wonders. He came to the field and looked for a tree but saw nothing. He turned around and looked in all directions—still nothing. Then he heard someone laughing. Looking up, he saw a big parrot sitting in a tree.

In an angry voice Pinocchio asked, "Why are you laughing?"

"Oh," said the parrot, "only because I just tickled myself under the wing. And because I always laugh at silly people who believe everything they are told."

"Do you mean me?" snapped Pinocchio.

"Yes, indeed, I mean you," said the parrot. "You are foolish enough to think that money can grow like beans or peas. Don't you know that to earn money honestly, you have to work with your hands and with your head?"

"I—I don't understand what you mean," said Pinocchio in a trembling voice.

"Oh, I think you do," said the parrot. "Why don't you check where you planted the money?"

Pinocchio did not want to believe the parrot. Still, he bent down and began to dig the dirt out of the hole where he had planted the money. He dug and he dug and he dug until he had made a hole as big as himself. But the money was not there. Every piece of it was gone. And Pinocchio knew, as well as you know, who took it.

Sadly, Pinocchio walked back to the village. On his way he passed a small cottage, and there, standing in the door, was a beautiful blue-haired fairy. "Pinocchio," she called out. "What happened to your gold coins?"

"I, uh, you see, well, I lost them. Yes, that's it, I lost them," stammered Pinocchio.

No sooner had he said this than his nose grew longer, longer, and longer!

"Pinocchio," said the fairy, "I hope you've learned your lesson." Then she called in a flock of woodpeckers, who pecked on his nose until it was back to its old size. But from then on, you could always tell whenever Pinocchio was lying, for his nose would grow and grow.

## More Adventures of Pinocchio

Pinocchio has many more adventures. He meets a naughty boy named Lampwick. They sneak away from school to go to the Land of Toys. But when Pinocchio leaves the Land of Toys, he finds that he has grown the ears and tail of a donkey! The blue-haired fairy helps Pinocchio, and he decides that he wants to become a real boy. Before he does, he goes through some very hard trials—he is even swallowed by a giant shark! In the end, Pinocchio is reunited with Geppetto, and his wish comes true: He is no longer a puppet but a real boy.

## The Princess and the Pea

*(From the story by Hans Christian Andersen)*

Once upon a time, there was a prince, and he wanted to marry a princess—but not just any princess. He wanted to marry a real princess. So he traveled all over the world looking for a real princess.

He went from kingdom to kingdom and he met plenty of princesses. Of course, they were all beautiful, talented, graceful, and kind. But never did the prince feel that he had found an absolutely, totally, completely real princess. There was always something missing. So, sad and disappointed, the prince returned home.

Back at the castle, his mother, the queen, asked him, "Did you find a princess?"

"Oh, I found plenty of princesses," the prince replied, "but I never felt sure that I'd found a *real* princess."

That night there was a terrible storm. Lightning flashed. Thunder crashed. The wind howled, and the rain pounded down. During the storm, there was a knock at the palace door. The king and queen opened the door and there, standing in the rain, was a princess. And, oh my, she was a mess! Her hair was dripping, her clothes were torn and muddy, and water poured out of her shoes.

"Who are you?" asked the queen.

"I am a princess," she said.

"Humph!" said the queen, and she thought to herself, "We'll see about that!" The queen went into a bedroom and took all the sheets and blankets off the bed. Then she put one tiny pea on the bed, and on top of that she piled twenty mattresses, and on top of those, twenty pads filled with feathers.

"Here is where you will sleep tonight," the queen said to the princess.

"Thank you," said the princess.

The next morning at the breakfast table, the queen asked the princess, "Did you have a good night's sleep?"

"No," said the princess. "I'm afraid I did not. I tossed and turned all night. Something in the bed was so hard and lumpy—why, I'm bruised black and blue

**New Word**
Does your child
know what
**delicate** means?
Delicate means
fine, dainty, or
easily damaged.

all over." So she had felt the pea through the twenty mattresses and twenty pads! The queen smiled at her son, and he smiled back at her. They were both thinking the same thing: surely, only a real princess could be so **delicate** and sensitive.

So the prince married the princess. And as for the pea, it was placed in a museum, where it may still be seen, if nobody has taken it.

And that, children, is a real story!

## Puss-in-Boots

Once upon a time there was an old miller, and when he died, he left his three sons all that he owned—which was not much. To the oldest son, he left his mill. To the middle son, he left his mule. And to the youngest son, he left only his cat.

With a sad sigh, the youngest son looked at the cat and said, "What can I do? My brothers can take care of themselves, but what can I do with only a cat? I suppose I could eat you and sell your skin, but then what?"

Now the cat heard all this, though of course, like all cats, he pretended to be paying no attention at all. And when the young man had finished speaking, the cat spoke up and said, "My good master, there's no need to worry. Just bring me a big bag and a pair of boots and I'll fix everything, you'll see."

"What can a cat do?" said the young man. But then he thought, "What have I got to lose?" After all, he had seen this cat play many clever tricks in order to catch mice. So he got the cat a bag and a pair of boots.

Puss pulled on the boots—and looking down at his booted paws, he had to admit that he did look rather handsome in them. Then he put some grain into the bag. He held the bag in his two front paws and went to a place where he knew there were many rabbits. He put the bag on the ground and left it wide open, with a little grain showing. Then he stretched himself out nearby and lay very still, as though he were dead. Soon a plump rabbit smelled the grain and hopped right into the bag. Quick as a wink, Puss jumped up and caught the rabbit.

Now Puss, bag in paws, went to the palace and asked to speak to His Majesty, the king. He was brought before the king, where he made a low bow and said, "Sire, I have brought you a fine plump rabbit, a gift from my noble master, the Marquis of Carabas." Puss purred with satisfaction at the fancy-sounding title that he had made up on the spot for his master.

"Tell your master," said the king, "that I accept his gift and am well pleased with it."

"Yes, Your Majesty," said Puss, and after bowing low again, he walked out in his boots.

A few days later, Puss used his same trick to catch some partridges, and he brought the bag of birds to the king, who was again well pleased. And so things went on for some time. Every few days Puss brought something he had caught to the king, and each time Puss offered it as a gift from the grand and noble Marquis of Carabas. The king began to think of this marquis as a famous hunter and a generous man, though he was, as you and I know, only the poor miller's youngest son!

Now it happened one day that Puss heard about the king's plans to go for a ride in his coach along the riverbank. And with the king would be his daughter, who was, of course, the most beautiful princess in the land. When Puss heard this, he went to his master and said, "Master, if you will do just as I tell you, your fortune is made. All you must do is go and wash yourself in the river, in a spot that I shall show you, and leave the rest to me."

"Well, it seems strange, but all right," said the young man. He did as the cat

told him, though he did not know why. While the young man was washing in the river, the king's coach passed by. And just at that moment Puss cried out, "Help! Help! My master, the Marquis of Carabas, is drowning! Save him, save him!"

The king heard the cries and looked out the window. When he saw it was the cat who had brought him so many gifts, he ordered his guards to run and help the Marquis of Carabas. While the guards pulled the young man out of the river, Puss ran up to the king's coach, his fur all puffed out. "Your Majesty!" he said in a breathless voice. "Thieves! Thieves! They robbed my master, and stole his clothes, and threw him into the deepest part of the river! He would have drowned if you had not come by with your men, just in time!"

The king told one of his guards to ride back to the palace and bring a fine suit of clothes for the Marquis of Carabas. When the young man had put on the clothes, he was dressed more finely than he had ever been in his life and really did appear to be a handsome fellow. So the king invited him into his coach, where who should be waiting but the princess. The young man and the princess exchanged a few silent glances, and, as Puss had planned, this was all it took for them to fall in love.

Meanwhile, Puss hurried on ahead of the coach. He came to a field where some people were picking corn, and he spoke to them. "Good people," said Puss, "the king approaches. You will tell him that this field belongs to my master, the Marquis of Carabas. For if you do not," Puss hissed, "you'll be chopped up like vegetables for a pot of soup!" Then the cat ran on to an even larger field where people were working and again ordered them to tell the king that the field belonged to the Marquis of Carabas, and again he hissed, "Or else you'll be chopped up like vegetables for a pot of soup!" And on and on Puss went, stopping at each field to give the same command and make the same warning.

As the king passed by the fields, he leaned out of his coach and said, "These are fine fields. Who owns them?" And the people, who had been greatly frightened by Puss, said, "The Marquis of Carabas." The king was amazed and said to the marquis, "You own a great deal of very fine land!" And the marquis replied, in a somewhat sleepy voice, as though he had heard such comments all his life,

"Yes, Sire, it is a lot, isn't it?" And the princess began to think even more of the handsome fellow.

Meanwhile, Puss had run ahead until he came to a grand castle. In this castle lived the real owner of all the fields. He was a mean, cruel ogre, and he had a most amazing power: He could change himself into any animal he wanted to be. Puss had learned of this power from some of the workers in the fields, who were scared of their cruel master. At the castle Puss said, "I have come to pay my respects to the owner of this great castle and all these lands, for I have heard that he is a man of great talents."

The ogre allowed Puss to come in. Puss bowed low before him and said, "I have been told that you have the power to change yourself into any kind of animal—even, they say, a lion or an elephant."

"That is true," the ogre grunted.

"Oh, is it?" said Puss.

"What? Do you not believe me?" the ogre roared. "Watch this!" And suddenly Puss saw before him a fierce lion. Filled with fear, Puss gave a loud "MEE-YOWL!" He leaped away and hid. When the lion changed back into an ogre, Puss came out of his hiding place and said, "That was most frightening. Truly, your powers are amazing! But I have heard that you can do something even more amazing. People say that you can turn yourself into a creature as small as a mouse. But surely that is impossible."

"Impossible!" cried the ogre. "Just you watch!" And with that he changed himself into a mouse and began to skitter around on the floor. Quicker than you can say "cheese," Puss jumped on the mouse and made a meal of him—and that was that!

By this time the king's coach had come to the gates of the castle. Puss scampered down, and as he opened the great doors, he announced, "Your Majesty is welcome to this castle, the home of my master, the Marquis of Carabas."

"What!" exclaimed the king. "Does this castle belong to you, too? I never saw anything so fine. I should really like to enter."

"Your Majesty is most welcome!" said the young man, bowing low. Then he gave his hand to the princess and they went up the steps, all following Puss, who danced along in his boots, with his tail twitching.

It will not surprise you, I am sure, if I tell you that the Marquis of Carabas married the princess, and that they were very happy together, and that Puss, the clever cat, lived in great comfort and never had to chase mice again—except, of course, where he wanted to.

## Rapunzel

*(A tale retold from the Brothers Grimm)*

Once there was a couple who, more than anything in the world, wished to have a baby. Finally, one day they learned that their wish would come true. The wife discovered that she was pregnant, and she and her husband were as happy as a couple could be.

Now, at the top of the couple's house, in the back, there was a little window. And from this window you could see a garden full of beautiful flowers and fresh vegetables. But around the garden was a high wall. And no one dared to enter the garden, because it belonged to a wicked witch.

One day the wife stood at the little window looking down into the witch's garden. In the garden she saw rows of lettuce, spinach, and rapunzel. The rapunzel plants looked particularly delicious. The leaves were so fresh and green that she felt that she simply must have some. Day after day she longed for a bowl of the rapunzel. She wanted it so desperately that she grew sad and pale.

When her husband saw her looking so sad, he began to worry. He asked her what was bothering her.

"Oh," she answered, "I long to eat some of that delicious-looking rapunzel from the garden behind our house. I have such a craving for it!" Her husband loved her very much, and he thought, "I must get my wife what she desires. I will get some of that rapunzel, no matter what."

That night he climbed over the wall into the witch's garden. He filled a sack with rapunzel and brought it back to his wife. She ate the leaves with delight. But she liked them so much and they tasted so good that the next day she longed for rapunzel twice as much as she had before. So, that night, the husband climbed the wall again and picked more rapunzel. Just as he was getting ready to climb back over the wall, he saw before him the gleaming, angry eyes of the witch.

"How dare you climb into my garden, you thief," she growled. "How dare you steal my rapunzel! You will pay dearly for this!"

"Oh, please," said the terrified man, "be merciful. I only did this because I had to. My wife, you see, is having a baby, and she was looking out the window and saw your rapunzel, and she felt that she had to have some."

"Well, then," the witch said, "you may have as much rapunzel as you want—on one condition. When your wife has the child, you must give it to me. I will take care of the child and raise it as my own."

The man was so flustered that he said "yes" and then tried not to think any more of it. But later, after his wife gave birth to a lovely baby girl, the witch appeared and reminded him of his promise.

The new parents begged the witch not to take their child. But the witch would not be denied. She took the baby girl to live with her and named her Rapunzel.

Rapunzel grew up to be a beautiful girl. When she was twelve years old, the witch took her deep into the forest. There she locked her in a tower with no steps and no door, only a small window near the top. Whenever the witch wanted to be let into the tower, she would call out from the ground below, "Rapunzel! Rapunzel! Let down your hair!"

Rapunzel had beautiful, long hair that shone like gold. When she heard the witch calling, she would open the window and let her hair fall down, down, down to the ground far below. Then the witch would hold on to the hair and climb up to the tower window.

Rapunzel had spent a few years in her tower when, one day, the king's son was riding through the forest and came upon the tower. As he came near, he heard a voice singing so sweetly that he stood still and listened. It was Rapunzel trying to drive away her loneliness by singing. The prince thought her voice was the most beautiful he had ever heard. He wanted to go inside to see her, so he looked for a door in the tower, but he could not find one. He rode home, but the song had entered into his heart, and he went back to the tower the very next day, hoping to hear the mysterious singer and her sweet songs.

Once, as he was standing behind some trees, who should come up to the tower but the witch. The prince watched, amazed, as the witch called out, "Rapunzel! Rapunzel! Let down your hair!" Then he saw how Rapunzel let down her long hair and how the witch climbed up it and went into the tower. "So that

is the ladder!" he whispered to himself. "Well, then, I too will climb it." The next day, as dusk fell, he came to the tower and cried, "Rapunzel! Rapunzel! Let down your hair!" Rapunzel let down her hair, and the prince climbed up.

Rapunzel was frightened when she saw the prince, for she had never seen a man before. But he spoke kindly to her and told how her singing had entered his heart and how he felt he could have no peace until he had seen her. Then Rapunzel forgot her fear, and when he asked her to be his wife, she put her hand in his hand and said, "I would gladly go with you, but I have no way to get out of this tower. The next time you come here, bring a bundle of silk. Bring some with you each time you come, and I will make a ladder of it. When the ladder is finished, I will use it to climb down from this tower, and then you will carry me away from here on your horse." They agreed that he would come to her every evening, since the witch came only in the daytime.

Things went on this way until one day Rapunzel made a mistake. Without thinking what she was saying, she said to the witch, "Why do you climb up so slowly? It takes the king's son only a moment."

"Oh, you wicked child!" screamed the witch. "I thought I had you hidden here from all the world. But now I see that you have betrayed me!" In a rage, the witch grabbed a pair of sharp scissors and cut off poor Rapunzel's hair. Then the witch drove Rapunzel away, leaving her to wander the forests, alone and miserable.

Later that day, when evening fell, the prince came and called out, "Rapunzel! Rapunzel! Let down your hair!" The witch lowered the cut-off hair, and the prince climbed up. But instead of seeing his dear Rapunzel at the top, he saw the gleaming eyes of the witch. "Aha!" she cried, and laughed at him. "You came to see your darling, but the sweet bird is no longer in its nest. You will see her no more!" Filled with horror and sadness, the prince fell from the tower. The fall did not kill him, but the thorns on which he fell cut his eyes and blinded him.

So, blind and alone, he wandered in the forest for several years, eating only roots and berries, and weeping over the loss of his dear Rapunzel. At last he came to a place in the forest where Rapunzel herself was wandering. He heard a sweet voice that he thought he had heard somewhere before. When he went toward the sound, Rapunzel saw him. She ran to him, wrapped her arms around his neck, and wept. When Rapunzel's tears touched the prince's eyes, he could see again. He was overjoyed and amazed; he had thought he would never see her again.

And so the prince took Rapunzel to his kingdom to be his bride, where she was welcomed with great joy. They were soon married, and they lived happily ever after.

# Rumpelstiltskin

*(A tale from the Brothers Grimm)*

Once upon a time there was a poor miller who had a beautiful daughter. She was so beautiful and clever that he could not help boasting about her. One day the miller happened to come before the king, and to impress the king, he began boasting about his daughter. And before he knew it, he found himself saying that his daughter was so amazing and so wonderful, why, she could even spin gold out of straw.

"That," said the king, "is a talent worth having. Bring your daughter to me, and let us see what she can do."

When the girl was brought to the palace, the king led her to a room that was almost full of straw. He pointed to a spinning wheel and said, "Get to work, and if by early morning you have not spun this straw into gold, you shall die."

The poor miller's daughter! Of course, she could not spin straw into gold. What could she do? She could think of nothing, and in the end she sat down and began to cry.

And that's when, all at once, *ka-lick,* the door opened and in walked a little man. "Good evening, miller's daughter," he said. "Why are you crying?"

"Because," she answered, "I must spin all this straw into gold before morning, and I don't know how."

Then the little man came close to her and whispered, "What will you give me if I spin it for you?"

"Why, I, I'll give you my necklace," she stammered.

The little man took the necklace, seated himself at the spinning wheel, and, *whirr, whirr, whirr,* he spun and he spun, and by sunup all the straw had been spun into gold. And when the king arrived, he was amazed. But the sight of all that gold made the greed for more grow in him. So he took the miller's daughter to a larger room, filled with yet more straw, and told her that if she valued her life, she must spin all this into gold in one night. Again the girl did not know

**Talk and Think**

There was also a miller in the story "Puss-in-Boots." How is the character in this story like the character in "Puss-in-Boots"?

what to do and sat down to cry, when, *ka-lick*, the door opened and in walked the little man.

"Crying again, I see," he said. "So, I suppose you have to spin all this into gold, too. What will you give me if I do it for you?"

"The ring from my finger," answered the girl.

So the little man took the ring, seated himself at the spinning wheel, and, *whirr, whirr, whirr,* he spun and he spun, and by sunup all the straw had been spun into gold. When the king arrived, he was overjoyed at the sight but hungry for still more gold. So he took the miller's daughter to an even larger room filled with straw and said, "Spin all this in one night, and if you succeed—well, then, you shall be my wife."

The king had hardly left the room when, *ka-lick*, the door opened and in came the little man, asking, "What will you give me if I spin all this straw for you one more time?"

"I have nothing left to give," the girl answered sadly.

"Then promise me this," said the little man. "Promise me that when you are queen, you will give me your first child."

The miller's daughter thought there was really very little chance that she would ever be queen, and so she promised, and the little man set to work at once. By morning the gold was piled so high that it reached the ceiling. When the king arrived, he was pleased to see all the gold he wanted. He married the miller's daughter and made her queen.

In a year's time, she brought a fine little baby into the world. She thought no more about the little man or her promise to him. Then one day, as she sat alone in her room rocking her baby, *ka-lick*, the door opened and in walked the little man, who said, "Now give me what you promised me."

The queen, filled with fear, clutched her baby tightly. "Please," she said, "I will give you all the riches of the kingdom, only leave me my child."

But the little man said, "No. I would rather have a living thing than all the treasures in the world." Then the queen began to weep and wail, and the little man felt pity for her. "I will give you this chance," he said. "In three days, if you can guess my name, then you may keep your child." Then he was gone as quickly as he had come.

The queen lay awake all night thinking of all the names she had ever heard. She sent a messenger to ride through the land and collect all the names that could be found. And when the little man came the next day, she tried all that she had been able to think of: Alexander, Balthazar, Casper, Doolittle, Eggleston, Ferdinand, and many more. But after each, the little man only said, "That is not my name."

The next day the queen sent servants all around the kingdom to find the most unusual names, and when the little man came, she tried them. "Are you called

Sheepshanks? Roast-Ribs? Snickerdoodle? Groucho? Winklehopper?" But after each, the little man only said, "That is not my name."

On the third and last day, the queen was worried sick. She held her child tight and was wondering what to do, when, *ka-lick*, the door opened and in walked—no, not the little man but the messenger the queen had sent in search of names. He bowed to the queen and said, "My lady, as I passed through the woods last night, I came to a high hill, and near it was a little house, and outside the house a fire was burning, and around the fire danced a funny little man, and as he hopped up and down he sang,

*'Today I brew, tomorrow I bake,*
*And then the fair queen's child I'll take.*
*And no one can deny my claim,*
*For Rumpelstiltskin is my name.'"*

The messenger left, and almost as soon as he had gone, the little man arrived. The queen greeted him by asking, "Is your name Jack?"

"That is not my name."

"Then are you called Harry?"

"That is not my name."

"Then perhaps," said the queen, "your name is—*Rumpelstiltskin!*"

"The devil told you that! The devil told you that!" cried the little man. And in his anger he stamped with his right foot so hard that he went into the ground up to his waist. Then he grabbed his other foot and pulled in such a fury that he split in two. And the queen and her child never feared him again.

## Sleeping Beauty

*(A tale from the Brothers Grimm)*

Once upon a time a king announced a great feast to celebrate the birth of his first child. He gave orders that all of the nobles in the land were to be invited to this feast—and all the fairies as well. For you see, there were thirteen fairies who made their home in his kingdom. The king wished to invite all of these fairies to the feast, so that each of them might look kindly upon his baby girl and perhaps give her a special fairy gift. But as the king had only twelve gold plates for the fairies to eat from, it was decided that one fairy would have to be left out.

The feast was held, and what a wonderful celebration it was. As it drew to an end, the fairies came forward to give the child gifts. One said to the child, "I give you the gift of virtue, so that you may be good." Another said, "I give you the gift of wisdom, so that you may be wise." A third fairy gave the child the gift of beauty. A fourth gave her riches. And on it went, with each fairy giving the child something wonderful, until the tiny infant had all that a human being could desire.

Eleven of the fairies had given their gifts, and the twelfth was just about to speak when, suddenly, in came the thirteenth fairy—the one who had been left out. She was very angry, and she cried out in a loud voice, "When the princess is fifteen years of age, she shall prick herself with a spindle and die!"

Without another word, the angry fairy left the hall. Everyone was terrified at what she had said. Then the twelfth fairy came forward and said, "I cannot undo this evil spell, but I can soften it. Here, then, is my gift to the child. The princess shall not die; instead she will fall into a deep sleep for a hundred years."

The king was determined to protect his child. "Surely," he said, "my daughter cannot prick herself with a spindle if she never sees one." So he gave an order that every spindle and every spinning wheel in the kingdom should be burned.

The princess grew up, and all the fairies' gifts to the child were plain to see: She was good, wise, kind, and beautiful. Everyone who saw her loved her.

On the day that the princess turned fifteen, the king and queen were away from the palace. The princess was left on her own, and she wandered about the palace, looking into all sorts of places and peeking into rooms that she had never explored before. She climbed a narrow winding stair until she came to a little door with a rusty key sticking out of the lock. She turned the key, and the door opened, and there in a little room sat an old woman with a spinning wheel, busily spinning away.

"Good day," said the princess, entering the room.

"Good day!" said the old woman.

"Excuse me," said the princess, "but would you be so kind as to tell me what you are doing?" for she had never seen a spinning wheel before.

"I am spinning," said the old woman.

The princess stretched forth her hand and asked, "What is this thing that spins around so merrily?" But hardly had she spoken when she pricked her finger on the spinning wheel's spindle, and in that very moment she fell into a deep sleep.

At the same time, sleep fell upon everyone in the palace. The king and queen, who had just come home and were in the great hall, fell fast asleep. The horses in their stalls, the dogs in the yard, the pigeons on the roof, and the flies on the walls—all fell asleep. Even the fire on the hearth went out. The wind stopped, and not a leaf fell from the trees.

In time, a hedge of thorns began to grow around the castle. The hedge grew taller and thicker every year, until at last it swallowed up the castle. Nothing could be seen of the once-famous building, not even the flags on the highest towers.

As the years passed, stories spread throughout the land. They told of a beautiful princess who slept behind the wall of thorns. Many a young prince came to seek the princess, but none could break through the thorns.

Finally the hundred years came to an end, and a worthy prince appeared to waken the princess. When the young man drew near the hedge of thorns, it changed into a hedge of beautiful flowers, which bent aside to let him pass. When he reached the castle yard, he saw the horses and dogs lying asleep, and on the roof the pigeons were sitting with their heads under their wings.

As he entered the castle and climbed the steps, the prince saw everyone still

asleep—the king, the queen, the cook, the maids, everyone. All was so quiet that he could hear his own breathing.

At last, the prince went up the narrow winding stairs and came to the room where the princess was sleeping. When he saw her looking so lovely in her sleep, he could not turn his eyes away. He bent down and kissed her. The princess opened her eyes and smiled at the prince. Together they went down the stairs, and they saw the king and queen waking up and all the people in the castle waking up and looking at one another in great surprise. The horses in the yard got up and shook themselves. The dogs sprang up and wagged their tails. The pigeons on the roof flew into the fields. The flies on the wall began to buzz. Even the kitchen fire leapt up and blazed.

A few days later the wedding of the prince and princess was held. The kingdom had never seen such feasting and rejoicing, and the prince and princess lived happily together for the rest of their days.

## The Tale of Peter Rabbit

*by Beatrix Potter*

Once upon a time, there were four little rabbits, and their names were—Flopsy, Mopsy, Cotton-tail, and Peter.

They lived with their mother in a sand-bank, underneath the root of a very big fir-tree.

"Now, my dears," said old Mrs. Rabbit one morning, "you may go into the fields or down the lane, but don't go into Mr. McGregor's garden: Your father had an accident there; he was put in a pie by Mrs. McGregor. Now run along, and don't get into mischief. I am going out."

Then old Mrs. Rabbit took a basket and her umbrella, and went through the wood to the baker's. She bought a loaf of brown bread and five currant buns.

Flopsy, Mopsy, and Cotton-tail, who were good little bunnies, went down the lane to gather blackberries. But Peter, who was very naughty, ran straight away to Mr. McGregor's garden, and squeezed under the gate!

First he ate some lettuces and some French beans; and then he ate some radishes; and then, feeling rather sick, he went to look for some parsley.

But round the end of a cucumber frame, whom should he meet but Mr. McGregor!

Mr. McGregor was on his hands and knees planting out young cabbages, but he jumped up and ran after Peter, waving a rake and calling out, "Stop, thief!"

Peter was most dreadfully frightened; he rushed all over the garden, for he had forgotten the way back to the gate.

He lost one of his shoes among the cabbages, and the other shoe amongst the potatoes.

After losing them, he ran on four legs and went faster, so that I think he might have got away altogether if he had not unfortunately run into a gooseberry net, and got caught by the large buttons on his jacket. It was a blue jacket with brass buttons, quite new.

Peter gave himself up for lost, and shed big tears; but his sobs were overheard by some friendly sparrows, who flew to him in great excitement, and implored him to exert himself.

Mr. McGregor came up with a sieve, which he intended to pop upon the top of Peter; but Peter wriggled out just in time, leaving his jacket behind him. And rushed into the tool-shed, and jumped into a can. It would have been a beautiful thing to hide in, if it had not had so much water in it.

Mr. McGregor was quite sure that Peter was somewhere in the tool-shed, perhaps hidden underneath a flower-pot. He began to turn them over carefully, looking under each.

Presently Peter sneezed—"Kertyschoo!" Mr. McGregor was after him in no time. And tried to put his foot upon Peter, who jumped out of a window, upsetting three plants. The window was too small for Mr. McGregor, and he was tired of running after Peter. He went back to his work.

Peter sat down to rest; he was out of breath and trembling with fright, and he had not the least idea which way to go. Also he was very damp with sitting in that can.

After a time he began to wander about, going lippity—lippity—not very fast, and looking all round.

He found a door in a wall; but it was locked, and there was no room for a fat little rabbit to squeeze underneath.

An old mouse was running in and out over the stone doorstep, carrying peas and beans to her family in the wood. Peter asked her the way to the gate, but she had such a large pea in her mouth that she could not answer. She only shook her head at him. Peter began to cry.

Then he tried to find his way straight across the garden, but he became more and more puzzled. Presently, he came to a pond where Mr. McGregor filled his water-cans. A white cat was staring at some gold-fish; she sat very, very still, but now and then the tip of her tail twitched as if it were alive. Peter thought it best to go away without speaking to her; he had heard about cats from his cousin, little Benjamin Bunny.

He went back towards the tool-shed, but suddenly, quite close to him, he heard the noise of a hoe—sc-r-ritch, scratch, scratch, scratch. Peter scuttered underneath the bushes. But presently, as nothing happened, he came out, and climbed upon a wheelbarrow and peeped over. The first thing he saw was Mr. McGregor hoeing onions. His back was turned towards Peter, and beyond him was the gate!

Peter got down very quietly off the wheelbarrow, and started running as fast as he could go, along a straight walk behind some black-currant bushes.

Mr. McGregor caught sight of him at the corner, but Peter did not care. He slipped underneath the gate, and was safe at last in the wood outside the garden.

Mr. McGregor hung up the little jacket and the shoes for a scare-crow to frighten the blackbirds.

Peter never stopped running or looked behind him till he got home to the big fir-tree.

He was so tired that he flopped down upon the nice soft sand on the floor of the rabbit-hole and shut his eyes. His mother was busy cooking; she wondered what he had done with his clothes. It was the second little jacket and pair of shoes that Peter had lost in a fortnight!

I am sorry to say that Peter was not very well during the evening.

His mother put him to bed, and made some chamomile tea; and she gave a dose of it to Peter!

"One table-spoonful to be taken at bed-time."

But Flopsy, Mopsy, and Cotton-tail had bread and milk and blackberries for supper.

Check your library for many more wonderful stories written and illustrated by Beatrix Potter, including *The Tale of Benjamin Bunny, The Tale of the Flopsy Bunnies, The Tale of Squirrel Nutkin, The Tale of Two Bad Mice, The Tale of Mrs. Tittlemouse*, and more.

## Why the Owl Has Big Eyes

*(An Iroquois legend)*

**PARENTS:** Like many Native American stories—indeed, like many folktales from different people around the world—this story tells how something came to be. (For an example of this kind of story from West Africa, see "All Stories Are Anansi's," page 54.)

Raweno, the spirit who makes everything, was busy creating animals. This afternoon, he was working on Rabbit. "May I have nice long legs and long ears like Deer's?" Rabbit asked. "And sharp fangs and claws like Panther's?"

"Certainly," Raweno said. But he had gotten no further than shaping Rabbit's hind legs when he was interrupted by Owl.

"Whoo, whoo. I want a nice long neck like Swan's," Owl demanded. "And beautiful red feathers like Cardinal's, and a long beak like Egret's, and a royal crown of plumes like Heron's. I want you to make me into the swiftest and the most beautiful of all birds."

"Be quiet," Raweno said. "You know that no one is supposed to watch me at work. Turn around, and close your eyes!"

Raweno shaped Rabbit's ears, long and alert, just like Deer's.

"Whoo, whoo," Owl said. "Nobody can forbid me to watch. I won't turn around and I certainly won't close my eyes. I like watching, and watch I will."

Then Raweno became angry. Forgetting Rabbit's front legs, he grabbed Owl from his branch and shook him with all his might. Owl's eyes grew big and round with fright. Raweno pushed down on Owl's head and pulled up on his ears until they stood up on both sides of his head.

"There!" Raweno said. "Now you have ears that are big enough to listen when someone tells you what to do, and a short neck that won't let you crane your head to watch things you shouldn't watch. And your eyes are big, but you can use them only at night—not during the day, when I am working. And finally, as punishment for your disobedience, your feathers won't be red like Cardinal's but ugly and gray, like this." And he rubbed Owl all over with mud.

Then he turned back to finish Rabbit. But where was he? Poor Rabbit had been so frightened by Raweno's anger that he had fled, unfinished. To this day, Rabbit must hop about on his uneven legs, and he has remained frightened, for he never received the fangs and claws he had requested. As for Owl, he remained as Raweno shaped him in his anger—with big eyes, a short neck, big ears, and the ability to see only at night, when Raweno isn't working.

Here are some more stories from different Native American peoples that tell how things came to be. Check your library for:

*Coyote: A Trickster Tale from the American Southwest* by Gerald Mc-Dermott (Harcourt Brace, 1994).

*Crow Chief: A Plains Indian Story* by Paul Goble (Orchard Books, 1992).

*Quillworker: A Cheyenne Legend* retold by Terri Cohlene (Watermill Press, 1990).

## Drama

Do you like to pretend? Maybe sometimes you and your friends pretend to be knights and princesses, or space explorers, or cops and robbers. Maybe you like to play with dolls and dress them up and speak for them.

When you do this, you are playacting. Another word for playacting is *drama*. Many television shows and movies are drama. Have you ever seen or been in a play, with actors in costume on a stage? That's drama too.

You and some friends can perform your own drama. You can be the actors and actresses. You can put on costumes. You can decorate the stage with scenery to show where your play is taking place. You will need to remember some words to speak; those words are called your lines. All the lines for the actors and actresses to say are written in the script. The script also gives some special directions, such as telling you when to come on the stage and when to go off.

Speak your lines in a big clear voice so that the people watching the play—the audience—can hear you. When you're acting onstage, people are watching you, but you have to act as if they're not there!

Here is a script for a play called *The Boy Who Cried Wolf*. It's a drama based on one of Aesop's fables (which you can read in this book on page 48). What kind of costumes will you use? What kind of scenery will you make?

> **Do it Yourself!**
> Put on your own drama using the script from *The Boy Who Cried Wolf*, on pages 148–52.

## The Boy Who Cried Wolf: A Drama

**Cast of Characters**

Announcer

John the Shepherd Boy

Farmer Brown

Second Farmer

Third Farmer

The Wolf

Sheep

(Note: Boys or girls can play any of these parts. If a girl plays the shepherd, you can change the name if you want.)

*The curtain opens. The Announcer comes onstage and talks directly to the audience.*

**ANNOUNCER:** Hello. Our drama is called *The Boy Who Cried Wolf.* This play comes from a fable by Aesop. A fable is a story that teaches a lesson. We hope you enjoy the play. Thank you.

*[The Announcer leaves the stage. Enter from opposite sides of the stage Farmer Brown and John the Shepherd Boy. They meet in the middle.]*

**FARMER BROWN:** Good morning, John. What are you doing out so early?

**JOHN:** Good morning, Farmer Brown. I'm going to the pasture to watch the sheep for my father. I've been watching them all summer.

**FARMER BROWN:** That's a big job for a young boy! I'm sure your father is very grateful to you.

**JOHN:** Oh, yes, he is. But I wish that I had someone to talk to or play with. There's no one around but the sheep.

**FARMER BROWN**: Do you see that valley way over there? *[Points to one side of the stage.]* I will be working there with my friends for a few weeks. We will be working very hard, so we cannot play. But if any trouble comes up, you can come get us.

**JOHN**: Thank you, Farmer Brown. Goodbye.

**FARMER BROWN**: Goodbye, John. Take good care of your sheep.

*[They exit on opposite sides of the stage. Now the Sheep come onstage.]*

**SHEEP**: We are a flock of fleecy sheep,
Baa! Baa! Baa!
We like to eat and play and sleep,
Baa! Baa! Baa!
The shepherd boy keeps watch all day,
Baa! Baa! Baa!
He keeps the big bad wolf away!
Baa! Baa! Baa!

*[John enters. He moves the Sheep toward a back corner of the stage. Meanwhile, Farmer Brown and the two other farmers enter and stay at the opposite end of the stage, where they "work" by pretending to dig, hoe, pick crops, etc.]*

**JOHN**: Oh, I'm so tired of watching sheep! I wish I had someone to talk to. Nothing exciting ever happens here, not even a wolf. *[He looks across to where the three farmers are working.]* I wish Farmer Brown and his friends would come here. I know! I'll cry "Wolf!" and make them think a wolf is eating the sheep. Then they'll come running. *[He runs toward the farmers and cries loudly.]* Wolf! Wolf!

*[The farmers drop their work and come running.]*

**FARMER BROWN**: Where is he? Where's the wolf?

**SECOND FARMER**: Where did he go? I don't see him.

**THIRD FARMER**: Has he gone already? Are we too late?

*[The farmers suddenly notice that John is laughing but trying to hide it.]*

**FARMER BROWN**: Why are you laughing, John? What's so funny about a wolf?

**SECOND FARMER**: Are you playing a joke on us, boy?

**THIRD FARMER**: If you are, I don't think it's very funny.

**JOHN** *[embarrassed]*: There wasn't any wolf. I was tired of staying here alone, so I cried "Wolf" just for fun.

**FARMER BROWN**: John, you had better not play any more jokes like that.

**SECOND FARMER**: That's right. You'll be sorry if a real wolf comes.

**THIRD FARMER**: Come on, friends. We have work to do!

*[The farmers leave the stage. John lets out a big sigh, hangs his head, and exits on the opposite side of the stage. The Announcer enters.]*

**ANNOUNCER**: Do you think that John has learned his lesson? I am sorry to say he did not. A few days later, he played the same trick again. The farmers ran to help him, and when they found out there was no wolf, they were very angry. Now a few more days have passed. And once again John the Shepherd Boy is watching the sheep.

*[The Announcer exits. Enter the Sheep, followed by John, sighing loudly and looking very tired and bored. Also enter the farmers, who go to work in their field.]*

**SHEEP**: We are a flock of fleecy sheep,

Baa! Baa! Baa!

We like to eat and play and sleep . . .

**JOHN** *[interrupting the Sheep]*: Oh, blah, blah, blah! I don't think I can stand this anymore. Every day, the same old thing. *[As John talks, the Wolf creeps onto the stage, looking very dangerous. The Sheep start baaing nervously but quietly, so that John can be heard.]* I never get to see anyone, or talk to anyone, or play any games. I want to have fun. I want some excitement. I want a . . . *[The Wolf has pulled one sheep from the flock. As he does, that sheep lets out a loud "BAA!" just as John is speaking. John turns and sees the Wolf—and finishes his sentence.]* . . . wolf!

*[The Wolf pulls the sheep off the stage. All the Sheep are baaing in fear. John runs toward the farmers, crying loudly.]* Wolf! Wolf! Help, come quick!

**FARMER BROWN**: A wolf? Really and truly, John?

**JOHN**: Really and truly! Hurry, come quick!

*[Farmer Brown starts to walk toward John, but the Second Farmer stops him.]*

**SECOND FARMER**: Wait a minute. Don't let the boy make a fool of us again.

**THIRD FARMER**: That's right. He's already played the same trick twice.

**FARMER BROWN**: But what if it's a real wolf?

**SECOND FARMER**: Then that's the boy's fault. How can we trust him when he plays so many tricks on us?

**FARMER BROWN**: I guess you're right. Let's get back to work.
   *[The farmers go back to their work. John runs back to the Sheep. He walks around the flock, looking as though he has lost something and can't find it.]*

**JOHN**: Oh, I have lost a poor little lamb. Why wouldn't they come to help me? What did I do to deserve this? Why didn't they believe me? Why? Why?!

**SHEEP**: *[all turning to stare at John]*: BAAAAAAA!

**JOHN**: All right, I know, I know. I didn't tell the truth before, so they didn't believe me this time. I'll never do that again, I promise—really and truly!
   *[John leads the Sheep, baaing, off the stage. Curtain closes.]*

One of the best parts of being in a play is hearing people applaud when it's over. That's when it's time for you to come out and take a bow. Usually only one actor at a time comes out on the stage. For this play, you would come out in this order: The Wolf, Sheep (all together), Third Farmer, Second Farmer, Farmer Brown, and John. When all of you are onstage, you can take one last bow together. And enjoy all the clapping—it's for you!

# Familiar Sayings

**PARENTS:** Every culture has phrases and proverbs that make no sense when carried over literally into another culture. To say, for example, that someone has "let the cat out of the bag" has nothing to do with setting free a trapped kitty. Nor—thank goodness— does it ever literally "rain cats and dogs"!

The sayings and phrases in this section may be familiar to many children, who hear them at home. But the inclusion of these sayings and phrases in the Core Knowledge Sequence has been singled out for gratitude by many parents and teachers who work with children from home cultures that are different from the culture of literate American English.

For first graders, we have chosen to introduce a selection of sayings that are likely to have some connections to the child's world of experience.

## An apple a day keeps the doctor away.

People use this saying to mean that eating apples helps keep you healthy.

When she unpacked her lunch, Janet groaned, "An apple again!"

"But that's good," said her friend Mae. "An apple a day keeps the doctor away."

---

**Make a Connection**
Learn about the human body in the "Science" chapter, on page 402.

**Make a Connection**

How might the princess in "The Frog Prince" (page 65) learn from this saying?

## Do unto others as you would have them do unto you.

This saying is called the Golden Rule. People use it to mean: Treat people as you would like to be treated yourself. It comes from the Bible.

"Molly, stop drawing on Becky's picture," said the babysitter. "Would you like Becky to mess up your picture? Remember: Do unto others as you would have them do unto you."

## Hit the nail on the head.

When you use a hammer, you have to hit the nail right on its head to make it go in straight. So when someone says you "hit the nail on the head," they mean that you have said or done something just right.

Caitlin was frustrated with her costume for the play. "There's just something wrong with it, and I can't figure it out," she said.

"Why don't you take off the crown and use this feather instead?" suggested Sara.

"That's it!" cried Caitlin. "Thanks, Sara. You hit the nail right on the head!"

## If at first you don't succeed, try, try again.

People use this saying to mean: Don't give up; keep trying.

Peter fell every time he tried the skateboard. "You'll get the hang of it, Pete," said his brother. "If at first you don't succeed, try, try again."

## Land of Nod.

To be in the "land of Nod" means to be asleep.

"I can't sleep!" Cassie said to her big sister, Anne. Both girls had been in bed for half an hour. The room was dark and cool, and they could hear crickets chirping outside.

"Close your eyes, Cassie," said Anne, "and I'll sing you a lullaby." She began to hum a tune to her little sister, and it was not long before Cassie drifted off to the Land of Nod.

## Let the cat out of the bag.

If you "let the cat out of the bag," you tell something that was meant to be a secret.

"Jake let the cat out of the bag: He told Hannah about her surprise party."

## The more the merrier.

People use this saying to welcome newcomers to a group. They say this because it means: The more people who take part, the more fun it can be.

The house was full of kids playing. Still, when the doorbell rang, Mr. DeNiro opened the door and waved in more children, saying, "Come in, come in, the more the merrier."

**Never leave till tomorrow what you can do today.**

People use this saying to mean: Don't put off things you have to do.

"Let's clean up in the morning," said Heidi.

"No," said Tina, "let's clean up now. You know what Grandma always says: 'Never leave till tomorrow what you can do today.'"

**Practice makes perfect.**

People use this saying to mean: Doing something over and over makes you good at it.

"Mrs. Kim," asked Jennie, "we wrote capital letters yesterday. Do we have to do it again today?"

"Yes, Jennie. We'll write them again today and every day this week. Practice makes perfect!"

## There's no place like home.

People use this saying to mean that travel may be pleasant, but home is the best place of all.

"What a great trip!" said Yoshiko. "We saw the Statue of Liberty and went to the beach and visited great museums!"

"Yes," said her mother, "we did have a wonderful time, but I'm glad to be back. There's no place like home."

**Make a Connection**

Reread "Tom Thumb" (pages 91–95). Do you think Tom thinks "there's no place like home"?

See the Aesop fables in this book (pages 47–53) for more sayings:

- "A wolf in sheep's clothing."
- "Don't count your chickens before they're hatched."
- "Sour grapes."

# II
# History and Geography

# Introduction

For many years, American elementary schools (especially in kindergarten through third grade) have taught "social studies" rather than history. Social studies have typically been made up of lessons about the family, neighborhood, and community. This focus on the personal and the local can be of value, but it is only a beginning.

As anyone knows who has witnessed children's fascination with dinosaurs, knights in armor, or pioneers on the prairie, young children are interested not just in themselves and their immediate surroundings but also in other people, places, and times. In first grade, we can take advantage of children's natural curiosity and begin to broaden their horizons. An early introduction to history and geography can foster an understanding of the broad world beyond the child's locality and make her aware of varied people and ways of life. Such historical study can also begin to develop children's sense of our nation's past and its significance.

In the following pages, we introduce—let us emphasize, *introduce*—a variety of people and events, most of which will be treated more fully in later grades. The idea in first grade is to plant seeds of knowledge that can grow later. The purpose for the child is not to achieve deep historical knowledge but, rather, to become familiar with people, terms, and ideas in such a way that, in later years, when the child hears them mentioned or reads about them, she enjoys the satisfying sense that "I know something about that."

Learning history is not simply a matter of being able to recall names and dates, though the value of getting a firm mental grip on a few names and dates—such as 1607 and 1776—should not be discounted. First graders have not, of course, developed a sophisticated sense of chronology that allows them to appreciate the vast expanses of years between, say, the American Revolution, ancient Egypt, and the Ice Age—all of which, to the first grader, happened long, long ago. Nevertheless, the development of a chronological sense is aided by having at least a few dates fixed in mind and associated with specific events, so that later, as the child grows, he can begin to develop a better sense of what happened when.

While it's good to help children grasp a few important facts, for young children the best history teaching emphasizes the "story" in history. By appealing to children's naturally active imaginations, we can ask them to "visit" people and places in the past, for example, we take children on a trip down the Nile River with King Tut in ancient Egypt and let them spend a day as the Sapa Inca, ruler of the Inca Empire. We encourage parents and teachers to go beyond these pages to help children learn about history through art projects, drama, music, and discussions.

In this section we introduce children not only to ancient civilizations but also to topics in the history of world religions. Many people were consulted during the development of the *Core Knowledge Sequence* (see pages vii–viii), and they agreed that religion is a shaping force in the history of civilization and thus should be included in the curriculum. The pages on religion have benefited from the critiques of religious scholars and representatives of various faiths. In introducing children to the history of world religions, we focus on symbols, figures, stories, and places of worship. Our goal is to be descriptive, not prescriptive, and to maintain a sense of respect and balance. In this book we introduce Judaism, Christianity, and Islam. Later books in this series discuss other world religions, including Hinduism and Buddhism.

We suggest that you read the "World History and Geography" section of this book with your child first, as the "American History" section assumes some familiarity with terms introduced in World History.

# World History and Geography

## History: Everyone's Story

History. Listen closely to the word: "history." Do you hear another word in it? Do you hear the word "story"?

History is a story. It's the story of all the people who have lived before us. It helps us remember who we are and what we've done.

When you study history, you learn stories of great men and women who have done extraordinary things. In this book, you'll meet Egyptian pharaohs who built amazing monuments in the desert and explorers who cut a path through the wilderness. You will meet a man who was so important in American history that he is known as the father of his country and a woman who disguised herself as a man to fight for that same country.

History is not just the story of emperors and presidents. It's also the story of ordinary people, of farmers, builders, artists, sailors, soldiers, teachers, and children. Their stories are worth knowing. They are our stories. History is about how we have changed and how we've stayed the same. And so history is everyone's story.

## The Ice Age: Humans on the Move

Our story begins a long, long time ago, before your parents or grandparents or even their parents or grandparents were born—in fact, way before their parents and grandparents or even their great-grandparents were born. How long ago? Well, take a deep breath and say, "long, long, long, long . . ." over and over until your breath gives out—and that's about how long ago our story begins.

In this long-ago time, the Earth was colder than it is now, and life was harder in many ways. To stay alive, people hunted and gathered plants to eat. At night they took shelter in damp caves and huddled around fires to keep warm. They couldn't buy their clothes or food. They had to make or find everything they needed to live. They made tools out of sticks and stones. They made needles out of bones, and they used these needles to sew animal skins together and make clothes.

But their most important task was finding food. Just like you, they got hungry and they had to eat. Of course, way back then they couldn't go shopping at a grocery store! To get food, they picked the wild plants that grew around them and they hunted for animals to eat.

Because the early humans were hunters, they were always on the move from place to place. Why did they have to keep moving? Can you think of a reason? They kept moving because they were following the animals they hunted. In those long-ago days, great herds of woolly mammoths, bison, and reindeer roamed the land. As the animal herds moved on, the human beings followed because those animals were their breakfast, lunch, and dinner!

The animals kept moving because they were looking for food, too, and for greener grass and a warmer climate. Back then, the Earth was colder than it is now. It was so cold that much of the Earth was covered by huge sheets of ice called glaciers—which is why we call that long-long-ago time the Ice Age.

## Learning About the Ice Age

Modern scientists who are called archaeologists [ar-key-AHL-oh-jists] try to learn about people who lived long ago by finding things those people left behind. If they find writings that have survived from long ago, archaeologists can study those writings and use them to figure out how people lived in the past. But archaeologists cannot study writings from the Ice Age, because writing had not been invented back in the Ice Age. The Ice Age people talked and told stories, but they did not have a way to write messages to one another.

Scientists who study the Ice Age have to look for clues of a different sort. They study things like tools and weapons. They also study bones—both the bones of men and women who lived during the Ice Age and the bones of animals they hunted.

Archaeologists also study cave paintings. Ice Age people could not write, but they could draw, and scientists have discovered many paintings they created. What do you think these wandering hunters drew? Was it something they needed to stay alive? If you said "wild animals," you're right! Most of the cave paintings that have survived show wild animals. Sometimes they also show Ice Age hunters hunting those animals.

These cave paintings were found in Algeria, in Northern Africa. Can you see the people? What sort of animal do you think they are wrestling with?

## Ötzi the Iceman

In 1991, scientists who study how humans lived long ago got a big surprise. Two hikers who were out for a walk along the Austrian–Italian border in the Alps Mountains came upon the body of a man that was partly covered in ice. The hikers called the police, and it turned out that the man in the ice was a hunter who had died more  than five thousand years ago. The ice had covered his body and preserved it.

Scientists named the man Ötzi [ET-zee]. They studied the clothes he wore and the tools he carried with him. They took X-rays of his body and did all sorts of tests. They even examined the food that was in Ötzi's stomach when he died!

Here are some of the things they found: Ötzi's lungs were blackened, probably from many hours of sitting around a campfire. One of his last meals was deer meat. He had several cavities in his teeth. He had a tattoo. He wore shoes made out of animal skins. He carried an ax, a knife, and some arrows.

The photograph is a reconstruction that shows what scientists think Ötzi looked like at the time of his death.

We've come a long way since the Ice Age. Today most people don't have to hunt to survive. Most of us don't have to wander around. We can settle in one place for a while. People have learned how to farm and grow food, so we don't have to follow animals. We have built towns and cities, and we know how to write.

You can see that, since the time of the early humans, there have been a lot of big changes in the way people live—changes like settling down in one place, learning how to farm, building cities, and communicating by writing. These changes are all part of what we mean by "civilization." That's a big word: Try saying it a few times. And as you say it, think of some of the things that make civilized people different from those Ice Age hunters long ago: things like living in one place, farming, building cities, and writing messages.

The first civilizations began in Africa and Asia. Can you find those continents on a globe or world map? Now let's learn about two of the earliest civilizations. Let's go first to **ancient** Egypt.

## Egypt: Gift of the Nile

Egypt is in Africa. It is located mostly within a giant desert called the Sahara. Do you know what the weather is usually like in a desert? It's dry. It doesn't rain much at all.

Even though they lived in a desert, the ancient Egyptians were among the first people to learn to farm. Now, wait a minute: How could that be? To grow crops, you need enough water. How could they farm in Egypt, with all that burning sun and so little rain?

**New Word**

When you hear the Egyptians or other people in this book described as **ancient**, it doesn't mean that they grew to be very old. It means that the people were part of a civilization that existed a long, long time ago. Ancient Egypt is the civilization that existed in Egypt thousands and thousands of years ago.

**Make a Connection**

Read more about what it is like in the desert in the "Habitats" section of the "Science" chapter, on page 385.

The Sahara Desert

**Talk and Think**

Sometimes children think that rivers flow *down*—toward the bottom, or the south, on a map. Remind them that rivers flow from high land to lower land. Find the Nile on a map or globe and trace the river's flow from its source in the mountains to its mouth on the Mediterranean.

In fact, the Egyptian soil wasn't as dry as you might think. Egypt had very little rain, but it had a great treasure—a fantastic flooding river called the Nile.

The Nile is the lo-o-o-ongest river in the world. Do you see it on the map? It begins high in the rain-soaked mountains of central Africa and drips down the mountainsides. It twists and splashes into calm lakes and beautiful waterfalls. The Nile travels north for thousands of miles, and when it finally reaches the desert, this river does more than flow. It floods!

Once a year the Nile overflows its banks. The river's yearly flood turns one of the driest parts of the world into fertile ground ("fertile" means that plants can grow there very easily). After the Nile floods, for about ten miles along either side of the river, the soil turns a rich black. It's full of minerals and other good things that help crops grow.

Five thousand years ago, the Nile's gift of rich black soil meant so much to the early Egyptians that they named their country "Black Land." We call such moist, rich soil "silt." If you mix silt, sunshine, and seeds together, plants will grow. Along the banks of the Nile, warm breezes blew wild barley seeds into the soil, and food crops sprang from the ground.

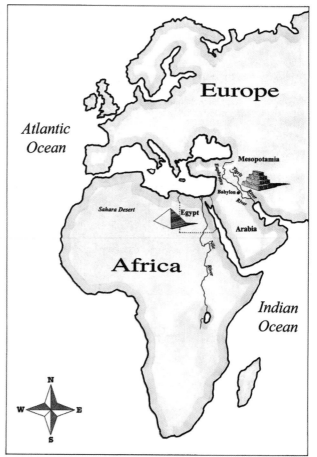

The Egyptians didn't just wait for nature to blow the seeds into the soil. They began planting seeds on purpose along the banks of the Nile. They grew big crops of grains like barley and wheat, whose seeds can be ground up into flour. We still grow these grains today. They are used in foods like cereal and bread.

When the Egyptians began to grow crops they could eat, then they didn't have to hunt as much. They began to stay in one place in order to be near their fields and take care of their crops. They began to build villages and cities. They began to build a civilization.

An Egyptian village on the banks of the Nile River

## Fantastic Pharaohs and Marvelous Monuments

The Egyptians built an amazing civilization. They built enormous buildings and monuments that are still among the biggest ever made. They built huge stone temples and pyramids. Why did they do it?

Well, one reason was that the pharaohs [FAIR-ohs] ordered them to do it. Who were the pharaohs? They were the rulers of ancient Egypt. The pharaohs had wonderful names that are fun to say—Rameses [RAM-uh-sees], Amenhotep [ah-men-HOE-tep], Tutankhamen [toot-awn-KAH-men], and Hatshepsut [hat-SHEP-soot]. They were like kings and queens, but in some ways they were even more powerful than kings. The people of ancient Egypt thought the pharaoh was divine—which means the people thought he was not just a powerful person but also a god. This belief in the pharaoh as a living god-king made his commands very powerful indeed!

The pharaohs wanted to inspire and amaze people with their greatness. Each pharaoh wanted to show his people that he was even more powerful and important than the god-king who had come before him.

Imagine for a moment that you're the pharaoh. You are very proud and boastful. To show everyone how powerful and important you are, what would you

A statue of Rameses II

do? Would you have someone write a story about the great things you've done? Would you have artists make huge statues of yourself for everyone to see? Those ideas occurred to the pharaohs too.

**Make a Connection**

Read about how ancient Egyptians used art to demonstrate their wealth and power on page 266.

The pharaohs ordered thousands of enslaved people to build great monuments to them and to the gods they worshipped. They ordered workers to carve large images of their faces in stone. Now, imagine for a moment that you're one of the workers: You sweat and strain in the sun as you drag huge, heavy stones across the hot sand. Maybe you don't think as highly of the pharaoh as he does of himself!

One very important pharaoh, Rameses II, thought he was so great that he even erased from the monuments the names of many pharaohs who had come before him. He made sure only his stories were written on the walls of the buildings!

## Hieroglyphics: Picture Writing

Do you remember the reason we know only a little about the early humans in the Ice Age? It's because those early humans did not have a way to write anything about themselves. But we know a lot more about the ancient Egyptians. Why do you think we know more?

Did you say it is because the Egyptians knew how to write? If so, you got it right! The Egyptians had an interesting form of writing. Instead of writing with letters, as you're learning to do, they used picture writing. This picture writing is called hieroglyphics. Archaeologists have figured

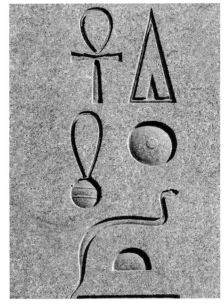

Hieroglyphics carved in stone

out what many of the hieroglyphics mean, so we can learn a lot about the Egyptians from what they wrote.

When Rameses II ordered his workers to tell his stories, they carved hieroglyphics in stone. Each picture—whether of a falcon, a snake, or a shepherd's staff—stood for a sound or had a meaning. One of the reasons we know so much about Rameses is that his workers wrote a lot about him.

## The Rosetta Stone

For a long time, nobody knew how to read hieroglyphics. People knew that hieroglyphics meant something, but they did not know what. Then some soldiers found a large stone called the Rosetta Stone. What was special about the Rosetta Stone was not that it had hieroglyphics carved on it— there were already lots of stones with hieroglyphics on them. What was special about it was that it had the same message written in three different languages, and one of those languages was ancient Greek. Since people knew how to read ancient Greek, they were able to figure out what the hieroglyphics were saying. Nowadays scholars can read most Egyptian hieroglyphics.

## A Journey Down the Nile

Are you ready for an adventure? Imagine you can travel back thousands of years to ancient Egypt. We're going for a trip down the Nile!

There's a boat floating on the river, and, look, there's a young man wearing a fancy headdress. He's nodding to you. You're lucky to have him as your host. Although he's young—only a teenager—he is very important. In fact, he's the pharaoh!

His name is Tutankhamen. Let's call him "King Tut" for short. Come on, hurry up—pharaohs aren't used to waiting for anyone.

In a very dignified voice, King Tut says, "Welcome aboard. I am so pleased that you can join us for the crocodile hunt."

"Crocodile hunt?!" you sputter. "But I don't even know how to fish!"

"Do not worry about a thing," King Tut responds. "My servants will spear the creatures for you." You look around and see that there are many people on the boat who are ready to wait on the young pharaoh's every need. They bow very low before him. You wonder what their lives are like: Are they afraid of this young pharaoh? Do they get tired of having to wait on him and do whatever he asks?

A servant brings King Tut a fruit drink and offers you one, too. You sip your drink and enjoy the sights as the boat floats along the Nile. "Look over there," says King Tut. "Do you see that enormous statue—that huge figure with the body of a lion and the head of a human? That is the Great Sphinx. The Sphinx is like the pharaoh: The pharaoh rules as a man, and he is as powerful as a lion.

The Great Sphinx (Its nose was accidentally knocked off about 200 years ago.)

Two pyramids

"And look there," says Tut, "near the Sphinx. Do you see the pyramids?"

How could you miss them? They're huge! The biggest pyramid covers a space on the ground as big as thirteen football fields (of course, they didn't play football way back in Tut's time)! You look at the young pharaoh and ask, "Why did you build the pyramids, King Tut? What are they for?"

Tut laughs and says, "Oh, I did not build them! Those pyramids have been around for hundreds of years. They are the sacred tombs of the god-kings who ruled before me. They are the burial places of ancestor pharaohs from long ago."

"But, King Tut," you ask, "why do you go to all that trouble to bury someone?"

"For us," the young pharaoh explains, "it is not a simple matter of just putting a pharaoh in the ground after he dies. No, what is important to us is the way the pharaoh lives after he dies."

Tut can tell that you're puzzled, so he goes on. "You know," he says, "that Egyptian pharaohs are god-kings. We believe that after our bodies die, our spirits keep on living—if we make the necessary prepa-

**Do It Yourself!**

Invite your child to draw a pyramid and decorate it with hieroglyphics of his or her own creation. Encourage your child to make a key that shows which letter, sound, or word each hieroglyphic stands for.

rations. First, our bodies must be well preserved, because the body provides a home for the spirit after death. So our priests prepare the bodies of dead pharaohs in a special way. They take out some of the organs. They wash the body and rub it with fragrant spices and special oils. One of the last things they do is wrap the body in rolls of white cloth, to make a mummy."

"Did you say *mommy*?"

"No, 'mummy.'" Tut goes on: "The mummy is very important. It's a home for the pharaoh's ever-living spirit. If the mummy is damaged, the spirit cannot live. So the mummy must be kept safe. That is why the pyramids were built. The pyramids are very safe places to protect the pharaoh's mummy."

"Still," you ask, "why do the pyramids have to be so big?"

"Oh, there is much more in the pyramid than just a mummy," Tut answers. "The pyramids are filled with different chambers and passageways. The room where the mummy lies contains everything the pharaoh needs in the afterlife."

"What does he need?" you ask.

"Why," says Tut, "his spirit needs almost everything he needed in his earthly life—food, furniture, jewelry, games, and much more."

Tut leans over and motions for you to come very close. Then he whispers to you, "If you can keep a secret, I'll tell you where I am to be buried."

"You can trust me," you whisper back. "Where?"

"There," he says, as he points up the Nile toward some distant hills.

"Is that where you'll have your pyramid built?" you ask.

This illustration, from the Egyptian Book of the Dead, shows the preparation of a mummy.

"No, no," says Tut with a frown. Then he explains that pharaohs aren't buried in pyramids anymore, because too many robbers, who have no respect for the dead, have broken into the monuments of the great pharaohs and stolen all the treasures. So, when Tut dies, he will be buried in a tomb hidden underground in a faraway place called the Valley of the Kings.

Thinking about tombs has made Tut very serious. In a friendly but firm voice, he tells you, "It is time for you to go now." You're just about to speak up and point out that you haven't caught a crocodile yet, but then you remember: It's not a good idea to talk back to a pharaoh!

## A Woman Pharaoh

Were all the pharaohs of Egypt men? Most were, but once there was a woman pharaoh named Hatshepsut. She didn't want to be called "queen." She wanted to be known as "pharaoh." She led armies into battle, and she ordered the building of great monuments. Here you can see a statue of Hatshepsut.

## The Treasures of King Tut

King Tut was a real pharaoh who lived thousands of years ago. He did a very good job hiding his tomb. It wasn't so very long ago—in 1922—that a hardworking archaeologist, after searching for five years, finally found Tut's tomb in the Valley of the Kings. As he entered the tomb, his eyes opened wide in amazement: It was in almost perfect condition! The tomb was full of decorated chairs, shining jewelry, fancy clothes, and thousands of other objects that had been buried with the pharaoh.

Here you can see two of the treasures from King Tut's tomb: a beautiful golden mask and a throne.

## Animal Gods

The ancient Egyptians believed in many gods. They often pictured their gods as having human bodies with the heads of animals, such as lions, rams, or crocodiles! The god of the sun, called Amon (sometimes Amon-Ra), had a ram's head. The sky god, Horus, had the head of a bird called a falcon.

## Mesopotamia—Another Gift

**Do It Yourself!**

Locate the Tigris and Euphrates rivers on a map or globe and trace the direction of their flow. Explain that "Mesopotamia" means the land between two rivers.

In Egypt, the Nile flooded every year. East of Egypt, on the continent of Asia, two other rivers flooded yearly. These neighboring rivers are called the Tigris [TIE-gris] and the Euphrates [yoo-FRAY-teez]. Like the Nile, when these rivers flooded, they gave the gift of rich soil. That meant people who lived beside or between the rivers could farm, grow plenty of food, and build their homes.

This warm and pleasant region has a long name, Mesopotamia [MESS-uh-puh-TAY-me-uh]. What happened between the Tigris and Euphrates rivers? A lot!

Mesopotamia is known as "the cradle of civilization" because history was born here. Remember, history is a story: So when we say history was born in Mesopotamia, we mean that it's the place where people first

The cuneiform writing developed in ancient Mesopotamia used wedge-shaped symbols.

began to write down the story of human lives. Even before the ancient Egyptians started writing with hieroglyphics, the early people of Mesopotamia had begun to write. We call their kind of writing cuneiform [KYOO-nee-uh-form]. It's a strange-sounding word, and it means wedge-shaped, which is exactly what cuneiform was: a thin, triangular, wedge-shaped kind of writing.

## A Great Mesopotamian Story

Not so long ago, archaeologists were digging in this cradle of civilization. They found twelve clay tablets covered with cuneiform. The tablets were more than five thousand years old! They told an exciting story—perhaps the world's oldest story. We do not know what the people of Mesopotamia called it, but we call it the Epic of Gilgamesh [GILL-guh-mesh].

An epic is a long story filled with the adventures of a hero. The Epic of Gilgamesh tells the story of a mighty king named Gilgamesh. In the beginning of the story, Gilgamesh is a harsh ruler. He forces his people to build high walls and tall monuments and never lets them rest. But this changes when Gilgamesh meets another hero, named Enkidu. Although they begin as enemies, Enkidu and Gilgamesh eventually become friends. Enkidu teaches Gilgamesh what it means to rule wisely.

Because the Epic of Gilgamesh was written down, we can learn a lot from it about how the people in long-ago Mesopotamia saw the world. It tells us what they admired in a hero, what gods they worshipped, and how they thought the gods wanted them to behave.

This statue shows Gilgamesh fighting a lion.

A ziggurat

## What's a Ziggurat?

Like the ancient Egyptians, the Mesopotamian people worshipped many gods. They prayed to a sky god, a sun god, a water god, a storm god, and many more. From what you know about ancient peoples and the importance of growing crops, why do you think weather gods were so important to them?

To honor their gods, the people of Mesopotamia built temples called ziggurats [zig-UH-roughts]. Ziggurats were enormous monuments with sides that looked like stair steps. They were not quite as tall as the pyramids, but if you saw one today, you'd feel very tiny standing next to it!

The people of Mesopotamia believed in a powerful goddess they called Ishtar. To honor Ishtar, they built a wall around their largest and most important city, Babylon [BAB-uh-lon]. The wall had a beautiful gate called the Gate of Ishtar. This gate was decorated with golden bulls and lions, the favorite animals of Ishtar. In this way, the people of Babylon warned their enemies, "Do not mess with us, for we are protected by Ishtar!"

The Gate of Ishtar

## A Leader and the Laws

In early Mesopotamia, the people did not have pharaohs as rulers. They had kings. One very important king was named Hammurabi [ha-muh-RAH-bee]. He ruled over Babylon. He also ruled the land around the city, because he had sent his armies out to conquer it. He was known for miles around as a strong and fair king.

Hammurabi decided that, to make Babylon strong, the kingdom needed to have good laws. Do you know what "laws" are? Laws are the rules we obey. Today, for example, we have laws that say that all cars have to stop when a school bus is loading or unloading children. Do you know of any other laws?

Of course, Hammurabi lived a very, very long time before school buses. In fact, he lived in a time when people were just beginning to understand why it's important to have laws.

Hammurabi collected laws from as many kingdoms as he could, and then he put together the Code of Hammurabi. This was a very long list of laws, and some of them seem strange or cruel to us today. For example, one law said that if a doctor operated on a patient and the patient died, then the doctor's hand should be chopped off!

This is definitely not the way we would do things today. But not all of Hammurabi's laws were so harsh. In fact, many of his laws protected those who could not protect themselves. For example, one law said that if a man was poor, a doctor should charge him less than he would charge a rich man for the same operation.

This carving shows Hammurabi with the sun god Shamash. Hammurabi's Code of Laws is carved below.

**Talk and Think**
Why do people need laws? What would happen without them?

**Talk and Think**
Justice is an important idea. Hammurabi was one of the first people to recognize how important laws are. Although we would not agree with some of the harsh laws he made, we share Hammurabi's concern with an idea called justice. Justice is a big and important idea. When we think about justice, we think about what is fair for everyone. And we ask, what can we do to make life in our communities more just—better and fairer—for everyone? What rules do you have in your house or community for fairness?

## Religions: What Different People Believe

Have you noticed that when we talk about early civilizations, we keep mentioning "the gods"? When we talk about the gods, or God, that people believe in, we are talking about their religion.

For thousands of years, different religions have helped many different people try to answer some big questions. These are not only questions that people asked long ago in ancient times. People still ask these questions today, questions like: How did the world begin? Where did people and animals come from? Why is the world the way it is? How should people behave?

Today there are many religions in the world. Let's find out more about three religions that have been important to many people for thousands of years. These three religions are called Judaism, Christianity, and Islam. Today each of these religions has millions of followers. But thousands of years ago, they were just getting started. We're going to look back to those long-ago times and learn about how Judaism, Christianity, and Islam began.

But first, think about this: Do you remember that people in ancient Mesopotamia and ancient Egypt believed in many gods? They believed in gods of nature, such as a sun god and an Earth god. They believed in many other gods, such as a god of the dead and a god to protect the city. Well, there's a big difference between the ancient Mesopotamian and Egyptian religions and the religions you're going to learn about now. Followers of Judaism, Christianity, and Islam do not believe in many gods. Instead, all of these religions believe in just one God. (When you refer to just one God, you spell the name with a capital "G" because that's how you begin a name, with a capital letter, right?) Thousands of years ago, this belief in just one God was a new idea. And this new idea came first from the religion called Judaism.

# Judaism

The followers of Judaism today are called Jews. The Jewish people believe in one God. Although this does not seem strange to most people today, it did seem strange to many people in the ancient world. As you know, most people in the ancient world believed there were many gods.

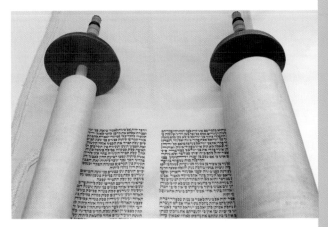

Copies of the Torah are often written on scrolls like the one shown here.

The holy books of the Jewish people are gathered together in a big book called the Hebrew Bible. These books were written a long time ago in Hebrew, a language that is still spoken by many Jews today.

The first part of the Hebrew Bible is called the Torah. The Torah tells the early history of the Jewish people and their God.

> **New Word**
>
> When Jewish people worship, they go to a place called a "synagogue" [SIN-uh-gog]. A synagogue is a place where Jews can worship God and study the Torah. Jewish children may go to a synagogue to study the Torah with a teacher called a rabbi, like the one shown here.

## The Story of Moses

One of the most important stories in the Torah is the story of Moses. Moses was a great leader of the Jewish people. Way back in the time of Moses, the Jewish people were known by another name: They were called Hebrews. Sometimes the Bible also calls them Israelites or the Children of Israel. Here is some of the story of Moses, as told in the Hebrew Bible.

The story of Moses begins in Egypt more than three thousand years ago. It was an awful time for the Hebrews because they were forced by the Egyptians to work as slaves. The Hebrews had to work long and hard in the hot sun, carrying the heavy rocks used to build the pyramids and other big monuments.

Now, the pharaoh of Egypt noticed something that bothered him. He saw that among the Hebrews, more and more children were being born every day. He began to worry that one day there might be so many Hebrews that they would rise up and fight against their Egyptian masters. And so Pharaoh gave a cruel command. He ordered that all boy children born to the Hebrew people should be drowned in the Nile River!

Just at this time, a Hebrew woman gave birth to a baby boy. She knew of Pharaoh's awful command. She decided she must do something to save her boy, but what? What could she do?

For a few months she did her best to hide him, but she could not keep him hidden forever. And so this is what she did. She wove a basket out of long strands of grass called bulrushes. She put tar on the bottom of the basket so that it would float. Then she carried her baby down to the Nile River and put him in the basket. She left the basket, with the baby in it, floating among the long grass by the riverbank. Hidden in the distance, the baby's older sister, named Miriam, watched the basket and waited to see what would happen.

Soon a group of women came walking along the riverbank. It was Pharaoh's daughter, along with the maidens who served her, coming to bathe in the river. Pharaoh's daughter saw the basket in the bulrushes, and she sent a maid to fetch it. When she looked inside, she saw a crying baby boy! "He must be one of the Hebrew children," she said. She felt sorry for the little child, all alone. She named him Moses, which, it is said, means "drawn out of the water."

Just then the baby's older sister, Miriam, came out of her hiding place. She approached Pharaoh's daughter and asked, "Shall I go and find a Hebrew woman to help you take care of the child?"

"Yes, do," said Pharaoh's daughter. Now, who do you think Miriam went to get? Moses's own mother! So, with two mothers to take care of him, Moses was raised as a prince in the palace of his people's enemies!

This stained-glass window shows Pharaoh's daughter discovering the baby Moses.

When Moses grew up, he saw something that upset him. He saw an Egyptian beating a Hebrew slave. Moses fought the Egyptian, and he killed him. And now Moses was in very big trouble. He had to leave Pharaoh's palace. He left behind his comfortable life and went far away and began to live as a shepherd.

The Hebrew Bible tells us that one day, as Moses was keeping watch over the sheep, he saw an amazing sight: It was a bush covered with flames, yet the bush itself was not burned by the flames. Then a voice spoke from the burning bush and said to Moses, "I am the God of your fathers. I have seen the suffering of my people who are in Egypt. I will send you to Pharaoh that you may bring forth my people out of Egypt to a good and broad land, a land flowing with milk and honey."

This stained-glass window shows God appearing to Moses in the burning bush.

Moses was afraid. He said, "O Lord, who am I to do this? Pharaoh will not listen to me. I am not a man of words. I do not speak well." Then God became angry and asked Moses who had given him the power to speak in the first place, and God told Moses, "I will teach you what to say."

So Moses, together with his brother, named Aaron, went to Pharaoh and said, "God has commanded you: *Let my people go.*" But Pharaoh said, "I do not know your God, and I will not let your people go." And Pharaoh made the Hebrews work even harder.

Then, says the Hebrew Bible, God punished the Egyptians. He sent a plague of frogs: The Nile River was filled with frogs, and the people found frogs in their beds and in their food bowls. Still, Pharaoh refused to let the Hebrews go. So God sent more punishments. The land was covered with gnats, and flies, and locusts. The crops died, and the cattle died. The people of Egypt found their skin covered with terrible sores. Thunder crashed in the sky as a terrible hail battered the earth.

Finally, Pharaoh had had enough. He decided to let the Hebrews leave Egypt. They gathered their few belongings and set off to the land that God had promised to Moses and his people, the promised land, "flowing with milk and honey."

The journey of the Hebrews out of Egypt is called the Exodus. It was a long, hard journey. Soon after they started, the Hebrews came to the shore of a sea, where they stopped to rest. They didn't know, however, that Pharaoh had changed his mind about letting the Hebrews leave. He wanted them back to work as slaves. So he sent his soldiers after them.

When the Hebrews saw Pharaoh's mighty troops approaching, they were ter-

Moses at the crossing of the Red Sea

rified. The soldiers, riding fast in their horse-drawn chariots, were coming at them from one side. On the other side was the sea. What could they do? They turned to Moses and cried out, "Have you brought us out of Egypt only to die here in the desert?"

But Moses raised his staff and a great wind began to blow. It blew so hard and so strong that the waters of the sea parted in two. The Hebrews were amazed to see a dry path between two walls of water! Moses led his people across this path through the sea. Not far behind came the soldiers of Pharaoh. But as they came across, the walls of water came crashing down, and all of Pharaoh's men were drowned.

The Hebrews were safe. Moses led them to their promised homeland, which is now called Israel. The escape of the Hebrews from Egypt is still celebrated by Jewish people today as an important holiday. That holiday is called Passover.

## Jewish Holidays and Symbols

Another important holiday in the Jewish religion is called Hanukkah [HAH-nuh-kuh]. Sometimes you will see it spelled Chanukah. This holiday is usually celebrated in December and is sometimes called the Festival of Lights. On each night for eight nights, a candle is lit in a special holder called a menorah.

One of the most important symbols of the Jewish people is a six-pointed star known as the Star of David. This star is named for King David, a mighty king whose story is told in the Hebrew Bible.

This menorah has a six-pointed Star of David built into its design.

# Christianity

The religion called Christianity began about two thousand years ago. It grew out of the religion you've just learned about, Judaism. Here's how it happened.

As you know, Moses led the Hebrews out of Egypt to their promised homeland, called Israel. But there were still many hard times ahead. More than once, the Jewish people were conquered and ruled over, as they had been by the Egyptians.

The Jewish people, as well as many other people, were conquered by the powerful Romans. The Romans had strong armies with thousands and thousands of soldiers. It was hard for the Jewish people to be ruled by the Romans. Many people in Israel hoped for a savior—a person who would come and save them. The Jewish people called this savior they hoped for the Messiah. Many Jewish people thought that when the Messiah came, he would lead the Jews against their Roman conquerors and make them free.

Into this world was born Jesus of Nazareth. Many people believe that Jesus was the Messiah the Jewish people were waiting for. These people are called Christians because they believed that Jesus was the Christ, or the chosen one of God.

Jesus was not the son of a king or a powerful warrior. His parents, named Mary and Joseph, were humble people. The story of Mary, Joseph, and the birth of Jesus is told in the holy book of Christians, called the Bible.

## The Christian Bible

The Christian Bible is divided into two parts: the Old Testament and the New Testament. The Old Testament contains books from the Hebrew Bible, which both Jews and Christians consider to be holy. The New Testament contains additional books that describe the life and teachings of Jesus. The New Testament is very important to Christians, but it is not part of the Jewish religion; it is the part of the Christian Bible that is new with Christianity.

### The First Christmas

Christians celebrate the birthday of Jesus each year on the day called Christmas. Here, from the Bible, is the story of the first Christmas.

In the city of Nazareth, there lived a young woman named Mary. She did not know that something amazing was going to happen to her.

The Bible tells us that one day Mary was visited by an angel sent by God, an angel named Gabriel. "Hail, O favored one!" Gabriel said to Mary ("hail" means hello). Mary was amazed and scared. "Do not be afraid," said the angel.

In this Italian painting, the angel Gabriel tells Mary that she will be the mother of Jesus.

But what Gabriel told her next made her more afraid and very excited. The angel said that Mary would have a son and that this son would be the Messiah, the promised one, the savior of Israel.

The angel told her that the baby would be sent from God and that her child would be called the Son of God.

Months later, Mary prepared to go on a trip with her new husband, Joseph. It was a hard time to travel, for Mary was now expecting a child, but they had to make the trip. The ruler of the Romans, called the "emperor," had sent out an order. The Roman emperor wanted to tax all the people he ruled (that means he wanted to get money from them). He ordered them to return to the town of their ancestors to pay their taxes.

So Mary and Joseph went to the town of Joseph's ancestors, the little town of Bethlehem. It was a hard journey. When they arrived, Mary could feel that it was time for her baby to be born, that very night. But they could not find a place to stay: There was no room at the inn. The innkeeper told them they could stay in the stable where the animals were kept. In there they would at least find some straw to rest on.

And there in the stable, with the cattle and other animals moving softly about, Mary gave birth to her baby son. And since there was no crib or bed, she placed him in a manger, which held the feed for the animals to eat.

Nearby there were shepherds in the field, keeping watch over their flocks by night. An angel appeared to them and said, "Fear not: for, behold, I bring you good tidings of great joy. For unto you is born this day a Savior, which is Christ the Lord."

The shepherds were amazed. For so many years their people had waited for a savior, a mighty leader. Could it be that their savior was born here, among such plain and humble people?

The shepherds hurried to Bethlehem to see the child.

This stained-glass window shows the shepherds visiting the baby Jesus while angels make music in the background.

They found Mary, and Joseph, and the babe, who was lying in a manger. The shepherds told Mary what the angel had said. Then they went to tell everyone the good news. But Mary remained quiet and thought deeply about all that had happened.

And that is what the Bible tells us of the first Christmas. Christians today remember and celebrate the first Christmas each year on the twenty-fifth of December by putting on special plays, by giving gifts, and by singing songs about Bethlehem, the angels, the shepherds, and the baby Jesus.

## Jesus the Teacher: The Parable of the Good Samaritan

When Jesus grew to be a man, he started teaching. People flocked to listen and Jesus attracted a group of followers. When Jesus taught people, he often told parables. A parable is a story that teaches a lesson.

Jesus taught that you should love your neighbor as you love yourself. Once, a lawyer asked Jesus, "Just exactly who is my neighbor?" To answer this question, Jesus told the parable of the Good Samaritan. (A Samaritan is a person from the region called Samaria.)

Once, said Jesus, a man was traveling along a road. Suddenly he was attacked by thieves. They robbed the man and beat him. He lay half dead by the side of the road. Soon a priest came along. He saw the man lying in pain but did not stop to help him. Then another man came down the road; he, too, walked right on by without helping. Then along came a Samaritan. When the Samaritan saw the half-dead man, he went to him and took care of his wounds. He took the man to a nearby inn. He told the innkeeper that he would pay whatever it cost to take care of the man.

When Jesus had told this story, he turned and asked the lawyer, "Which now of these three was neighbor unto him that fell among the thieves?"

And that, from the New Testament, is the story of the Good Samaritan. What do you think? Who was most like a neighbor to the man who was robbed and beaten? Why?

Today, people sometimes call anyone who goes out of his or her way to help someone in need a Good Samaritan.

This picture shows Jesus teaching.

## Easter

Many people listened to Jesus and believed him. But many others got angry with Jesus. They expected a savior who would lead them in a great fight against the Romans. Instead, Jesus said that people should forgive their enemies.

Although many people began to follow Jesus, other people became his enemies. His words made them angry and scared. And so they hurt Jesus, and eventually they killed him. He was put to death on a cross, so the cross has become the main symbol of Christianity.

Christians believe that on the third day after Jesus died, he rose from the dead; Christians celebrate his rising from the dead each year on the holiday known as Easter. Easter and Christmas are the two most important holidays and celebrations for Christians.

**New Word**
Christians worship in a place called a "church." Some churches are large, fancy buildings. Others are smaller and plainer, like the church shown here.

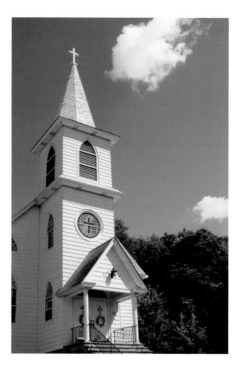

## Islam

A long time after Jesus lived—in fact, more than five hundred years later—a man named Muhammad was born in the land then called Arabia (look at the map on page 168). The religion of Islam began in the time of Muhammad. Followers of Islam are called Muslims (sometimes spelled Moslems).

Muhammad was a merchant: a person who buys and sells things for a living. He was a respected man in his hometown of Mecca (sometimes spelled Makkah). Many people called him al-Amin, which means "the trustworthy."

Because he was a merchant, Muhammad traveled a lot to buy and sell his goods. In his travels he met many different people. Some of them were followers of the two religions you've already learned about—Judaism and Christianity. From these Jews and Christians, Muhammad learned about the idea of one God. And from the Christians he learned about the teachings of Jesus.

Muhammad thought about what he learned during his life and travels. When he returned home, he looked around at what he saw in his own land and he became troubled. He saw that many of the people still worshipped many gods. He felt that too many people in the city of Mecca had become proud and greedy. He did not like the rich rulers of the city. He believed they fought too much and were too concerned with money.

Here is the story that Muslims tell about how their religion began. Muhammad liked to go off to sit alone in a quiet cave, where he could think about things that were worrying him. One day, when he was forty years old, he went to the cave and there he had a vision (a vision is like a dream, except you're awake). Muhammad saw an angel, the angel Gabriel. Is that name familiar to you? Gabriel is the same angel who, the Bible says, came to Mary to tell her that she would give birth to the baby Jesus.

Muslims believe that God spoke to Muhammad through the angel Gabriel. The angel told Muhammad to tell everyone in Arabia that there was only one God, whose name is Allah. "Allah" is the Arabic word for the English word

"God." So, you see, Muslims worship the same God that Jewish and Christian people worship.

Muhammad set out to tell people that they should worship only the one God, Allah. Some people listened to Muhammad's teachings and believed him. But most people were not very happy to hear what he said. He told them that their ideas about religion were wrong and that they should change what they believed and how they behaved. Some people got so mad at Muhammad that they even killed some of his followers and forced him to leave Mecca, the city that was his home.

But Muhammad was determined to spread his message. He continued to teach about Allah, and more people began to follow him. The people liked Muhammad's lessons about being kind to one another and about helping the poor. They prayed many times every day. They tried hard to live better lives.

The rulers of Mecca were still angry at Muhammad, and they were worried as more people began to follow him. More than once, the rulers of Mecca sent soldiers to attack the Muslims. But the Muslims fought back, and in the end they beat the soldiers of Mecca. Muhammad returned to his home city, and his many followers came with him.

Soon all of Arabia accepted Muhammad as the messenger of God.

Since the time of Muhammad, the religion of Islam has spread from Arabia to many other parts of the world.

Muslims everywhere study the Qur'an (pronounced core-ON and sometimes spelled Koran). The Qur'an is the holy book of Islam. It contains the teachings of Muhammad.

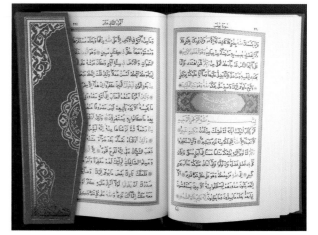

Muhammad, the prophet of Islam, came from the city of Mecca. Today this city is the holiest city in the Islamic world. Muslims are expected to make a hajj, or pilgrimage, to Mecca at some point in their life. Once there, they visit a holy site called the Ka'aba. Muslims worship in "mosques" [MOSKS]. Most mosques have at least one tall tower called a minaret. If you visit a city where Muslims live, you may hear men calling out from a minaret. These men are calling Muslims to come to the mosque for prayers.

This mosque has four minarets.

The Ka'aba in Mecca is one of the holiest sites in the Islamic world.

## Three Religions, One God

Jews, Christians, and Muslims have a great deal in common. All the followers of these religions believe in the same God, though they call this one God by different names. The holy books of the three religions tell some of the same stories. The Christian Bible contains many books from the Hebrew Bible of the Jews, and the Qur'an includes many stories that are also told in the Torah, such as the story of Noah and the flood and the story of Moses.

In later books in this series, you'll learn more about these religions, and you'll learn about some other religions too.

# American History and Geography

## Crossing the Land Bridge

Do you know the seven continents? Can you name them and point to them on the map? (If you want to read about the continents, you can look back at the "World History and Geography" section of *What Your Kindergartner Needs to Know*.)

Can you find North America and Asia on the map on page 200? Look way up to what is now the state of Alaska. Do you see how close Alaska is to Asia? They are separated by only a small body of water.

But that water wasn't always there. Thousands of years ago, way back in the Ice Age, there was a narrow strip of land that connected Asia and North America. It was like a bridge across the water—and that's why it is sometimes called the land bridge.

Do you remember learning about the Ice Age earlier in this book (see pages 164–67)? What do you remember about that long-ago time? Yes, it was cold! Do you remember how people lived then? They spent most of their time just trying to stay warm and trying to get enough to eat. Do you remember how the people back then got their food? They picked berries, and they hunted big animals like reindeer and woolly mammoths.

Well, those big animals didn't sit around and say, "Come get us, Ice Age hunters!" No, the animals kept on the move. Just like people, the reindeer, woolly mammoths, and other animals needed to eat too. So they kept moving, looking for food.

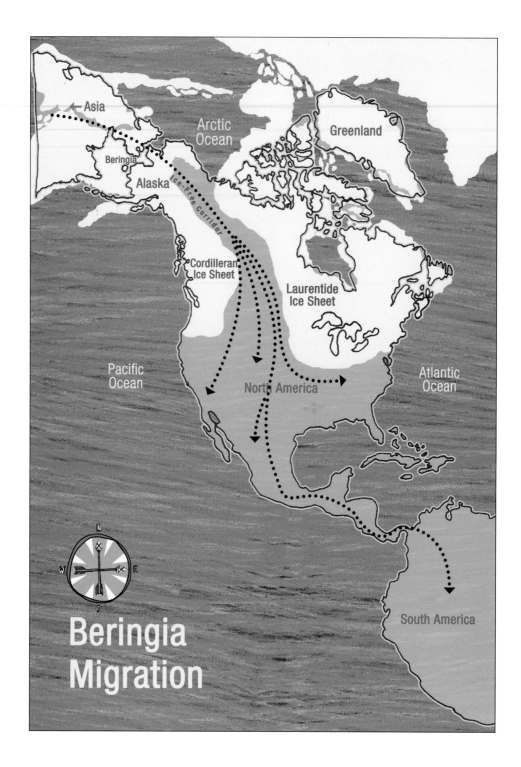

Beringia
Migration

"Stop! It's dinnertime."

From Asia, big herds of animals moved east and south. Some of them moved right across the land bridge that connected Asia and Alaska and came to what is now North America. And who else do you think was hurrying across the land bridge, following the animals? That's right, the people! Why did they follow the animals? They were following their food!

As the years passed—in fact, thousands of years—more and more people made their way from Asia to North America. We think many of them came across the land bridge that connected the two continents, but some of them may have traveled along the coast in boats. In any case, these people from Asia spread all over North and South America. They were the ancestors of the people we now call Native Americans, or American Indians.

For a long time, these early people kept alive by hunting, fishing, and gathering wild berries, nuts, and fruit. As time passed, however, some of these early Americans began to grow their own food, especially the people who lived farther south, where it was warmer and easier to grow crops. These crops, such as corn and beans, gave them plenty to eat. When people can grow enough food to eat, they don't have to keep moving around and chasing their dinner. They can stay put and make their homes in one place.

Little by little, the ancestors of the first Americans did what people in ancient Egypt and Mesopotamia had done thousands of years before. As they learned to farm and built their homes, the first American **civilizations** were established. They settled down, they founded towns and cities, they made works of art, and some of them learned to write.

Let's look back in history to learn about three early American civilizations: the Mayan civilization, the Aztec civilization, and the Inca civilization.

**Talk and Think**

If people from Asia were the ancestors of Native Americans, who were the ancestors of the people in Asia? Most scientists believe that the first humans came from Africa, more than half a million years ago. If those scientists are right, then all of us have ancestors who lived in Africa! Do you know where your more recent ancestors lived?

**New Word**

As you learn about these American **civilizations**, remind your child of the word "civilization." What are some elements of a civilization? What are some things that distinguish a civilization from the life of early humans? (Settlements, farming, government, writing.)

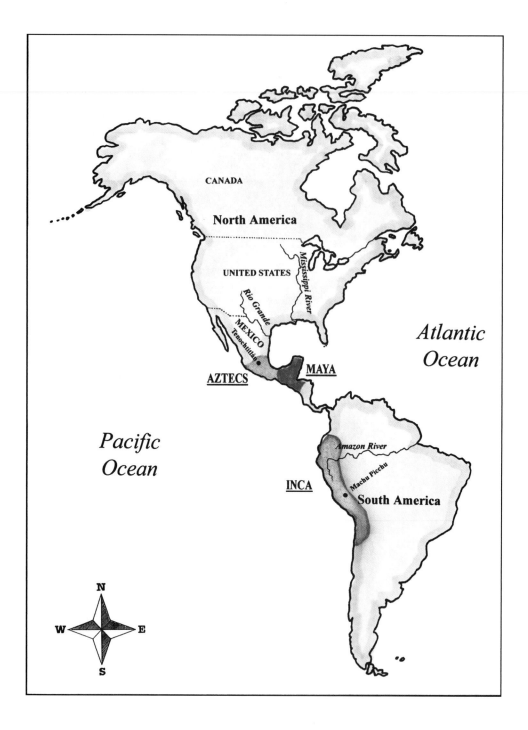

# Cities in the Jungle: The Maya

First you're going to meet a civilization that developed in Central America. You know where North America and South America are, but where is Central America? If you don't know, you can probably figure it out. It helps to know that the word "central" means in the middle. Look at the map on page 202. You can find the continents of North America and South America, right? Well, do you see how the land gets narrower as you move down from North America to South America? That area, which is in the middle, between the two continents, is called Central America.

Deep in the rain forests of Central America, the Mayan people made their home. In the moist jungle soil, the Maya grew corn, squash, and beans. And there, thousands of years ago, the Maya built their cities.

**Make a Connection**
You can learn more about rain forests on page 390 in the "Science" section of this book.

And what amazing cities they were, with big stone palaces and—what's this? Take a look: Here's a tall stone building, with stairs going up the slanted sides. Does this remind you of something? Something Egyptian? Like a pyramid?

Well, the Egyptians built their pyramids a long time before the Maya and in a different part of the world. So the Maya never knew about the Egyptians. Still,

A Mayan temple

like the Egyptians, the Maya buried their kings in big stone buildings that reach way above the tallest trees in the jungle. The stairs on the Mayan pyramids were for the priests, who would climb to the top to worship their gods.

Like other ancient people you've learned about, the Maya worshipped nature gods, such as gods of the wind and the rain. They also worshipped animal gods. They made pictures showing some of their gods partly in human form and partly in the form of a big, fierce jungle cat, the jaguar.

This Mayan animal god is part opossum.

The Maya knew how to write. You remember Egyptian hieroglyphics, don't you? The Maya had their own form of picture writing. They used their picture writing to make a kind of calendar and to tell stories of the lives, battles, and triumphs of the Mayan leaders. Sometimes they wrote in books made from the bark of trees. Sometimes they carved their stories on big stone pillars. Just imagine if you had to write by carving letters in hard stone! Aren't you glad you have pencil and paper?

You're learning to write in school, along with your friends and with children in schools all across the country and in other countries too. But did you know that the idea that everyone should be able to write is a pretty new idea in human history? In long-ago times, only a very few people learned to write. Only a few of the Mayan people knew how to write, and these few were called the scribes.

A stone decorated with Mayan hieroglyphics

## An Unsolved Mystery

Sometimes history is a mystery. We don't know about some very important things that happened in the past. We know that the Maya built great cities, and we know they lived in these cities for hundreds of years. But then they left and the cities were swallowed up by the rain forest. And that's the mystery: Why did the Maya leave their cities? Not even the Maya who still live in Central America today know the answers to these questions: Why, long ago, did the ancient Maya allow the jungle to spread over their buildings and monuments? What happened to their civilization? Was there a drought—a long time without rain—that

These buildings in the Mayan city of Tikal were once overgrown by rain forest.

killed the crops? Did they catch some awful disease? Was there a terrible war? We don't know the answers, but historians and archaeologists are working to find out. Maybe someday you can help solve this mystery!

## City in the Lake: The Aztec City of Tenochtitlán

Now let's meet another early American civilization. Like the Maya, these people also built great cities, but not until hundreds of years after the Maya. These people were called the Aztecs.

To see where the Aztecs lived, look at the map on page 202. The Aztecs built their greatest city in what is now the country of Mexico, at the place where you

**Make a Connection**
See pages 216–18 to learn more about Mexico.

can now find one of the biggest modern cities in the world: Mexico City. The Aztecs called their city Tenochtitlán [tay-nosh-tee-TLAHN].

The Aztecs chose an unusual location to build their city: in a lake! Actually, they built their city on islands in the lake, and then, to connect the islands, they built bridges as well as waterways called canals. They built huge stone temples devoted to the worship of their many gods. There was a temple for the rain god, a temple for the corn god, and a temple for the sun god.

This painting shows Aztec workers constructing the city of Tenochtitlán.

The Aztecs told a legend about why they picked such an unusual location for Tenochtitlán. They said their sun god had commanded them to keep moving until they saw an eagle sitting on a prickly pear cactus while eating a snake. There, they should build their city. According to the legend, the Aztecs traveled until they saw this strange sight at Tenochtitlán. In fact, "Tenochtitlán" means place of the prickly pear cactus. If you look at a flag of Mexico, you'll see that modern-day Mexicans still remember this legend.

After the Aztecs built their great city, they set out to conquer the people around them. "To conquer" means to defeat someone in war and to take over their land. The Aztecs believed in fighting and conquering other people. All boys had to serve in the army, and the army's job was to conquer. Other people feared and hated the Aztecs because they were always making war and taking prisoners.

The Aztecs built Tenochtitlán on the site where they found an eagle, with a snake in his mouth, perched on a cactus.

This serpent mosaic, created in Aztec Mexico, is carved from wood and decorated with turquoise and shells.

**Take a Look**

The Aztecs were not just fierce warriors. They were also very good craftsmen. They made wonderful sculptures. They made many beautiful things using turquoise stones, jade, gold, and other precious materials. The serpent shown here is a mosaic, made by Aztec craftsmen using tiny pieces of turquoise.

## Cities in the Clouds: The Inca Empire

On the continent of South America, there's a big, long mountain range. Look on the map on page 202. Run your finger up and down the Andes Mountains on the map.

High up in the Andes, the air is thin and cold. The mountains are steep, rough, and rocky, so it's not easy to get around—unless you're a sure-footed llama, or maybe a condor soaring above the mountain ledges.

A llama in the mountains of Peru

Does this seem like a place to start building a civilization? Maybe not, but that's just what the Inca people did.

The Inca built their cities high in the mountains of what is now Peru. How did they do it? They used something the Andes Mountains have plenty of: rock!

The Inca people were very skillful masons (masons are people who cut stone and use it to build). They cut and hauled huge blocks of stone. They put the big stone blocks together so exactly that you couldn't even slide a piece of paper between them! After they built beautiful stone walls and fortresses, they decorated the insides with gold and silver, which they found plenty of in the mountains.

One of the most amazing of the Inca cities is Machu Picchu [MA-chu PEE-chu], which sits atop a tall mountain. This city was almost completely forgotten for more than three hundred years. Now it is a popular tourist destination.

The Inca city of Machu Picchu

The ruler of the Inca Empire was a mighty emperor known as the Sapa Inca. The first Sapa Inca was thought to be a child of the sun god. The Inca Empire began to grow when the emperor and his warriors conquered some of the land around them. Later emperors added more land, and the Inca Empire eventually grew large and powerful.

The Inca emperors came up with a clever way to send messages. They set up a network of fast runners. These runners would carry messages from the Sapa Inca out to the various parts of the empire, traveling on roads built by Inca masons. The first runner would run several miles, until he got to a rest area, then he would pass the message to the next runner, who would carry it onward, like a runner in a relay race.

## Sapa Inca for a Day

**What About You?**

Remind students that an archaeologist is a scientist who tries to learn about ancient people by studying the things they leave behind. Ask your child to imagine that he or she is an archaeologist. Which of the ancient civilizations described in this book—Egyptian, Mesopotamian, Maya, Aztec, Inca—would your child choose to study? Why?

Are you tired of being a first grader? How would you like to be the Sapa Inca for a day? There is not much work involved. All of the hard work will be done by your servants. In fact, here come some of them now.

Good morning, Your Majesty! These servants have come to dress you.

Here are your shoulder pads, and here is your robe of the sun, studded with jewels and turquoise. Here is the man with your headdress fringed with gold. But let's not put that on until we have put on your earrings.

Yes, I know that the earrings are very heavy. That is as it should be. The Sapa Inca does not wear dinky little earrings. His

News flash from Peru: The Sapa Inca, Huayna Capac, will be replaced during today's trip by—you!

earrings must hang down almost to his shoulders. There. Now we can add the headdress.

Will we be going out today? Yes, we will.

Will you be walking? No, you most certainly will not be walking! The Sapa Inca does not walk anywhere. He is carried from place to place on his litter, as is fitting. Ah, here comes your litter now. Place your royal rump, very gently, here. That's it.

Your servants will carry you through the streets on this litter. Some of them will run ahead of you and sweep the streets to make sure there aren't any leaves or bits of trash in your path. Some of them will throw flowers on the road so everything smells nice, and some of them will play music. Does that sound satisfactory, Your Majesty?

What's the weather like outside? It is a bright, sunny day, Your Majesty.

What's that? Your mother makes you wear sunscreen when it's sunny? Well, that will not be necessary today. After all, you are a direct descendant of the sun god Inti, and he would never allow your royal skin to become sunburned. In addition, a servant will be covering you with a special cloth. You will be able to see through it, but other people will not be able to see you.

Shall we go, then?

## The Arrival of the Europeans

For many hundreds of years, the Mayan, Aztec, and Incan civilizations were strong. What happened to them?

We know that the Maya left their great cities, but we don't know why. It's a mystery.

What happened to the Aztecs and the Inca is not a mystery. What happened was the arrival of new people. These people dressed differently, and they spoke a different language. They came on ships, across the Atlantic Ocean, from the faraway continent of Europe.

One of the first Europeans to arrive was Christopher Columbus. In three

**All Together**

The date 1492 is worth remembering. Think back. In what year did Columbus make his voyage? There is a little jingle that can help you remember:

*"In fourteen hundred and ninety-two,*
*Columbus sailed the ocean blue."*

Encourage students to repeat and memorize the jingle.

small ships, he and his sailors made a bold and daring voyage from Europe to "the New World." At least, it was a new world for Columbus and other Europeans. For the Maya, Aztecs, Inca, and many other Native American peoples, it was home!

Do you remember the story of Columbus's voyage? If you've learned about Columbus in the kindergarten book in this series, or in other books, let's see what you remember. (Don't worry if you can't remember everything; most of us have to hear a story more than once before we can remember much about it!) Ready? Here goes.

It was hard for Columbus to find someone who would help pay for his voyage. He finally got help from a king and queen. Do you remember what country they were king and queen of? The king and queen of Spain helped Columbus. Their names were King Ferdinand and Queen Isabella.

Columbus set sail from Europe in three ships. Do you remember any of their names? They were the *Niña,* the *Pinta,* and the *Santa María.* The voyage across the Atlantic Ocean was hard and sometimes stormy. Some of the sailors grew scared; they wanted Columbus to turn back. But he kept on, and finally they reached land.

When Christopher Columbus came to America, he claimed the lands he visited for Spain.

They landed on a little island in a group of islands now called the Bahamas. They were greeted by the friendly people who lived there. The people were part of the Taino [TIE-no] tribe. But Columbus and others called them "Indians." Do you remember why? Because Columbus thought he had landed in Asia, which the Europeans also called "the Indies." Columbus thought he was in the Indies, so he called the people he met there Indians. Even though the name was a mistake, it is still used today. Many descendants of these early people in America still call themselves American Indians, and they are also called Native Americans. ("Descendants" are people who come from other people: You are a descendant of your parents, your grandparents, your great-grandparents, your great-great-grandparents, and so on.)

So Columbus thought he was in Asia (or "the Indies"). He didn't know that he had bumped into land near North America and South America. He and other Europeans didn't know that these continents existed!

Columbus wasn't interested in finding any new continents. Neither were Queen Isabella and King Ferdinand. Well, then, what did they want from this voyage? Mainly two things: They wanted to spread their religion; they wanted the people Columbus met to become Christians. And, even more, they wanted to find valuable stuff like gold and spices.

You know that gold is valuable, but spices? Yes, spices were valuable back then—even spices like pepper, which you probably have in your kitchen today. In those days the people in Europe did not have many spices, and they were willing to pay lots of money to get them. Remember, people long ago didn't have refrigerators to keep their meat from rotting. They wanted the pepper because they thought that it and other spices would help keep the meat fresh and would certainly make their meals taste better!

When Columbus landed on that island in the Bahamas, he put up a Spanish flag and claimed the land for Spain. If you say, "I claim this," you are saying, "This belongs to me." Did the land belong to Spain? No. The Taino people already lived there. And not too far away, in parts of Central America and South America, there were already great civilizations (though Columbus never saw them), such as those of the Aztec and Inca peoples.

But Europeans like Columbus didn't think much about the people already living in the lands they found. Back then the Europeans thought that everything was "finders keepers." When Columbus arrived in the New World, he thought, "I've found it. I am sailing for the King and Queen of Spain. So I claim this land for Spain."

**Take a Look**

If you have access to a world map or a globe, help your child use his finger to trace Columbus's route and identify significant locations. Have him move his finger from Spain across the Atlantic Ocean to the Bahamas. Have him find the continent of Asia so that he can appreciate just how far away Columbus landed from his intended destination. Explain that Columbus did not know about North and South America. He thought he could sail all the way around to Asia. In fact, he thought he *had* done so.

## The Spanish Conquerors

Soon after Columbus, more and more people from Spain came to North and South America. Many of them came hoping to find gold and other riches. Both the Aztecs and the Inca had a lot of gold and other riches that the Spaniards wanted. And the Spaniards would fight to get them.

Do you remember what it means to "conquer" someone? Not long ago, you learned that the Aztecs went to war against many people around them and conquered them. But now the Aztecs themselves would be conquered by the Spanish.

The Spanish word for conqueror is "conquistador" [kon-kee-stah-DOR]. That is what we call the Spanish explorers who conquered the Native Americans. One conquistador, named Hernán Cortés [core-TEZ], led the Spanish against the Aztecs.

This image shows Cortés and two other Spaniards being welcomed to Tenochtitlán.

The leader of the Aztecs at this time was named Montezuma [mon-teh-ZOO-mah]. You may also see Montezuma spelled "Moctezuma." Have you ever heard the song that begins, "From the halls of Montezuma"? It's the song of the United States Marines.

Montezuma had terrible dreams that something bad was going to happen to his people. That something bad turned out to be Cortés. Cortés and his soldiers marched to the city of Tenochtitlán. Montezuma welcomed them, but the peace did not last and the Spanish took him prisoner in his own home. The Aztec people fought back, but Cortés made an alliance with some of Montezuma's enemies and defeated the

Aztecs. Cortés and the Spaniards took all the gold and riches they could find and set themselves up as the new governors of Mexico.

Not many years later, the Inca people were defeated by another Spanish conquistador. His name was Francisco Pizarro. He forced the people he conquered to work as slaves, digging silver from mines in the ground.

## Why Did the Spanish Win?

The Aztecs were fierce warriors; they had conquered many people around them. The Inca, too, were a strong people. And there were many more Aztec and Inca people than there were Spanish soldiers. So why did the Spanish win?

The Spanish won because they had better weapons. They had swords, guns, and cannons. They also wore armor and helmets, which protected them from the spears and arrows of the Native Americans.

The Spanish soldiers rode horses too. The Native Americans had never seen a horse before. At first they thought the horse and rider were one animal. Think how frightened you would be to see such a strange creature!

But something even more powerful worked against the Native Americans: They caught diseases from the Spaniards. The Native Americans had never been exposed to the terrible diseases, such as smallpox, that had killed so many people in Europe. So, many of the Native Americans never had a chance to fight the Spanish soldiers, because they died from diseases like smallpox.

**Make a Connection**
Read about how vaccines protect people today from diseases on pages 408–10.

Because of Columbus, Cortés, Pizarro, and other explorers, Spain claimed a lot of land in North and South America. Some of this land is now part of the United States, including the states of California and Texas. Spain also claimed almost all of the land south of our country—and that's why, even today, most people in these countries south of the United States still speak Spanish.

## Mexico Today

Do you know the names of the three biggest countries on the continent of North America? Take a look at a globe or map. Find the United States of America. What country is to the north? Canada. What country is to the south? Mexico.

Mexico is south of the United States and north of the area called Central America. The capital of Mexico is Mexico City. Do you remember the Aztec city, Tenochtitlán? Mexico City is built on the site where Tenochtitlán stood, and it's one of the largest cities in the world, with more than eight million people.

Look at the map below: Can you find the river called the Rio [REE-oh] Grande? The name means large river. The Rio Grande forms the border (the dividing line) that separates the state of Texas from Mexico. The Rio Grande

flows into a body of warm water called the Gulf of Mexico. Can you find this on the map? Look at the map again: What ocean is on the other side (to the west) of Mexico? It's the Pacific Ocean.

If you were to take a trip from the Rio Grande and go south through Mexico today, you'd see a mix of land, people, and customs. You would drive by the giant Sierra Madre [see-AIR-ah MAH-dreh] Mountains, through dry deserts, and even through humid rain forests. You would meet a variety of people living everywhere from big cities to small villages.

The Sierra Madre Mountains

On the map, look at the southern part of Mexico. If you use your imagination, can you see the part that looks kind of like the tail of a whale? This area is called the Yucatán [yoo-kuh-TAN] Peninsula. What is a **peninsula**? It's a piece of land surrounded by water on three sides. Do you see the water on three sides of the "whale's tail"? The Yucatán Peninsula is a big rain forest. The ancient Maya lived there, and descendants of the Maya still live there today.

Many people who live in Mexico today are the descendants of both

**New Word**

The word **peninsula** comes from two Latin words that mean almost an island. That's a good way to think about what a peninsula is: It's *almost* an island, but not quite, because it is still connected to the mainland on one side. Invite your child to find peninsulas on a world map or globe.

**Talk and Think**
Does your child know any Mexican foods?

Spanish and Native American people. Most Mexicans speak Spanish. Many Mexicans enjoy foods that came from the Native Americans, such as tortillas [tor-TEE-yahs]. Tortillas are thin, round, flat breads made from ground-up maize ("maize" is another word for corn flour). Tortillas are like bread for many Mexicans; they can be eaten alone or filled with carne [CAR-neh] (meat) or frijoles [free-HO-less] (beans).

Many Mexicans celebrate holidays with fiestas [fee-ES-tahs] (festivals), which include singing, dancing, fireworks, parades, and a variety of food. Also, Mexican children love to play a game in which they put on a blindfold and swing a stick at a piñata [peen-YAH-tah], a colorful shape usually made out of papier-mâché. When someone hits the piñata, it breaks open and surprises like toys and candy fall out!

**Make a Connection**
Learn more about Mexican culture by looking at the painting called *La Piñata*, by the Mexican artist Diego Rivera (page 276). You can also make your own piñata by decorating sheets of paper and taping them together with transparent tape.

One of the most important holidays in Mexico is El Diez y Seis de Septiembre [el dee-ess ee-SAYS de sep-tee-EM-breh]. That means the sixteenth of September, and it is Mexico's Independence Day. Now, you may know that the United States fought to gain its independence from England—but which European country do you think Mexico wanted to be independent of? If you said Spain, you're right.

Corn tortillas are used in many Mexican dishes.

She is swinging at the piñata.

## And Then Came England

Let's go back in history again, almost five hundred years ago, to the time of the Spanish explorers and conquistadors. While Cortés, Pizarro, and others were claiming lands in the New World for Spain, people back in Europe were starting to tell stories. They said that the Spanish were finding incredible treasure in the New World, whole cities full of gold and silver. Now, this wasn't true, but people still told such stories. And the stories made people stop and ask themselves, "Why should the Spanish have all the gold and silver? Let's get some for ourselves too!"

Some people in England began to think of sending English settlers to the New World. Maybe they would find treasure too. So the queen of England, Queen Elizabeth, turned to one of her favorite people, the bold and handsome Sir Walter Raleigh. She asked Sir Walter to get together a group of Englishmen and send them to start a colony in North America. (Do you remember what a "colony" is? A colony is a place ruled by people living in another, often faraway, part of the world.)

Sir Walter Raleigh sent about a hundred Englishmen in several ships on a trip across the stormy Atlantic Ocean. They landed on an island off the coast of what is now North Carolina. They did not bother to grow food for the coming winter. Instead, they spent much of their time digging for gold—which they didn't find. To get food, they had to trade with the Native Americans. But then the English colonists—who thought they were much better than the Native Americans—started bragging about their cities and their religion. Soon the Native Americans refused to give them any food. So, tired and disappointed, the colonists went back home to England.

> **Talk and Think**
>
> There's a famous story about Sir Walter Raleigh and Queen Elizabeth. The story says that one day when the queen was out taking a walk, she came to a big puddle. Would you expect a queen to walk through a puddle and get her feet wet and dirty? Certainly not! What should be done? Sir Walter Raleigh did not hesitate. He took off his fine cloak and spread it out over the puddle for the queen to walk across. Now, that's good manners! How do you show your good manners?

## The Lost Colony

Still, Sir Walter Raleigh was not ready to give up. He brought together another group of people to go to the New World. This group included not just men but women and children too. On a fine June day, they set sail for America. But things went wrong from the start. They were supposed to land on the continent of North America, but the ship's captain refused to go any farther than the little island of Roanoke—the same island that the English colonists had left behind only a year before. Would these newcomers have better luck?

The colonists had been in the New World only a few weeks when a happy event occurred: One of the women had a baby. The baby, named Virginia Dare, was the first English child born in the New World. As Virginia grew up, did she like her new home? Did she have a happy childhood? We don't know! Why not? Because we don't know what happened to the colonists on Roanoke Island.

Here is what we do know. The ship that brought the colonists to the little island turned around and went back to England for more supplies. The ship was supposed to come back to the island within a year. But when the ship got back to England, England was in a war with Spain. So no English ship was able to return to Roanoke for three years! When a ship finally did get back to the island, the crew found no one there. Everyone in the colony was gone. The little colony on

The letters "CRO" were all that remained of "the lost colony."

Roanoke Island had disappeared; even today, people call it "the lost colony."

The English sailors found nothing but some letters carved into a tree: "CRO." What did "CRO" mean? There was an Indian tribe called the Croatan on a nearby island. Had the Croatan people attacked the colonists? Or had the colonists gone to live with the Croatan people? Some American Indians who live in North Carolina today say that they are descendants of both the Croatan Indians and the lost colonists. So maybe the colonists did find a new life after all. Or maybe something else happened. It's another mystery in our history!

## A Lasting English Colony: Jamestown

After these hard times, you might think the English would give up trying to start a colony in the New World. But the English did not want to let Spain take all the riches of the New World. They wanted to find gold. And they wanted some other things as well. They wanted to cut trees so that they could get wood to build ships. They wanted to catch the fish that swam in the waters off North America. So the English kept on trying.

In 1607, the English set up their first successful settlement in what is now Virginia. They named it Jamestown after the English king at the time, James I.

About a hundred men came to Jamestown in 1607—no women came on this trip (they would not arrive until twelve months later). Most of the men came because they wanted to get rich. They expected to find lots of gold. They had heard

This is what the fort at Jamestown probably looked like in 1607.

Captain John Smith

stories that in the New World you could walk around and pick up diamonds, rubies, and other riches that were just lying on the ground!

What they found was quite different. The settlers didn't know they had picked a dangerous place to build their fort. The ground was swampy. There were many mosquitoes, which carried a deadly disease called malaria. Even the water was unhealthy, and many of the settlers would get sick from drinking it. Eight months later, only thirty-eight of the original hundred colonists remained alive.

The Jamestown settlers had a strict leader: Captain John Smith. John Smith helped them get through some very hard times. He ordered them to stop looking for gold and to instead begin planting corn. Gold may be valuable, but you can't eat it.

Still, the settlers did not have enough food at first. Sometimes they took food from the Native Americans who lived in the area. Sometimes John Smith was able to trade with the Native Americans: He traded copper kettles and tools in exchange for corn and other food.

The most powerful Native American leader in the area was called Powhatan by the English settlers. His own people called him Wahunsonacock. He brought thirty tribes together under his leadership.

The settlers and the Native Americans didn't trust each other. Each suspected the other of wanting to do something bad. Sometimes they managed to get along peacefully. John Smith said that Powhatan once asked him, "Why should you take by force from us that which you can obtain by love?" Still, sometimes the settlers and Native Americans fought fiercely.

If you visit Jamestown today, you can visit a re-creation of the original fort and settlement and learn how the settlers lived. You can even walk on replicas of the ships on which the colonists arrived.

## Tobacco

The settlers at Jamestown struggled to find crops that would grow well in their soil. At last they found one that would—tobacco, the plant used to make cigarettes and cigars. The settlers at Jamestown thought tobacco was great, but King James did not agree. He called smoking a custom "loathsome to the eye, hateful to the nose, harmful to the brain, and dangerous to the lungs."

## Pocahontas

Once, John Smith was captured by the people of Powhatan. Nobody knows for sure exactly what happened next. But years later, John Smith wrote a book in

Pocahontas

which he said he was saved by a courageous Native American girl. This girl was Powhatan's daughter. You may know her name—Pocahontas.

In his book, John Smith said that he was about to be killed by the Native Americans when Pocahontas begged that his life be spared. But no one would listen to the young girl. Heavy clubs were about to come down on Smith's head when suddenly Pocahontas rushed forward. She took Smith's head in her arms and forced the Native Americans to choose between hurting her or saving Smith. Pocahontas's father chose to release John Smith.

John Smith might have made up this story. But it has been told over and over, and it became so popular in England that people wrote poems and plays about Pocahontas. The story of Pocahontas is still popular today.

## The Pilgrims

Jamestown was the first important English settlement in our country. But only thirteen years after the founding of Jamestown, another important English settlement was started in the north, in what is now the state of Massachusetts (see the map on page 229). It was started by the Pilgrims.

You may already know some things about the Pilgrims (if you've learned about them from the kindergarten book in this series or from other books). You might remember their hard voyage in 1620 on a ship called the *Mayflower*, as well as the story of the first Thanksgiving. Let's learn more now about who the Pilgrims were and why they came to this country.

The Pilgrims were Christians who believed strongly in living the way they thought the Bible said they should live. But the Pilgrims wanted to worship God in a way that was not allowed in England. Back in those days, many people did not have religious freedom. If you have religious freedom—which Americans do today—then you are free to make up your own mind

The Pilgrims arrive at Plymouth.

about what you believe and how you want to worship. But the Pilgrims did not have this freedom. No: Back then, in many places all over the world, kings and other rulers had the power to say, "You must worship my way or leave!"

Well, the Pilgrims left. In fact, that's why we call them "pilgrims." Pilgrims are people who go on a journey—often a religious journey. When the Pilgrims left England, they first went to the nearby country of Holland. They went there because the people in Holland had more religious freedom than the people in England.

But the Pilgrims, who were English, didn't feel at home in Holland, where the people spoke a different language. Then some of the Pilgrim leaders had a new idea—more than an idea, really, almost a dream! Maybe, they thought, just maybe, they could begin a new life in the New World—in America! Maybe in America they could make a new home and be free to worship the way they wanted to.

In 1620, the Pilgrims boarded a tiny ship called the *Mayflower*. They crossed the rough Atlantic Ocean. You may already know that when they arrived in America, their lives were terribly difficult, and many of them died. But they were courageous. They worked hard and started a small village called Plymouth Plantation. Here they could worship in their own way. For this, they were thankful.

**Talk and Think**

The first English people who came to America came here for different reasons. Why did people come to Jamestown? Why did the Pilgrims come to Plymouth?

## The Puritans

The Pilgrims were not the only colonists who settled in New England. Another group, which arrived a few years later, was called the Puritans. Like the Pilgrims, the Puritans were a deeply religious group of Christians. But even people of the same religion can disagree, and the Puritans did not agree with all the beliefs of the Pilgrims.

The Puritans settled along a **bay** near what is now the city of Boston, in Massachusetts (look at the map of the thirteen colonies on page 229). (Of course, there was no big city back then!) The Puritans worked hard and their colony grew quickly. It was called the Massachusetts Bay Colony. Soon many more Puritans came to America.

What was it like to grow up as a Puritan child? Puritan parents could be strict: They expected children to behave properly at all times. They knew their children couldn't always be perfect, but they expected them to constantly try to be their best. They also placed a great value on learning to read, because they felt it was very important to be able to read the Bible.

Puritan children would often learn their letters from a little book called a primer (the word rhymes with "swimmer"). You may still hear that word used today: A "primer" is a first book for a beginning reader.

One primer that many Puritan children used was named *The New-England Primer.* It taught a lit-

> **New Word**
> A **bay** is a body of water that is part of an ocean and surrounded by land on some sides. Often the water in a bay will be calmer and safer than the water out in the open ocean.

THE
*New-England*
PRIMER
Enlarged.

For the more eafy attaining the true
Reading of ENGLISH.

To which is added,

The Affembly's Catechifm.

PHILADELPHIA:

Printe and Sold by *B. Franklin*, and
*D. Hall*, in *Market-ftreet*, 1

The New-England Primer

tle rhyme to go along with each letter of the alphabet. Often the rhymes tried to teach a lesson. For example, next to the letter "B," children saw a picture of the Bible and this little rhyme:

*Thy life to mend,*
*This Book attend.*

There were also some warnings in the book. For the letter "F," children read:

*The idle Fool*
*Is whipped at school.*

You wouldn't want to be caught daydreaming in a Puritan school!

## Slavery Comes to the Colonies

The Pilgrims and Puritans, as well as the first settlers of Jamestown, came to America because they wanted to. But one group of people came to America because they were forced to.

What do you know about slavery? Have you learned about slavery from the kindergarten book in this series or from other books?

In 1619, a ship arrived at Jamestown carrying people from Africa. These people had been taken from their homes and forced to get on a ship that brought them to America. They were sold to the Virginia settlers, and they were made to work, usually on farms.

Africans were brought to North America until 1619 and were forced to work for the Virginia settlers.

As the years went on, big farms were started in Virginia and other Southern colonies. These farms were called plantations. The owners of these big farms needed lots of workers to grow crops like tobacco and rice. And so more and more people were taken from Africa and brought to America. Here, they were forced to work as enslaved people on the big farms.

Many of these people did not survive the terrible voyage across the Atlantic Ocean. This voyage was called the Middle Passage. Africans were chained together and jammed into ships that were dirty and unhealthy. Many of them died along the way.

In America, some people did believe that slavery was wrong. But from the time that the first Africans were brought to Jamestown in 1619, it would take more than two hundred years before slavery was ended in America. And it would take a terrible war to do this. (You'll learn about this war in the next book in this series.)

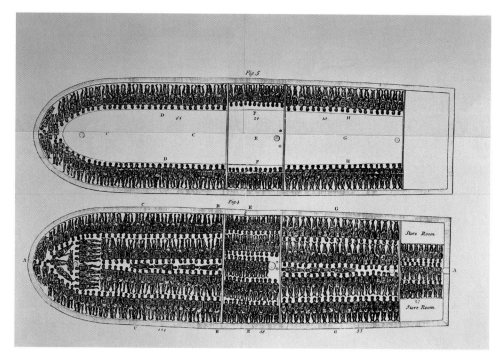

This image shows enslaved African people crowded together on a slave ship.

## Thirteen Colonies

Do you remember when the first English settlers arrived at Jamestown? (In 1607.) How about Plymouth? (In 1620.) Over the next century—that's one hundred years—more and more people moved from Europe to America. Of those who came willingly, most came from England, but others came from France, Holland, Germany, and other countries. Some people came to the Virginia and the Massachusetts Bay colonies. Other people started new colonies: The Dutch (who came from Holland) started a colony in what is now New York.

As the years passed, thirteen colonies grew up in the eastern part of the country near the Atlantic Ocean. Later, these thirteen colonies would become the first states of the United States. Can you locate and name the thirteen colonies?

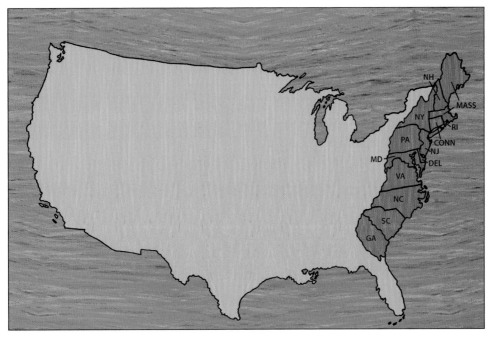

The thirteen colonies

A colony, you may remember, is an area ruled by the government of a faraway country. The thirteen colonies in America were ruled by the king of faraway England. How did these thirteen colonies break away from England and become the first thirteen states of a new country called the United States of America? That's what you're about to find out!

## The Colonists and the King

Let's move ahead many years to the 1760s: That's about one hundred fifty years after the first settlers arrived at Jamestown. In the 1760s, the thirteen English colonies in America were ruled by King George III. They were so proud that they even named towns and colleges after the king, like Georgetown and King's College.

King George III

But then things started to change. King George started to do things that worried the colonists. He had the **British** Parliament pass laws the colonists did not like. And he ordered the colonists to pay taxes on things like sugar, stamps, and paper, which meant that when the colonists bought some paper, they had to pay whatever the paper cost, of course, but then they had to pay some extra money. This extra money was a tax.

A tax is money that a government charges people to pay for things the government does—things like building roads or paying for soldiers and what the soldiers need to fight a war. The taxes the American colonists paid went straight to the British government. At this time, King George needed lots of money because England had just fought a very expensive war against France.

> **New Word**
>
> Sometimes people use the word **British** the same way they use the word "English." Are "British" and "English" the same? Not quite, but they're close. "British" comes from the name Great Britain. A long time ago, the little country of England took over some other nearby lands, including Wales and Scotland. The English used the name Great Britain for their own country of England and for the lands that England had taken over.

## The Boston Tea Party

As King George made more laws and charged more taxes, many colonists got worried and upset. Some colonists spoke out: "The king is way across the ocean in England," they said. "He doesn't really know what's good for us here in the American colonies." But many colonists still liked the king. They said, "If we just explain our worries to the king, he will understand."

So the colonists tried to explain. And they kept on explaining, but things didn't change. The colonists got more worried. They thought, "If we have to keep paying taxes, and if the king keeps making laws we don't like, pretty soon we won't have any money left and we won't be free to do anything!"

Then King George placed a new tax on something that almost every colonist bought a lot of: tea. Well, for many colonists, that was the last straw. Some angry colonists in Boston said, "The king doesn't understand! He needs to be shown that we colonists are not kidding." So they planned a "tea party"—but, as you'll see, it was a very strange party!

On a cold day in December, a ship arrived in Boston Harbor. It was carrying a load of tea. Many colonists were angry. They did not want to pay taxes on this tea. So, that night, a group of colonists dressed like Mohawk Indians tiptoed onto the docks at Boston Harbor. They quietly boarded the ship that brought the tea. They worked quickly. What did they do? They dumped two hundred fifty chests of tea into the **harbor**. They would show the king what they thought of his taxes!

That was the Boston Tea Party. It was a strange kind of tea party because nobody drank any tea!

**Talk and Think**

Ask your child if he knows what the "last straw" means. The phrase describes the moment when things have gone too far one way and just have to change. It comes from a legend about a man who piled straw on his camel's back until it was to much to hold. Sometimes you hear, "It was the straw that broke the camel's back."

**New Word**

A **harbor** is a place along the coast where there are no dangerous rocks and the water is deep enough for ships to sail right up to the land. If people build a town next to a harbor, that town can be a "port," a town where boats dock to load and unload goods.

The Boston Tea Party

## A Fight with Mother?

When the British heard about the Boston Tea Party, they were angry—no, they were furious! King George decided to punish the colonists. He closed the port of Boston, and that hurt the colonists. Many people depended on the ships going in and out of Boston. The ships carried away things that the colonists wanted to sell to other countries, and the ships brought in things that the colonists needed or wanted from other countries. So, closing the port meant that the colonists lost money and jobs.

The British government did other things that made the colonists angry. The people in Boston were not allowed to come together in town meetings. British soldiers were sent to keep order. Soon British soldiers were everywhere. They wore uniforms that were bright red, and many colonists began to refer to them angrily as "the Redcoats."

Americans started to think that maybe they would have to fight Britain, their own mother country, to be free! Maybe they would have to do battle with the Redcoats!

A Redcoat and a Minuteman

This was a scary idea, and at first most people did not agree. Over time, however, more and more people began to think it was a good idea. In Massachusetts, the colonists formed groups of men who agreed to be ready to fight the British, if it came to that. These men were called Minutemen because they could be ready to fight with a minute's notice. The colonists also gathered weapons and ammunition. They hid them outside Boston in Concord, Massachusetts.

Of course, the British soldiers didn't like this at all. They decided to find the colonists' weapons and take them away. But the colonists were ready. They had spies keeping watch to see when the Redcoats would make their move.

**New Word**

While many colonists wanted to break free of England, others did not. These people were called loyalists or Tories. The Tories were colonists who were still on the side of—or loyal to—King George and the government of Great Britain.

## The Midnight Ride of Paul Revere

Well, eventually, the British did make their move. They sent Redcoats to capture the guns and ammunition that were being kept in Concord. But one colonist, a silversmith named Paul Revere, knew they were coming. How did he know? He had already made plans with a friend in Boston who was keeping an eye on the British soldiers. If and when the Redcoats started to move toward Concord, then Paul Revere was to send a signal from high in the steeple of a church tower. The signal was: "One if by land, two if by sea." That meant: Light one lamp if the British troops were marching by land from Boston to Concord. But light two lamps if the British were coming in boats across the bay.

On a clear spring evening, Paul Revere got word that the British were coming by sea, so he lit two lamps in the steeple of the Old North Church. He got into a small boat with two friends and rowed silently past a large British warship in Boston Harbor. Although it was a bright night, they made it safely to the other

Paul Revere alerting the Minutemen

side without the soldiers spotting him. There Paul Revere borrowed a fine horse and galloped off to Lexington to warn his friends, Samuel Adams and John Hancock, that the British were coming.

Along the way he shouted his warning, "The Redcoats are coming! The Redcoats are coming!"

Now, you may find this hard to believe, but as Paul Revere shouted his warning, someone actually shouted back, "Quiet down! You're making too much noise!"

"Noise!" said Paul Revere. "You'll have noise enough before long!" And Paul Revere was right. Following his warning, American Minutemen were getting dressed and grabbing their muskets.

## A Nation Is Born

The very next day, at Lexington and Concord, the Minutemen were waiting for the Redcoats. The Redcoats came. A shot was fired; more shots rang out. A

Minutemen fighting British Redcoats

famous poem says that first shot was "the shot heard 'round the world." No, not because it was loud but because it was important, very important. It was the beginning of a war that would lead to a new nation.

We call that war the American Revolution, or the Revolutionary War. One meaning of the word "revolution" is a really big change. The American Revolution was certainly a big change. It turned out to be more than just a little fight between the colonists and their mother country over weapons and taxes. It became a big fight about being free, about whether the colonies would be allowed to make their own country and to rule themselves.

In 1776—a year after the first shots were fired at Lexington and Concord—the colonists took a very big step. They told King George that they wanted to be free and start their own country—a country called the United States of America.

Thomas Jefferson is on the nickel.

On July 4, in the year 1776, many American leaders signed the Declaration of Independence. That's why we still celebrate every Fourth of July as Independence Day, the birthday of our nation. Do you remember (from the kindergarten book in this series) who wrote the Declaration of Independence? His face is on the nickel: His name is Thomas Jefferson.

The Declaration of Independence said:

We hold these truths to be self-evident,
that all men are created equal,
that they are endowed by their Creator
with certain unalienable rights.

What did Jefferson mean when he said that some "truths" are "self-evident"? He meant: Anyone can plainly see that these things are true. And what were those things? Jefferson laid out two of them:

1. that "all men are created equal" (back then, "men" was sometimes used to mean "people");
2. that all men have "certain unalienable rights."

Let's look at the first of Jefferson's claims. To say that "all men are created equal" was a bold statement at the time. In most countries, there were kings and dukes and noblemen, who were treated, and expected to be treated, as better and more important than farmers and peasants. No one had ever started a country before based on the idea that "all men are created equal."

The second claim was also a bold one. To say that all people have "certain unalienable rights" is to say that people have some rights that nobody—not even a king—can take away. Jefferson said that people have the right to be free and to decide how to rule themselves. He said, "King George, we are not going to listen to you anymore. We have the right to decide for ourselves how to rule our own country!"

How do you think King George III felt about these ideas? Do you think he agreed that he and his subjects were "created equal" and that the colonists had certain rights not even he could take away? He certainly did not. He thought the colonists were starting a rebellion, and he was determined to defeat them.

Thomas Jefferson and his fellow Americans knew they were doing something new, something big, something revolutionary. They were starting a new nation.

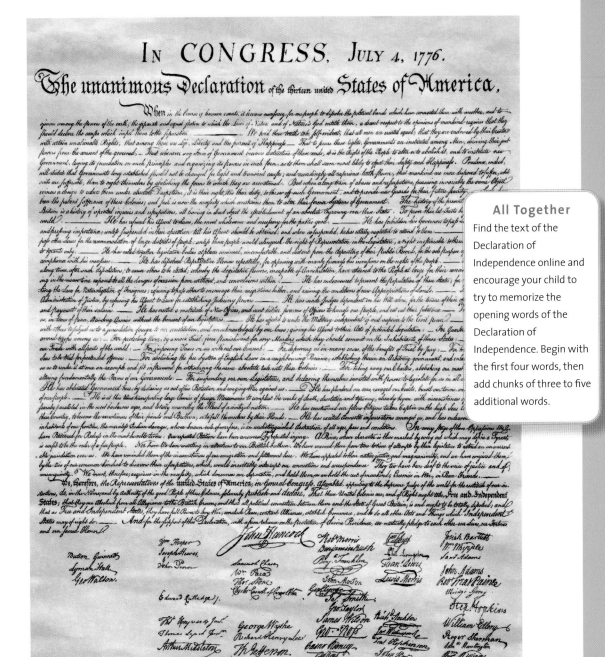

The Declaration of Independence

If you had been in the city of Philadelphia on July 4, 1776, you would have heard the sound of a big bell ringing—the Liberty Bell. From the town hall, the Liberty Bell rang out to tell the people of Philadelphia that the colonies had declared their independence.

Why would people use a bell to announce important news? Do you think they had radio, telephones, or television back then?

When the bell rang, the people of Philadelphia gathered to hear the first reading of the Declaration of Independence. After independence was won, the bell was rung on special occasions. Almost sixty years later, it cracked. But it still remains a symbol of our country. You can see the Liberty Bell if you go to Philadelphia.

They were establishing a new government. Could they make it work? Were they ready for a democracy—a government by the people, not by a king?

Jefferson thought Americans were ready. He said other people around the world would look to America to see if we could make democracy work. But first the United States had to win the war against Great Britain.

The Liberty Bell

## George Washington and the War for Independence

After declaring independence, the colonists had to select a leader for their army. They chose a planter from Virginia named George Washington. You may have heard about him if you read the kindergarten book in this series. Sometimes he is called "the father of his country." George Washington may have done more than anyone else to help win the American Revolution.

When the war for independence started, there was no American army. Each of the thirteen colonies sent men who wanted to help fight for liberty, but these men were not soldiers. They were farmers, blacksmiths, shoemakers, carpenters, and shopkeepers. Who would turn these men into an army and lead them in battle? George Washington. It was Washington who taught the American sol-

diers how to fight together, and it was Washington who kept them from losing hope when it seemed like the Americans might be defeated.

There were lots of reasons why the Americans might have lost hope. The British had more soldiers, more ships, and more guns, and the British soldiers were well trained and well equipped. The Americans, on the other hand, had lots of problems. The new government did not always have enough money to pay the soldiers. Sometimes it didn't even have enough money to buy them food.

But still the Americans did not give up. They fought hard for what they believed in. They fought for their dream of a free country where the people could

George Washington

rule themselves. And one of the reasons why they did not give up is that their leader, General Washington, stayed with them through all of the hardships they had to bear and refused to quit.

# The Flags They Fought Under

During the Revolutionary War, the Continental Congress decided that the official flag of the United States would have thirteen stripes—one for each of the thirteen colonies—and also thirteen stars. However, the congress did not say how the stars were to be arranged, and for a while different flag-makers used different designs. Some flags had the stars arranged in lines; others had them arranged in a circle. The design shown here is sometimes called the "Betsy Ross" flag because it was thought to have been created by a woman named Betsy Ross. Scholars today think the Betsy Ross story may be a legend rather than real history, but you will still hear people talk about Betsy Ross and the U.S. flag.

## George Washington and His Men

There's a story about George Washington that says a lot about the kind of leader he was. The story goes like this:

One day during the Revolutionary War, some soldiers were struggling to lift a huge log into place. One of the soldiers was giving orders to the others. Now, in the army, people have different ranks, such as sergeant, captain, and, at the top, general. People of higher rank are in charge and can give orders to people of lower rank. So, on this day, a man with the rank of corporal—which is not a very high rank—was giving orders to the soldiers trying to lift the heavy log. "Heave-ho, men!" the corporal shouted. "Come on! Put your backs into it!"

Just then a stranger rode up on a horse. The stranger was not wearing a military uniform. The stranger asked the corporal, "Why don't you help your men?" The corporal looked at the stranger with amazement. Then he said, in a very proud voice, as though he were a great king or emperor, "Sir, I am a corporal!"

"You are?" replied the stranger. Then he got down from his horse, took off his hat, and bowed to the corporal. "I beg your pardon, Mr. Corporal," he said. The stranger helped the soldiers lift the heavy log. He pushed and pulled and sweated with the soldiers until finally they got the log in place.

Then the stranger turned to the corporal and said, "Mr. Corporal, when you have another job and do not have enough men to do it, send for your general and I will come again to help you."

The corporal's mouth fell open: The man who had helped move the log was General Washington!

## From Valley Forge to Yorktown

One of the low points for George Washington and the colonial army came early in the war, when they spent a long, cold winter in Valley Forge, Pennsylvania. It was freezing cold, and the soldiers were in terrible condition. Their clothes were

Washington and his men endured a terrible winter at Valley Forge.

in tatters. Many of them had to march through snow with no shoes. They wrapped their feet in rags. There was not enough food to feed the soldiers, and many of them died during the winter.

When the spring came, however, things began to improve. The weather warmed up. A new drill instructor arrived from Europe to help Washington train the men. Also, the nation of France decided to support the Americans in their struggle for independence.

With help from the French, the American army began to win more battles. A few years later, in 1781, Washington and his army trapped the main British army at Yorktown, Virginia. With the Americans on one side and the French on the other, the British soldiers were boxed in, and eventually they were forced to surrender. That meant that the Americans had won the war, and that the United States of America would become a free and independent country.

Did you know? In this famous drawing the British general (on the right) is offering his sword to General Washington (on the left) as a sign of surrender. Actually, though, the British general, who was humiliated, refused to appear at the ceremonial sword offering and sent a representative instead. George Washington responded by sending his own representative.

## "And Called It Macaroni"

Here's part of a song you may know.

Yankee Doodle went to town,
A-riding on a pony.
Stuck a feather in his cap
And called it macaroni.

Have you ever sung "Yankee Doodle"? Did you know that the lyrics of this song come from the American Revolution? Here's some more of the song:

Father and I went down to camp
Along with Captain Gooding,
And there we saw the men and boys
As thick as hasty pudding.

And there was Captain Washington
Upon a slapping stallion,
A-giving orders to his men,
I guess there was a million.

Yankee Doodle, keep it up,
Yankee Doodle dandy,
Mind the music and the step,
And with the girls be handy.

It was the British who came up with the name Yankee Doodle. They used it to make fun of the Americans. "Yankee" was their word for an American, and "doodle" was a word meaning fool or simpleton. But the Americans said, "Fine! Go ahead and call us Yankees! We like the name, and we'll sing the song too!" And "Yankee Doodle" has been a favorite song of the American people ever since. (By the way, "hasty pudding" is a thick pudding made of cornmeal or oatmeal.)

## A Courageous Woman: Deborah Sampson

Most of the soldiers who fought in the Revolutionary War were men, but there were also a few women who fought in the war. One of them was Deborah Sampson.

Deborah Sampson was a young woman with big dreams. When the Revolution started, she helped on her family's farm and worked to get food to the American soldiers. But Deborah wanted to do more. She wanted to fight the British and help the Americans win the war.

In those days, women weren't allowed to fight in the army. People wanted to protect women from the dangers of war, and some people thought women were too weak to fight. But not Deborah Sampson. She thought of a plan. She dressed up like a man. She called herself "Robert Shurtleff," and she joined the American army!

Deborah (or "Robert") was well liked by her fellow soldiers, and nobody suspected she was a woman. This may have been partly because she was taller than most women of her day. She fought bravely in several battles, and once she was wounded in the leg. Sampson hid her wound so that no doctor could treat her and find out she wasn't a man! Her leg wound got better, but later

Deborah Sampson disguised herself as a man and fought bravely for her country.

she was wounded again and ran a high fever. Her captain put her in the hospital in Philadelphia. When the doctors discovered she was a woman, they said, "Really, Miss Sampson, we think you should go home now."

Deborah Sampson did go home. But for almost a year she had managed to fool everyone—and to serve her country.

# A Poet for Freedom: Phillis Wheatley

Phillis Wheatley was born in Africa and brought to America on a slave ship when she was only eight years old. She was sold to a merchant in Boston named John Wheatley. Mr. Wheatley and his wife did something very unusual. They taught Phillis to read and write—which was something that almost no enslaved people were taught to do.

The poet Phillis Wheatley

Phillis Wheatley studied hard. She used her knowledge and talents to write poetry. She wrote very good poetry, and people began to notice her. In 1773, just a few years before the colonists declared independence, she published her first book of poems.

In some of her poems, Phillis Wheatley asked the colonists to think. How could they demand freedom from England, she asked, but at the same time make people like herself live as slaves? How could people say, "We have a right to be free!" and then say, "You people from Africa must continue to be slaves"?

Phillis Wheatley was luckier than many Africans who were brought to America. She did not remain enslaved for her whole life. The Wheatleys freed her, and she married a free black man and kept on writing.

# Benjamin Franklin

One man who played a key role in the American Revolution was Benjamin Franklin. Or perhaps it would be better to say that this one man played several key roles.

Do you remember when the Continental Congress met in Philadelphia and decided to declare independence? Benjamin Franklin was one of the men who voted for independence.

Do you remember when Thomas Jefferson wrote the Declaration of Independence? Benjamin Franklin was one of the men who helped him. Franklin read what Jefferson wrote and made several suggestions for improvement.

Do you remember when the French decided to help the Americans in their war for independence? Well, it was Benjamin Franklin, more than anyone else, who was responsible for that. As ambassador to France, it was his job to persuade the French to send soldiers to America. Franklin did this, and the troops the French sent helped the United States win the war.

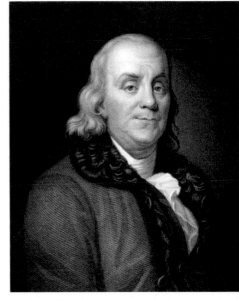

Ben Franklin

Benjamin Franklin, bottom center, went to France to persuade the French to help the colonists.

## The Wisdom of Benjamin Franklin

Ben Franklin was a man of many talents. When he was still a young man, he started a printing business, published a newspaper, and taught himself to read four different languages.

For many years, Franklin printed a book called *Poor Richard's Almanack*. An "almanac" is a book that comes out every year and is filled with lots of information about the weather, about growing crops, and about all sorts of other things.

In *Poor Richard's Almanack*, Ben Franklin included many bits of advice on how to live a successful and happy life. Some of these bits of advice have become famous sayings. See if you have heard any of the sayings below, and spend a few minutes thinking about what each of them might mean:

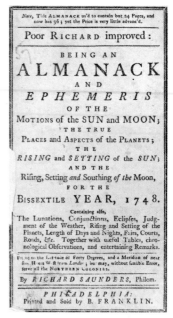

*Poor Richard's Almanack* for 1748, printed and sold by Benjamin Franklin

### Do It Yourself

Make a poster that illustrates one of the proverbs from Franklin's almanac or one of the sayings and proverbs on pages 153–57 of this book; for a more ambitious project, make several pages, each illustrating a proverb, then staple the pages together to make a collection of proverbs and sayings.

- Early to bed and early to rise makes a man healthy, wealthy, and wise.
- Little strokes fell great oaks.
- Lost time is never found again.
- A friend in need is a friend indeed.
- There are no gains without pains.
- Blame-all and Praise-all are two blockheads.
- Three may keep a secret, if two of them are dead.

## Inventor and Scientist

Benjamin Franklin was also a great inventor. He enjoyed swimming and carved special hand paddles out of wood that helped him swim faster. He invented a new kind of stove that could heat more space while using less wood. He also invented the kind of glasses we call bifocals. Bifocals are glasses that combine two lenses—one that helps a person see things that are far away and another that helps the person see things up close.

Franklin also kept up with recent discoveries in science. In his day, people were just beginning to learn about electricity. Franklin had the idea that lightning might be a kind of electricity. To prove this, he flew a kite during an electric storm. He was trying to see if he could "catch" some of the electricity he thought was in the lightning. Today we know that Franklin was right: Lightning is a kind of electricity. But we also know that Franklin's experiment was very dangerous: There is so much electricity in lightning that it could have killed Ben Franklin.

Ben Franklin flew a kite during a thunderstorm to prove that lightning is electricity. Don't try this at home!

Ben Franklin won a lot of arguments in his life, but he lost some too. One of the arguments he lost was over which animal should be shown on the great seal of the United States. The bald eagle was eventually selected—and the bald eagle has been an important symbol of the United States ever since. Franklin, however, thought the bald eagle was a bad choice. He said that the bald eagle was "a bird of bad moral character" because it sometimes stole fish from other animals. Franklin thought the turkey was "a more respectable bird" and would have been a better choice!

## Washington as President

George Washington became the first President of the United States.

When the Revolutionary War ended, some people thought George Washington was such a great leader that he should be crowned King of America! But Washington didn't like that idea. He said he didn't fight the British for all those years just so the United States could have another King George! After the war he went back home to his farm, his wife, and his family.

But a little while later, Americans decided their new country needed a strong leader—not a king but a president. They wanted George Washington because they felt he was a popular leader. Now, part of George Washington wanted to stay at Mount Vernon, his home in Virginia, with his family. But another part of him felt that he had to do what was best for his country. And so George Washington became the first President of the United States.

George Washington served as president for four years. Then he was elected a second time and served for another four years. Because he did so much for the United States of America, George Washington is called the father of our country. Our nation's capital, Washington, D.C., is named after him. You can see him on the one-dollar bill and also on the quarter coin.

The Washington Monument in Washington, D.C., is one of the many monuments to the first President of the United States.

**Talk and Think**

Discuss how a person becomes president. Is a president like a king, who is born into a royal family? No: The American people choose the president. We vote for the person we want to lead our country. Ask your child if she knows the name of the current president.

**Make a Connection**

Read or reread the poem "Washington" on page 43 of this book. Hand your students a dollar bill and a handful of coins, including a quarter and a nickel. Ask them if they can find George Washington. Then repeat with Thomas Jefferson. See if students can recognize and remember anything about the other presidents shown on the coins.

## Freedom for All?

The American Revolution brought big changes, but it didn't change everything. Even though the Declaration of Independence stated that "all men are created equal . . . with certain unalienable rights," the American Revolution did not free the slaves. Nor did it give women equal rights with men. Women did not have the same rights as men, and enslaved people had no rights at all.

Sometimes the hardest thing to change is the way people think and act. People don't change all at once. It would take time for Americans to understand the "ideals"—that means the most important goals—behind the American Revolution, especially the ideal that "all men are created equal."

Still, with the Revolution, Americans took a big and daring step. They said, "We won't have a king. We, the people, will vote and decide!" That was a new idea—in fact, it was downright revolutionary!

## America Grows

Look on page 229 at the map of the original thirteen colonies. After the Revolution, these became the first thirteen states of the United States of America.

Do you see how all those states are on the coast of the Atlantic Ocean? But the United States is now a country that stretches from the Atlantic Ocean to what other ocean? That's right, the Pacific. So how did this happen? How did this country grow from east to west, "from sea to shining sea"?

It happened in many ways, over many years. It began even before the Revolutionary War, when Americans were still under British rule. More and more Americans kept moving away from the Atlantic Ocean. Can you guess which way most of them were moving? They were going west. They were going out to the "frontier"—into places without settlements or towns, places that were new and strange to them. Many of them didn't know exactly where they were going, or what they would find, but they were helped by trailblazers like Daniel Boone.

**Take a Look**

Use the map on page 229 to review directions on a map. Ask questions like, "Which colony is south of Massachusetts?" "Which colony is north of North Carolina?"

Do you know what it means to "blaze a trail"? A trail is a path through the wilderness. To make a path, sometimes you have to cut your way through a forest thick with trees and bushes and briars. Blazing a trail means marking trees with paint or small cuts so that others can follow where you have gone.

Daniel Boone was a trailblazer. He set out to find a path through the Appalachian Mountains that would lead him to good farmland in Kentucky. (Look at the map on page 255; can you find the Appalachian Mountains?) At first Daniel Boone couldn't find a way through the mountains: They just stood there, big and high and hard to get over. But then he found a Native American trail that led through a gap—a space—in the mountains.

Later, in 1775, just a year before the signing of the Declaration of Independence, Daniel Boone and some helpers set to work. They cut down trees and moved big rocks and turned the Native American trail into a road wide enough for families to travel on. This road was called the Wilderness Road. In just a few years, thousands of frontiersmen and frontierswomen were heading west on the Wilderness Road. They were looking for land they could farm and build their homes on.

Do your parents ever disagree about whether it is time to stop and ask for directions? Well, be glad your mother didn't marry Daniel Boone. Boone never admitted he was lost; however, he did admit that, on one occasion, he was "confused for several weeks." The Wilderness Trail that he blazed helped many settlers who came after him make their way west without getting lost.

Daniel Boone helped open the West for settlers.

Daniel Boone and the settlers who followed him often fought with the American Indians. For the Indians, these settlers meant trouble, because they were making their farms and homes on the land where the Native Americans hunted. How would the Native Americans live if the settlers scared away the animals the Native Americans needed for food and many other uses? But, for the most part, the settlers were not concerned with what the Native Americans needed. They knew what they wanted: land, and lots of it. So, they kept coming—thousands of them. They built homes, forts, and towns, including Boonesboro, which was named after the trailblazer who opened the way west.

## What a Bargain! The Louisiana Purchase

> **New Word**
>
> Have you ever heard your parents or a friend say, "I got a bargain"? That means, "I got a great deal! I bought something and paid a lot less money than it's worth!"

The United States got a really great **bargain** in the year 1803. At the time, Thomas Jefferson was president—our country's third president, by the way. (Do you remember what he wrote at the beginning of the American Revolution?) President Jefferson wanted to buy some land that was claimed by France. The land was on the Mississippi River and included the small city of New Orleans (which is now a big city).

It turned out the French did not want to sell the little bit of land that Jefferson wanted. Instead, they wanted to sell all of the land they claimed in North America! It was so much land, and for such a low price, that Jefferson said, "Yes!"

This bargain was called the Louisiana Purchase ("to purchase" means the same thing as to buy). Louisiana is the name the French gave to the land, in honor of the King of France, King Louis [LOO-ee]. Overnight, the Louisiana Purchase made our country more than twice as big! Take a look at the map on the facing page and see.

Thomas Jefferson was excited about the new land he had purchased for the United States. But he didn't really know what it contained. He wanted to know how far west the land went. He wanted to know what Native American people lived there and what kinds of animals and plants were there. So he sent a group

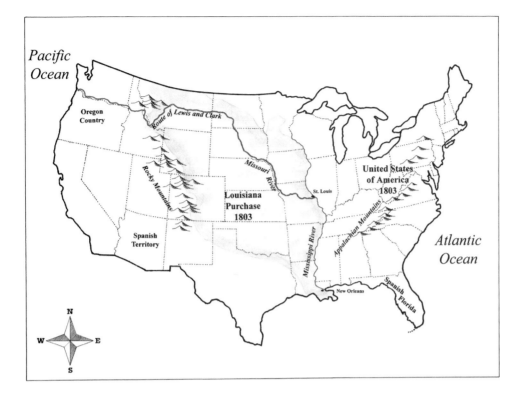

of men to explore it. They were led by Lewis and Clark. That's two men, Meri-
wether Lewis and William Clark. With their men and supplies, they set off on

boats, heading west on the Missouri
River. (Find this river on the map shown
above.)

Lewis and Clark didn't have modern
equipment like cameras or tape recorders.
So, to collect the information that President Jefferson wanted, every day they
wrote descriptions of what they saw. They
drew lots of pictures and made many
maps. They saw animals they had never
seen before, including huge herds of buf-
falo, prairie dogs, and ferocious grizzly
bears.

Lewis and Clark explored the land of the Louisiana Purchase.

Sacagawea served as a guide for Lewis and Clark.

Lewis and Clark met many American Indians along the way. They traveled through the lands of the Cheyenne, Crow, Nez Perce, Chinook, and others. They met a young woman named Sacajawea, of the Shoshone tribe. She helped guide them on part of their journey through the rough Rocky Mountains, and she spoke for them when they met other Native Americans.

Sacajawea did not go with Lewis and Clark to the end of their journey, which finally took them all the way to the Pacific Ocean. But when they reached the Pacific, Lewis and Clark knew that without her help, the two explorers might not have made it.

## Looking Ahead

You know how some books have chapters? Well, if you imagine American history as a big book, then what you've learned so far is like the first chapters. You've learned about the early Native American civilizations, the Spanish conquerors, and the English settlers. You've seen how thirteen colonies of England declared their independence and fought to become a new country, the United States of America. And you've seen how that country started to grow "from sea to shining sea."

There are many more exciting chapters ahead in the story of American history. In the second-grade book in this series, you'll learn about how the new nation, the United States, decided—after lots of arguments!—to make laws and govern itself. You'll find out about how the Americans got into another war with England—a war that gave us our national anthem ("Oh, say, can you see by the dawn's early light . . ."). You'll follow more settlers as they move west, and you'll learn about how this affected the Native Americans. You'll read the story of a terrible war with a good result. It was terrible because Americans fought against Americans, and many people died, but it led to the end of slavery in this country. And you'll learn how America has grown and changed as many people from countries all over the world have become part of this country.

## Suggested Resources

*RECOMMENDED FOR READING ALOUD*
*A Little History of the World* by E. H. Gombrich (Yale University Press, 2008)
*The Story of the World* by Susan Wise Bauer, 2 vols. (Peace Hill Press, 2002)

*EGYPT*
*Bill and Pete Go Down the Nile* by Tomie dePaola (Puffin, 1996)
*Cleopatra* by Diane Stanley (HarperCollins, 1997)

*The Hundredth Name* by Shulamith Levy Oppenheim (Boyds Mills Press, 1997)

*I Wonder Why Pyramids Were Built and Other Questions About Ancient Egypt* by Philip Steele (Kingfisher, 2011)

*Mummies Made in Egypt* by Aliki (Thomas Y. Crowell Co., 1979)

*Tut's Mummy: Lost . . . and Found* by Judy Donnelly (Random House, 1988)


### JUDAISM, CHRISTIANITY, ISLAM

*Celebrate: A Book of Jewish Holidays* by Judith Gross (Grosset & Dunlap, 2005)

*The Nativity* by Julie Vivas (Houghton Mifflin Harcourt Books, 2006)

*The Story of Hanukkah* by David A. Adler (Holiday House, 2011)

*Under the Ramadan Moon* by Sylvia Whitman (Albert Whitman, 2011)

*What You Will See Inside a Mosque* by Aisha Karen Khan (Skylight Paths, 2008)


### AMERICAN HISTORY

*Benjamin Franklin* and/or *George Washington* by Ingri D'Aulaire (Demco, 1987, 1996)

*The Flame of Peace: A Tale of the Aztecs* by Deborah Lattimore (HarperCollins, 1987)

*If You Sailed on the Mayflower in 1620* by Ann McGovern (Scholastic, 1991)

*Let It Begin Here! Lexington and Concord: First Battles of the American Revolution* by Dennis Brindell Fradin (Walker Children's, 2005)

*Lewis and Clark: Explorers of the American West* by Steven Kroll (Holiday House, 1996)

*Lewis and Clark for Kids: Their Journey of Discovery with 21 Activities* by Janis Herbert (Chicago Review Press, 2000)

*Rain Player* by David Wisniewski (Houghton Mifflin Harcourt, 1995)

*The Sad Night: The Story of an Aztec Victory and a Spanish Loss* by Sally Schofer Mathews (Houghton Mifflin Harcourt, 2001)

*Sam the Minuteman* by Nathaniel Benchley (HarperCollins, 1987)

*Samuel Eaton's Day: A Day in the Life of a Pilgrim Boy* by Kate Waters (Scholastic, 1996)

*MEXICO*

*Count Your Way Through Mexico* by Jim Haskins (Lerner, 1989)

*P Is for Piñata: A Mexico Alphabet* by Tony Johnston (Sleeping Bear, 2008)

*GEOGRAPHY*

*National Geographic Kids Beginner's World Atlas* (National Geographic, 2011)

# III
# Visual Arts

## Introduction

First graders should experience art primarily by *doing:* by drawing, painting, cutting and pasting, working with clay and other materials. Planned activities are great, but spontaneous art is just as important, a wonderful way for a child to understand and identify with art.

Reading this section aloud together will help your child become comfortable talking about art while getting to know some great works of art. In this way, your child experiences art by *seeing* and *thinking* as well as by *doing*. The experience comes full circle: Seeing and thinking about art will enrich your child's natural enjoyment of making art.

## People Have Been Making Art for a *Very* Long Time

Do you like to draw pictures? Do you use a pencil, or crayons, or a marker? Did someone teach you how to draw? Probably not. You probably started drawing simply for the fun of it.

People enjoy drawing. Sometimes they draw for pleasure, and sometimes they make drawings to share with other people. Sometimes people just scribble, or they make designs, and sometimes they make drawings of people and things and places they know. What kind of drawing do you like to do?

People have been making art for a long, long time. How do we know that? Because there are works of art that are very, very old—works of art that were made before anyone had paper or pencils, works of art that were made before anyone even wrote things down! We call those works of art "prehistoric," which means they are so old, they come from a time before people started writing things down. They might not have written down words, but they did make art. Here is a story about some boys who discovered some of the most famous prehistoric art in all the world.

## The Boys Who Found the Cave Paintings

One fall day in the country called France, which is part of the continent of Europe, four boys and their dog, Robot, went walking in the forest. They had heard people say that the forest had hidden **caves** and tunnels that led underground to a treasure. The boys really wanted to find those caves.

Suddenly Robot started barking. The boys went to

see what got their dog so excited. A big tree had fallen over and, near its roots, a big hole had opened up. One boy dared to climb through the hole. The others worried about him, but then they heard him call out, "Follow me! Bring the lantern!" They each crawled through the hole and found themselves in a cave big enough to stand up in. They had found a secret tunnel!

By the light of the lantern, they looked around. There on the walls of the cave they saw drawings of animals—cows and bulls and horses—in red and

black and brown. They had never seen anything like it.

The boys climbed back out and ran to tell their parents what they had found. They also told their teacher, who knew a lot about history, and he followed them down into the cave again.

"You boys have found something rare and amazing," their teacher told them.

"These cave paintings are very old. They were made thousands and thousands of years ago! In fact, they are some of the oldest works of art in the world."

People came from far away just to see the ancient cave paintings. The boys decided that Robot had indeed led them to a treasure. It wasn't gold or jewels. It was these beautiful works of art, made by people who lived a long, long time ago.

## Art That Is Very Old

The pictures on the cave walls in France were drawn by people so long ago that it's hard to imagine—almost thirty thousand years ago! Prehistoric cave paintings have been found in France, Spain, and the United States. Since those people did not write anything down, we don't know why they made these cave paintings, but we can guess.

**Do It Yourself**

Find a *really* big cardboard box, like an appliance box. Set it on its side, with an opening your child can crawl into, and encourage your child to pretend it's his or her cave, with walls for making drawings on the inside.

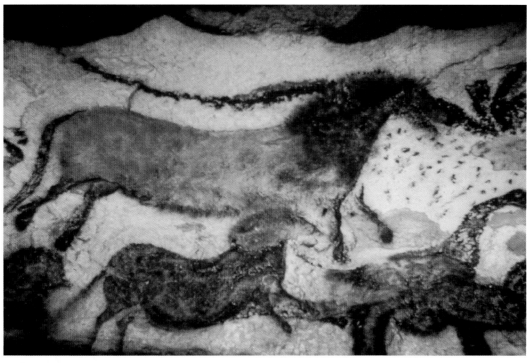

Wall paintings, Lascaux, France

What do you see in the cave paintings? Why do you think these early people drew pictures of animals? Were the animals important to these early people? Maybe they hunted these animals for food. (You can find out more about these long-long-ago people in the "World History and Geography" section of this book; see pages 164–67.)

## Art from Ancient Egypt

People have been making art for a long, *long* time. Long after people made cave paintings, but still thousands of years before you were born, people in ancient Egypt made beautiful and amazing works of art.

The ancient Egyptians thought that art was a way to show great wealth and power and to express their ideas about religion.

The ancient Egyptians considered their "pharaohs," or kings and queens, to be gods. The god-kings and god-queens lived special lives, with many servants. When they died, their servants made them into **mummies** and buried them in beautiful coffins with all their favorite things, like jewelry, food, and even pets. They made a very fancy place called a tomb in which to put all those things, because the Egyptians thought their god-kings and god-queens were going to live a special life after they died and they needed to take those things with them.

> **New Word**
> Egyptian **mummies** are not the same as "mommies"—or "daddies"! The ancient Egyptians made mummies by wrapping cloth around and around a body before burying it. They even made their cats into mummies.

When the king named Tutankhamen [toot-awn-KAH-men] (Tut for short) was buried in his tomb, his mummy was placed inside this fancy golden box. This mummy case is like a sculpture of King Tut, with his eyes open, his special pharaoh's headdress on, and his arms crossed.

Here is a different kind of ancient Egyptian work of art. It is a bust—a sculpture of the head and shoulders—of a queen named Nefertiti. She is wearing a special queen's headdress and a dress with a collar of jewels. The sculpture makes her look beautiful, calm, and happy. Does she look like a real person to you?

**Make a Connection**

Read more about ancient Egypt in the "World History and Geography" section of this book, pages 167–77. The pyramids introduced there contained the ornate tombs mentioned here.

Bust of Nefertiti

## A World of Color

What colors can you name? Do you have a favorite color? Artists love color. They love to see colors in the world, and they love to use colors in their art.

Artists call red, yellow, and blue the "primary" colors. They are the three basic colors we start with. We can mix them to make other colors. But no matter how hard you try, you cannot start with other colors and mix them together to make red, yellow, or blue. That's why they are called primary.

red     yellow     blue

But you can mix red, yellow, or blue together and come up with other colors. Here's what you get:

**Do It Yourself**

Help your child use watercolors, tempera, or craft tissue to combine primary colors and make secondary colors. Once your child has these formulas down, invite further experimentation with color combining.

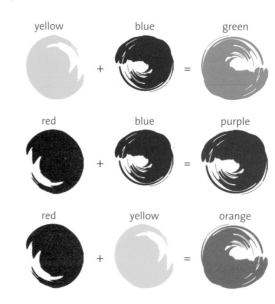

yellow + blue = green

red + blue = purple

red + yellow = orange

*Field of Tulips in Holland*, Claude Monet

Let's learn about the French artist Claude Monet [moe-NAY] and see how he used color. Monet loved light and color. He liked to go outside in the bright sunlight. He would set up his easel and look around and paint the colors that he saw. Sometimes those colors surprised him!

Here is a painting by Monet. What do you see in the painting? The sky and some clouds. Big fields, with what in them? Colorful flowers! Let's look for the three primary colors in Monet's painting. The flowers are red and yellow, and the sky is blue. Tulips are a kind of flower that grows in Holland.

The name of this painting is *Field of Tulips in Holland*. Holland is a country in Europe, near France, where they have a lot of buildings like the tall one here, called a windmill.

*Arrangement in Grey and Black, No. 1*, James Abbott McNeill Whistler

Not all paintings are filled with bright colors. Some artists decide to leave bright colors out of their paintings. Take a look at this painting by the American artist James McNeill Whistler. What colors did he choose to use in this painting?

Whistler called his painting *Arrangement in Grey and Black, No. 1*. Many people call it *Whistler's Mother*—because it is a painting that the artist made of his mother.

When you look at the painting, what kind of person do you think Whistler's mother was? Does she look like a happy, fun-loving person, ready to get up and dance around the room? Does she seem young or old? How would you describe the expression on her face?

Can you find any colors other than gray and black in Whistler's painting?

## Line Up!

Take a pencil or crayon and make a dot on a sheet of paper. Put your pencil or crayon on the dot and let it wander away from it. Now you have a "line." A line starts with a dot and then goes somewhere.

Lines come in all types—straight, curved, zigzag, wavy, and spiral.

Lines can be fat or skinny, smooth or jagged, long or short. Use a sharp pencil and you can make a thin line. Use a fat crayon and you can make a broad line. A line made with chalk on a sidewalk often turns out rough and jagged. A line made with finger paints usually comes out curved.

Here is a drawing made by another French artist, Henri Matisse [on-REE ma-TEECE]. He used just a few lines to draw this animal—can you recognize it? It is a swan, with a long neck, opening up its two big wings.

What type of lines does Matisse use for the neck of the swan—straight, jagged, or curved? Can you see other curved lines in Matisse's drawing? Curved lines make this swan look graceful.

*The Swan*, Henri Matisse

**All Together**

Gather together some plain paper and several different drawing utensils: pencils, markers, chalk, crayons, pens. Have fun with your child, using the utensils to make different lines: straight, curved, wavy, zigzag, spiral. Together, say the word over and over as your child makes that kind of line.

Here is a painting by the American artist Georgia O'Keeffe. She called her painting *Shell No. 1*. What kind of line did O'Keeffe use more than any other? She made a curve go around and around, inside itself—we call that line a spiral. Put your finger at the center of the shell and trace the spiral, around and around and outward. Can you think of other things that are shaped in a spiral?

Georgia O'Keeffe loved beautiful things from nature, like flowers, bones, and shells. She painted them very carefully, and she often made them much bigger than they really were, to make people look more closely. For example, the little shell O'Keeffe painted was only an inch or two across, but in this painting she made it the size of a beach ball.

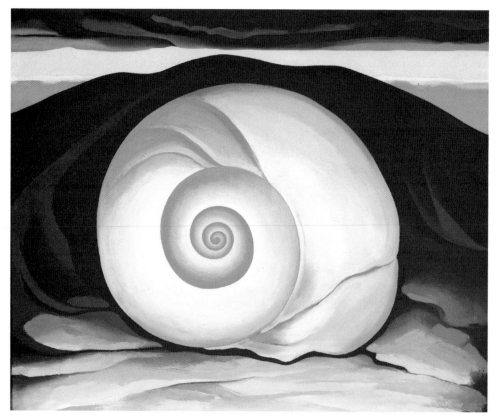

*Shell No. 1*, Georgia O'Keeffe

## Get in Shape!

A line that you draw with a crayon on a big piece of paper can go around and around and around and up and down and around again, and it's still one line! Drawing that kind of line makes lots of shapes inside. Any time you cut something out, or draw lines that connect, you are creating a *shape*.

Some shapes have names. Take a look at these three shapes. Can you name them? Circle, square, and triangle.

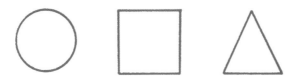

Here are three more shapes that have names. Can you name these? Rectangle, oval, and diamond.

Here is a picture of a shape that someone cut out of construction paper. Does it look like something to you? It looks sort of like the shape of a person, with a head, two arms, and two legs. Even though it doesn't look exactly like any real person, we can still tell that it's shaped like a person.

Different shapes can make you feel and think different things. Look again at the circle and the square. Which one makes you think of something moving? Circles roll: Think of wheels, marbles, balls. Squares and rectangles seem to rest in one place: Think of a big rectangular object, like a refrigerator. Triangles have points, and the points

> **Do It Yourself**
>
> Help your child make a shapes collage. You'll need colored construction paper, a piece of white paper, scissors, and glue. Ask your child to cut out a square, rectangle, triangle, diamond, circle, semicircle, and oval from the colored construction paper. She can cut more than one of each shape, in different colors and sizes. Now she can make a work of art by pasting the shapes onto the white paper. You can use this as a way to practice naming the basic shapes as well as a fun art project.

can make you think of something moving in a certain direction, like a rocket rising into the sky.

Artists always pay attention to shapes. Let's try something: We're going to look at a picture and try to pay attention to just the shapes in it. That means we won't think about the colors or what the picture shows you, but instead we will be looking at the basic shapes the artist used in his painting.

Have you ever been up so high, in an airplane or a Ferris wheel, that when you looked down everything seemed like little shapes, like squares and triangles and circles? That's the kind of feeling you get when you look at this painting, called *Stone City, Iowa,* created by the American artist Grant Wood. Imagine you are flying over this place. What do you see?

Let's look for shapes in this painting. Look at the houses: They look like rectangles with triangles on top. Their roofs look like diamonds. What shape did Wood use for the trees? They all look like ovals and circles, don't they? But some of them are round, fat circles and others are tall, thin ovals.

*Stone City, Iowa,* Grant Wood, 1930, oil on wood panel, 30.25 × 40. Art © Figge Art Museum, successors to the estate of Nan Wood Graham/Licensed by VAGA, New York, NY

*Parade,* Jacob Lawrence

Let's look at shapes in another painting. This one, called *Parade*, was made by the African American artist Jacob Lawrence. Lawrence used different shapes to make the bodies of the people in his painting.

Here is an experiment, a way to figure out what shapes Lawrence used for the people in this painting. See the man dressed in black in the middle of the painting? Put your finger on the top of his hat. Now make your finger move down to his foot in back, then across to his foot in front, and back up to the top of his hat. What shape did your finger draw? A shape with three sides: a triangle.

Can you find other people in the painting whose bodies seem shaped like triangles? What about other shapes? Some of the people in front, watching the parade, seem to be shaped more like rectangles, don't they? Do you see any circles?

# Looking Closely at Art

**Make a Connection**

Before you discuss the art elements in this painting, talk with your child about what it portrays. Start with the title, *La Piñata*. Does your child know what that means? Piñatas are described in the section on Mexico in "American History and Geography," pages 216–18. It's worth noting for your child that the subject and the artist of this painting both come from Mexico.

As we have been looking at works of art, we have noticed colors, lines, and shapes. Now let's look at all three in this painting, called *La Piñata*, by the Mexican artist Diego Rivera [dee-AY-go ree-VAIR-ah].

Let's start with colors. What colors do you see in this painting? Do you see the primary colors—red, yellow, and blue?

Now what about lines and shapes? Use your finger to trace some of the lines in the painting. It is not like Matisse's swan, drawn only with lines, but there are some strong lines in this painting. Where are curved lines? Are there any straight lines? Any circles? Triangles? Rectangles?

Now let's talk about what is happening in this painting. It tells a story. What are these children doing? What happened just before the scene in the painting? What might happen next?

*La Piñata*, Diego Rivera

## Texture: Oh, What a Feeling!

Imagine that you're holding a kitten. How does it feel? You might say it feels "soft" or "furry."

Now imagine that you're holding a frog. How does it feel? Not the same as a kitten, does it? You might say it feels "slippery" or "smooth" or even "slimy."

Every one of those words—soft, furry, slippery, smooth, slimy—describes "texture." When you talk about the way something feels when you touch it, you're

talking about its *texture*. Everything that you touch has some sort of texture. A rock could be "rough" or "hard" or "bumpy." An apple might be "shiny" and "hard" outside but "juicy" and "soft" inside when you take a bite. When you lie in the grass, it might feel "scratchy" or "wet."

Some works of art have texture because you can actually imagine holding and touching them with your hands. Take a look at this mask, for example. It was made by an Iroquois Native American. The mask maker weaved dry corn husks in a tight pattern to make the face, and added loose corn husks around the outside.

This mask was worn during agricultural ceremonies. Imagine putting this over your face as a mask. What does it feel like? What is the texture? Do you feel the smoothness of the husk where it is woven? Do you feel the prickly loose pieces?

Artists use texture even when they make things you are not going to touch and hold. In fact, when you visit art museums, there are usually

> ### Talk and Think
> Have fun with your child coming up with as many words describing texture as you can. Gather everyday items with different textures, for example: leaves, marbles, nuts and bolts, cereal, a sponge, a blanket, cotton balls, wood, aluminum foil, shells. Feel each object and ask your child what words describe its texture. Help if necessary, and then go back to compare and contrast the objects and their textures, using the words again.

signs all around that say: PLEASE DO NOT TOUCH THE ARTWORKS. But you can always imagine the texture of a work of art without actually touching it.

For example, take a look at this sculpture, made more than a hundred years ago by a French artist named Edgar Degas [day-GAH]. What does the sculpture show? It's a girl dressed to do ballet. The name of this sculpture is *The Little Dancer of Fourteen Years.*

The body of the dancer is made of a metal, so her face, arms, and legs have a smooth, hard texture. But Degas added materials to give the sculpture other textures. The dancer has a satin ribbon in her hair, and she wears a tutu, or ballet skirt, made of cloth called muslin. So, along with the hard metal, Degas added a shiny ribbon and a soft skirt.

When people in France first saw this sculpture, they were shocked. They were used to statues made only of hard substances like metal or stone. Degas

*The Little Dancer of Fourteen Years (La Petite Danseuse de Quatorze Ans)*, Edgar Degas

surprised them by dressing a statue in shiny and soft materials—clothing that a real person might wear!

Even paintings and drawings can have texture. Artists can paint a tabletop that looks smooth or a mountainside that looks rough. You might not be able to touch them, but you can imagine how they feel.

Look at this painting called *Young Hare* by the German artist Albrecht Dürer [AL-brekt DUR-er]. He used short lines and a combination of colors, especially brown and white, to give the rabbit's fur a soft, fluffy texture.

Did Dürer give a different texture to other parts of the rabbit? What about the whiskers? The claws? What about the eyes? Each of these parts of the animal has a different texture, thanks to the way the artist painted them.

*Young Hare,* Albrecht Dürer

## Portraits Are Pictures of People

Have you had your picture taken at school? Or is there a picture of you on a wall or shelf at home? Maybe your family has a scrapbook with pictures of you when you were a baby. Every one of those pictures of you is called a portrait. A portrait is a picture of a person. It can be taken with a camera, or it can be drawn or painted. Perhaps the most famous portrait in the world is this one, called the *Mona Lisa*. It was painted by the Italian artist Leonardo da Vinci [dah VIN-chee] about five hundred years ago.

For hundreds of years, people have wondered about the woman in this portrait. Is she happy? Is she looking at you or at something else? What might she be

*Mona Lisa*, Leonardo da Vinci

thinking? No one is sure of the answers to those questions. No one even knows who this woman is. Still, her portrait is very famous.

Portraits can tell a lot about a person and the times in which he lived. Here is another portrait, painted by the Spanish artist Francisco Goya [GOI-yuh] more than two hundred years ago.

What do you see in this portrait? You might think this is a little girl, or even a doll, because of the child's long hair, red lips, and fancy costume. But this is the portrait of a little boy whose parents were very wealthy—wealthy enough to hire an artist to paint a portrait of their son! This little boy's name is Manuel, which is what the caption at the bottom of the painting tells us.

*Don Manuel Osorio Manrique de Zuñiga*, Francisco de Goya

Let's look at some of the decisions the artist made. What is the brightest color in the entire portrait? Certainly the bright red of the boy's clothing. Much of the rest of the painting is quite dark, but do you notice that Goya made the wall behind the little boy's head lighter, sort of like shining a spotlight on his face?

What textures do you see in this portrait of Manuel? There is the smooth, shiny cloth of his sash and his shoes, and the frilly cloth of the collar around his neck. His brown hair looks soft and his skin looks smooth.

This portrait tells a story as well. Manuel is holding a string. Where does it go? Trace the line of the string with your finger, from one of Manuel's hands to the other hand and then down to—what? The leg of the bird. That bird must be Manuel's pet. The cage has more pet birds in it too.

But what's that sitting in the darkness behind the bird? Cats! And what are the cats looking at? Manuel's pet bird! What might happen? Does Manuel seem worried?

## Self-Portraits: Take a Good Look at Yourself

When an artist paints a picture of another person, it's called a portrait. But when an artist paints a picture of himself or herself, it's called a self-portrait.

Just like a portrait, a self-portrait tells you a lot about the person and his or her times. Self-portraits don't all look like photographs. You can paint yourself in many different ways. You could make a happy self-portrait or a sad self-portrait, an angry self-portrait or a silly self-portrait.

The Dutch painter Vincent van Gogh [van GOH*] painted many self-portraits. He painted the one on the facing page when he was thirty-six years old.

How does van Gogh look in this self-portrait? Does he seem calm or worried? Look closely at the colors that he used to paint his face. Are you surprised by the color of the shadows under his eyes? It makes his skin look green! But those patches of green contrast with the brownish-red color of his hair and beard.

Can you tell whether van Gogh was sitting in a room or in a park when he painted this self-portrait? You can't really tell, because the artist decided to paint swirling lines of blue and green in the background of his picture. It looks more like a design than a room or a park. Where else do you see curving blue lines in this painting?

**Do It Yourself**

Start with four different pieces of paper and ask your child to draw four different kinds of self-portraits: happy, sad, angry, silly (or scared, brave, sleepy, excited). Write the word that each self-portrait conveys at the bottom of the picture with your child's name. Then go back over all four of them, emphasizing the concept of a self-portrait each time.

* You may also hear his name pronounced van KHOKH, especially outside the United States.

*Self-Portrait*, Vincent van Gogh

## Still Life: A Beautiful Arrangement

A painting of a person is called a portrait. Now let's look at another kind of painting: a *still life*. What do those words make you think of? "Still" seems like nothing is moving, but "life" sounds like the scene may be in a place where people live. A still life is a painting of objects that don't move. It can be a pitcher of water, or a vase of flowers, or a bowl of fruit, or a crumpled cloth napkin. People are never included in a still life, because after a while they would move!

*Irises*, Vincent van Gogh

**Talk and Think**

Have fun practicing sorting skills with your child. Cut out magazine photos that could be called either a portrait (a picture of a person) or a still life (a picture of objects). Use at least six of each. Place them, faceup, on the floor or table and mix them up. Now ask your child to put the portraits together and the still lifes together. Talk through each grouping when your child is done.

Let's look at two still-life paintings. The first is called *Irises*. It shows a bouquet of flowers called irises in a pitcher on a tabletop or counter. If you look closely—look especially at the tabletop—you can see the paintbrush strokes made by the artist. Do these energetic brushstrokes remind you of another painting you've seen? *Irises* was made by Vincent van Gogh, whose self-portrait we just looked at. Van Gogh liked to paint still lifes of flowers, such as irises and sunflowers. Can you point out the curved and straight lines in this painting?

*Still Life with Apples and Oranges*, Paul Cézanne

The other still life is called *Apples and Oranges*. It is by a French artist named Paul Cézanne [say-ZAHN]. What shapes do you see in this painting? What colors? What did Cézanne do to make the circular shapes of the fruit stand out? He outlined them in a dark color, he placed them against white things, and he made sure that they had the brightest colors of all in his still life.

## Murals: Paintings on Walls

Most of the paintings you make are made on paper, and most of the paintings we have seen in this book were painted on canvas, a white cloth. Paintings on paper or canvas can be framed and hung on a wall. But what about painting the wall itself?

**Take a Look**

Pause to talk about the size of this mural, so your child understands that this is a small photograph of a huge painting. Point out the floor and the guardrail in front of the painting, explaining to your child that he or she would stand about as tall as that railing.

When an artist makes a work of art right on the wall, it is called a "mural." A mural is a large painting done on a wall, either inside or on the outside of a building. Are there any murals painted on walls where you live?

Here is a mural painted by the Mexican artist Diego Rivera. (He painted *La Piñata*, on page 276, as well.) This mural was painted in 1953 on the wall of a hospital in Mexico City.

The name of Rivera's mural is *The History of Medicine in Mexico*, and it tells many stories all in one. The mural is divided clearly into two parts.

What do you see on the right? These are people from the ancient Aztec civilization in Mexico (which you can learn about in this book, on pages 205–7). They have simple clothes. Some even have special costumes, like robes and capes. They are holding and healing sick people in the way they did long ago.

*The History of Medicine in Mexico: The People's Demand for Better Health,* Diego Rivera

And what do you see on the left? There are doctors and nurses, working the way they do in hospitals today. They are also healing sick people.

In the center of this mural is the Aztec goddess who was believed to make things clean by touching them. Why do you think Rivera chose to put this figure in a mural about medicine?

**Make a Connection**

As you and your child talk about this painting, turn back to review the content and images in the sections on the Aztecs and on modern Mexico, pages 205–7 and 216–18. Rivera created a mural that represented those two periods of Mexican history.

## Suggested Resources

*ART ACTIVITY BOOKS*

*EcoArt! Earth-Friendly Art and Craft Experiences for 3- to 9-Year-Olds* by Laurie Carlson (Williamson Publishing, 1992)

*Kids' Art Works! Creating with Color, Design, Texture & More* by Sandi Henry (Williamson Publishing, 1999)

*The Kids' Multicultural Art Book: Art and Craft Experiences from Around the World* by Alexandra Michaels (Williamson Publishing, 2007)

*Mudworks: Creative Clay, Dough, and Modeling Experiences* and *Scribble Cookies and Other Independent Creative Art Experiences for Children* by MaryAnn F. Kohl (Bright Ring Publishing, 1985 and 1989)

*My Art Book: Amazing Art Projects Inspired by Masterpieces* by Dorling Kindersley (DK Children, 2011)

*BOOKS THAT REPRINT ARTWORKS FOR CHILDREN*

*Come Look with Me* series by Gladys S. Blizzard (Charlesbridge Publishing), including *Come Look with Me: Enjoying Art with Children* (1990); *Come Look with Me: Animals in Art* (1992); *Come Look with Me: World of Play* (1993); *Come Look with Me: Exploring Landscape Art with Children* (1992)

*I Spy: An Alphabet in Art* by Lucy Micklethwait (Greenwillow, 1996)

*Museum ABC* by The Metropolitan Museum of Art (Little, Brown, 2002)

*Vincent's Colors* by Vincent van Gogh (Chronicle Books, 2005)

# IV
# Music

# Introduction

A wealth of musical experiences can be shared with your child—singing songs, listening to all kinds of music, dancing around at home, attending local musical performances. By doing these, as well as reading this section together, you will help fine-tune your child's understanding and enjoyment of the music that weaves through our world in so many ways.

Best, and probably easiest, is to *sing with your child*. We suggest some favorite songs in this section (see pages 315–25). Try to shake off any adult lack of self-confidence about your voice. Remember that in your own home, you're the star! It's fine to play recordings for your child (we suggest some at the end of this chapter), but the more you sing together, the more music becomes an integral part of your child's education.

In the previous book in this series, *What Your Kindergartner Needs to Know*, we introduced music activities and the basic elements of music, such as rhythm, pitch, and tempo. We encourage you to continue these activities with your first grader.

In this book, we introduce many kinds of music, including jazz, classical music, and opera, as well as different kinds of dance. We suggest ways to become familiar with great composers. We introduce some basic terms and concepts, such as melody, harmony, and rhythm, and the notion that music can be written down and read. Later books in this series will introduce musical notation in greater detail.

Some families will choose to provide lessons that will lift children to a level of musical competence beyond what we describe in the following pages. Different children will develop musical appreciation and skills at different rates and to different degrees. It's important for everyone to enjoy music, and we hope this section of the book will increase enjoyment through experience and understanding.

## Melody, Harmony, and Rhythm

What's your favorite song? Let's sing it together.

Now, let's hum it.

When you hum, you don't sing any words. You just sing the music. You can call that music the "melody," or the tune, of the song.

Have you ever heard a choir sing? Different people's voices sound different, and when they sing together, even though they are singing different notes, the music they make sounds good.

In music, some sounds go together well. But some don't. It's kind of like clothing: Some clothes go together and some don't. If you put on a red-striped shirt with purple-and-green-checked pants, your clothes don't match. But if you put on that shirt with red pants, they go well together.

Music can be like that too. When the sounds match, or go well together, we say they make harmony. Instruments can make harmony, voices can make harmony, and voices singing together with instruments can make harmony too.

**Do It Yourself**

Play Name That Tune together. Think of a song your child enjoys. Hum just a few notes of it to begin with. Can she "name that tune"? If not, hum those notes and add a few more. Keep doing that until she can guess the song and you can sing it together. Now switch places and have her hum a tune for you to name.

Do you ever hear music that makes you want to clap your hands or stamp your feet? Or maybe you like to dance to your favorite music. When you clap or move along with the music, you are hearing its "rhythm."

Let's think about some musical rhythms that you might know. What's the rhythm of a marching band? *Boom-baboom-baboom! Boom-baboom-baboom!* The big drum plays the beat and the band members step in time.

What's the rhythm of a lullaby? Would it be like a marching band? Not at all! *Loo-lee, loo-la. Loo-lee, loo-la.* It will be slow and smooth and calm, just like you are when you rock a baby to sleep in a cradle.

### All Together

Explore the natural beat of a song you like singing together. First, invite your child to clap along as you sing. Let him try it naturally. Then do it together, but this time really emphasize the words that get the strong beat. Now just clap and say (not sing) the words of the song together, still putting the same stress on the words as you do when you sing. You can point out that what you are doing is paying attention to rhythm.

## Meet a Great Composer

Lots of people like to sing. Some people like to make up new songs and music. When they do, they write it down to share with others.

A person who writes music is a "composer." There is a lot of wonderful music that was written by composers long before you, your parents, or even your grandparents were born. But because that music is so wonderful, people still play it on instruments or sing it, and others still enjoy listening to it.

One of the greatest composers of all—someone whose music many, many people have enjoyed for hundreds of years—is Wolfgang Amadeus Mozart [VULF-gahng Ah-mah-DAY-us MOTE-sart]. That's a long name, so we can just call him Mozart. Mozart lived long ago in a country in Europe called Austria. He did not live a long life—he died when he was only thirty-five years old—but he wrote more than six hundred pieces of music. Some had words for people to sing, and some was instrumental music composed for people to play together.

Mozart started writing music when he was just a little boy. He was an amazing child, a real genius. In fact, his entire family was very musical. His father, Leopold Mozart, played the violin in the orchestra at the court of the prince-archbishop, who was the ruler of all of Salzburg, the city where they lived. His mother had a beautiful voice and loved to sing. His older sister, whom he called Nannerl [NAHN-uhl], was learning to play the clavier [CLAV-eer], which was an instrument in those days like a small piano. Here is a story about Mozart when he was a little boy.

> **Do It Yourself**
>
> The most important way to help your child get to know Mozart is by listening to his music! There are many good recordings. A good work to start with is called *A Little Night Music*. A convenient collection of favorite works is a compact disc called *Mozart: Greatest Hits* (Sony Classical MLK 64053).

# Mozart the Wonder Boy

Nannerl was having a music lesson. Her father, Leopold, was teaching her how to play the clavier. Little Wolfgang Mozart was watching and listening to every note she played. When her lesson was over he asked, "Please may I have a lesson, Papa?"

"You are too little, Wolfie!" said Father Mozart.

Wolfgang waited until his father and sister had finished her lesson. Then he tiptoed up to the clavier and pressed the keys. He could just barely reach them. But playing music made him smile. It sounded beautiful.

His father heard the sounds and came and watched quietly from the doorway. It was amazing! Wolfgang was playing the music that Nannerl had just been practicing, and he was playing every note cor-

rectly. He had listened, and he remembered, and he could play the piece by heart. Leopold Mozart decided to give his little boy music lessons right away.

Soon Wolfgang was playing the violin as well as the clavier. He learned to read music and then learned to play pieces by memory very quickly. He enjoyed composing his own music, too. First he would play

it, and then he would write it down. His mother and father were surprised and delighted. No one could believe that a little boy of five years old could write such beautiful music.

Leopold Mozart decided to take Nannerl and Wolfgang to the big city of Vienna, where they could perform for many more people. He wanted to introduce his children to princes and kings. In those days, the only way a musician could make a living was to find a patron, a rich and powerful person who would pay him to perform and compose. Leopold Mozart dreamed that he could find patrons for Nannerl and Wolfgang in Vienna.

It was a long trip. They traveled in a coach pulled by horses. When they arrived in Vienna, Father Mozart made an appointment for the talented little Mozart children to appear at court and play music for the family of the emperor, the most important man in all of Austria. They dressed in their best clothes and rode in the royal coach on the way to the concert.

The emperor, the empress, and the royal children were waiting to hear the Mozart children. First Nannerl and Wolfgang played a duet. Then Nannerl played a piece by herself. When Wolfgang stood up to perform on his own, the emperor spoke to him directly.

"What are you going to play, little one?" he asked, smiling.

"I shall play my 'Allegro in B-flat major,'" Wolfgang replied, giving the name of one of the pieces he had composed.

"Very good," said the emperor, "but let's see how well you know your keyboard." He held up a large white cloth. Everyone in the room gulped. The emperor draped the cloth over the clavier's keyboard, so Wolfgang could not see the instrument he was playing.

But Wolfgang just sighed. It made no difference to him. He could play the clavier without looking. He placed his hands on the keyboard, underneath the cloth, and even looked the emperor in the eye—and played his Allegro perfectly.

"Well done!" cried the emperor and empress, applauding. They were so impressed, they rewarded Leopold Mozart with money and asked him to give music lessons to their children. They invited Nannerl and Wolfgang to come back and perform often for them.

After that, Leopold Mozart took Nannerl and Wolfgang to many different countries. One trip lasted three years and five months! Wherever they went, they gave concerts. Everyone admired them and gave them presents. They called Wolfgang "Mozart the Wonder Boy"!

## Mozart, a Famous Composer

**Do It Yourself**

Listening is a skill best practiced for the fun of it. Your child will likely enjoy *Classical Kids* (BMG Music; produced by Susan Hammond), an award-winning series of recordings available on CD or as MP3 files, with stories about composers, their works, and musical performances. The series includes *Mozart's Magic Fantasy, Beethoven Lives Upstairs,* and *Mr. Bach Comes to Call.* Each title mixes fact and fiction and weaves familiar musical selections into the telling of a lively and engaging story.

Wolfgang Mozart grew up to become one of the greatest composers of all time. He wrote music for the clavier (we now play those pieces on the piano). He wrote music for people to sing. And he wrote music for the orchestra, in which many people play different instruments but they make the same music. Even today, people all over the world love to perform and to listen to his wonderful music.

Mozart is one of many famous composers whose music is still played and enjoyed today. Sometimes we call music written long ago but still enjoyed today classical music. Mozart is a classical music composer.

## Reading and Writing Music

If you have a tune that you made up in your head, and you want to share it with others, what do you do? You could just sing it for others, but you might want to write it down. To write music down, you need to use special marks that tell other people about the melody and harmony and rhythm.

Here is the music for a song you know. We can point to the music as we sing it.

Twin-kle,  twin-kle,  lit-tle  star,  How I  won-der  what you  are!

Reading music is like reading words—it takes time and practice!

Words are made of letters, like A, B, and C. When you write music, you use special marks that stand for the sounds of the music. Here are three of those special marks.

whole note    half note    quarter note

These are called musical notes, and this kind of writing is called musical notation. Each kind of note has a name.

The first note is a "whole note." It looks something like a big O. The second note is a "half note." It's like a whole note with a tail sticking up. As its name suggests, a half note lasts half as long as a whole note. The third note is a "quarter note." It looks like a half note except that the O is colored in. A quarter note lasts half as long as a half note.

Composers around the world use this same notation to write their music down, so anyone who reads music can play it. Two people might live far away from each other and speak different languages, but they can play music together if they can both read music.

## Instruments and Their Families

Mozart first learned to play music on instruments called the clavier and the violin. They are both members of the string **family** of instruments.

Let's talk about four different families of instruments: the "percussion" family, the "string" family, the "woodwind" family, and the "brass" family. You can get to know each instrument in two important ways: by its shape and by the kind of sound it makes.

> **New Word**
>
> As you begin to talk about musical instrument families, pause to discuss what a **family** is. Who is in your family? Does everyone in your family look the same? But do people in your family look a little bit alike? Just like people who are in the same family, instruments in a family often look alike, but they are not exactly the same.

drum

bell

triangle

### The Percussion Family

Here are some of the members of the percussion family. These instruments are all fun to play. You shake them or you hit them with your hand, a stick, or a mallet. Do you recognize any of these instruments? Do you see a drum? A bell? A triangle? Some people call these "rhythm" instruments, because a lot of times that is what they do best: They beat the rhythm of the music.

One percussion instrument is named for its shape: It's called a triangle. When you hit it, it makes a *ding-a-ling-a-ling* sound. Another member of the percussion family looks like a pair of lids that go on top of two big pots. These are cymbals, and when you hit them together, they can make a loud *crash!*

cymbals

banjo

violin

## The String Family

Have you ever seen a musical instrument that has strings? How about a guitar? A banjo? A violin? These instruments don't look the same, but they all have strings. You can play some stringed instruments with a bow, like the one next to the violin, or with your hand, by strumming or plucking the strings with your finger, like the boy playing the guitar.

guitar

harp

cello

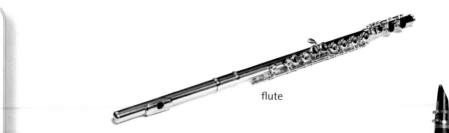

flute

**Do It Yourself**

While your child is learning about musical instruments, have some fun making your own. These two books show you how:

*Let's Make Music!* by Jessica Baron Turner (Hal Leonard, 1995)

*Making Music* by Ann Sayre Wiseman and John Langstaff (Storey Publishing, 2003)

Noise made on pots and pans can be music too, especially when you start talking about rhythm and accents with your child.

## The Woodwind Family

I'll bet if you think about the name of this family—"woodwinds"—you can guess how you would play one of them. You play these instruments by blowing air into them. It's kind of like hearing the wind whistling.

These instruments all used to be made out of wood, which is why they are called woodwinds, but some are made from other materials today.

Here are four different members of the woodwind family: a bassoon, a clarinet, a flute, and an oboe. Each one makes its own special kind of sound.

clarinet

bassoon

oboe

Here is a boy playing a recorder. Have you ever played a recorder before?

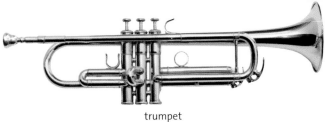
trumpet

French horn

## The Brass Family

If you've ever seen a band marching in a parade, you've heard members of the "brass" family: the French horn, the trumpet, the trombone, and the big, loud tuba.

Brass is a hard, shiny metal, and most instruments in the brass family are horns made of brass. Just as with the woodwinds, you play brass instruments by blowing air into them. Because they are shaped differently and because you blow into them differently, though, a brass instrument does not sound the same as a woodwind.

trombone

tuba

# The Orchestra

All the instrument families—percussion, string, woodwind, and brass—play music together in an "orchestra." It takes many musicians playing many instruments to make up an orchestra. They all play together, led by someone called a *conductor*. The conductor is a man or woman who stands in front of the orchestra and helps the musicians play well together. Some conductors just move their hands and arms, but others almost dance to the music. The conductor and all the musicians practice over and over many times, to be sure they get really good at playing a piece of music together before they perform for an audience.

When an orchestra plays music, it makes one big sound. But if you listen closely, you can sometimes hear one instrument or another. It is fun to learn to recognize the sounds of the different instruments as they play their parts in an orchestra.

**PARENTS:** Here are some other ways to get to know the instruments in an orchestra.

Listen to *Peter and the Wolf.*

The Russian composer Sergei Prokofiev [SAIR-gay pruh-KOF-yef] wrote this piece of music. Many fine recordings are available to buy or listen to online. It's a story of a boy and several different animals. Each character has its own song, played by a different instrument. Often, when it is performed, a narrator tells the story in words to go along with the music.

Read *Meet the Orchestra.*

This delightful picture book by Ann Hayes (Sandpiper, 1995; also available on Kindle) introduces many different instruments as an orchestra of animals prepares for a concert.

Listen to a concert in person, on television, or online.

If you can find an opportunity to go to a band or orchestra concert in person, do so. Next best, watch a performance on TV or online. You can point out how the seating of musicians is organized by instrumental family.

## Music Can Tell a Story

When we talk about a story, we usually think it will be told in words. But music can tell a story too, sometimes with words and sometimes without.

The verses of a song often tell a story. For instance, "Oh! Susanna" is a song that tells a story. Let's sing it and listen for the story it tells:

> I come from Alabama with a banjo on my knee;
> I'm goin' to Lou'siana, my true love for to see.
> It rained all night the day I left, the weather it was dry;
> The sun so hot I froze to death, Susanna, don't you cry.
>
> Oh! Susanna, don't you cry for me;
> I come from Alabama with my banjo on my knee.
>
> I had a dream the other night, when everything was still;
> I thought I saw Susanna dear, a-coming down the hill.
> The buckwheat cake was in her mouth, the tear was in her eye;
> Said I, I'm coming from the south, Susanna, don't you cry.
>
> Oh! Susanna, don't you cry for me;
> I come from Alabama with my banjo on my knee.

**Make a Connection**

See an image of a banjo on page 301. You can go online to find and listen to banjo and guitar music so your child can hear and recognize the different sounds.

## Dramas with Music: Opera

What would it be like if you woke up one day and everybody was singing instead of talking? Just imagine . . .

You're lying in bed, and you hear your mother singing (to the tune of "On Top of Old Smokey"):

> It's time to get up now,
> Get ready for school.
> Put on your red sweater
> 'Cause outside it's cool.

You go to school and, when you get there, your teacher sings to the class (to the tune of "Yankee Doodle"):

> All right, children, settle down,
> It's time to practice writing.
> Please make sure your pencil's sharp.
> Let's write something exciting!

Even you sing instead of talk! When you get home from school and your mother asks you how you are, you sing (to the tune of "Twinkle, Twinkle, Little Star"):

> I worked hard at school all day,
> Now I'm ready for some play.

That might be strange, if everyone was singing instead of talking, but it might be fun too, don't you think? It would be like living in an "opera."

An opera is a play with actors in costume

**Talk and Think**

Read "Hansel and Gretel" together in this book just before listening to or viewing one of several recorded versions of Engelbert Humperdinck's opera *Hansel and Gretel*. Experience the opera together, feeling free to stop the music to talk about how the sounds tell the story. Encourage your child to use adjectives—cheerful, sleepy, scary, happy—to describe different parts of the opera.

onstage, but instead of talking, all the actors sing. An orchestra plays music at the opera, and all the people in the opera sing, sometimes by themselves and sometimes together, in duets or even big choruses. Sometimes operas are written in other languages, but people still enjoy them because the music is beautiful even if they can't understand the words.

Operas are pieces of music that always tell stories. Some operas are funny; some operas are sad. Some operas tell stories you probably know. For example, two very famous operas are called *Cinderella* and *Hansel and Gretel*. Do you know those stories already?

## Musical Stories Without Words

Sometimes music can tell a story without using words. Close your eyes while you listen to music, and the sounds might help you see pictures in your mind. Listening to some music, you might imagine a bumble-bee buzzing around the flowers, or two people arguing with each other, or thunder and lightning during a big storm, or a baby falling asleep, or graceful swans swimming in a pond. One way to listen to music is to close your eyes and just imagine what the sounds remind you of.

Sometimes a composer will think about a favorite story and write music that still tells the story but without words. One example is a famous piece of music to be played by an orchestra, written by a French composer named Paul Dukas [doo-KAH], and is called *The Sorcerer's Apprentice*. Here is the story told by that piece of music.

## The Sorcerer's Apprentice

Once there was a young man who worked for an old, powerful wizard. He did many chores for the wizard and he watched and listened carefully, hoping one day to be able to do magic himself.

One morning the **sorcerer** left the **apprentice** all alone. There was a lot of work to do, carrying buckets of water from the river to their castle. The apprentice quickly grew tired of doing all the hard work and came up

**New Word**

When you introduce *The Sorcerer's Apprentice*, you may need to talk about two new words. A sorcerer is like a wizard or a magician. And an apprentice is a young worker who is helping and learning.

with a good idea! Maybe he could use magic to get his chores done. Then he could just relax.

So the apprentice tiptoed over and picked up the master sorcerer's powerful magic wand (even though he knew he was not supposed to do so). He spun around, waved the wand in the air, and pointed the wand toward an old broom resting against the wall in the corner.

The apprentice said some of the magic words he had heard the sorcerer say, and then to his amazement he watched as the broom came alive. Then it grew arms! It picked up a bucket, shuffled off, and returned with the bucket full of water. It dumped the water into a tub and turned around, ready to get more. The apprentice was delighted! His magic worked, and the broom was doing his work for him!

At first the apprentice was pleased, but then something went wrong. The broom wouldn't stop! It kept bringing more water, pouring bucket after bucket into the tub even after the tub was overflowing and water was spilling out all over the floor. The apprentice waved the wand and said all the magic words he could think of, but he could not get the broom to stop.

So what next? The apprentice grabbed an ax and—*whack!*—chopped the broom into splinters. He thought he had found the solution, but in fact he had made matters worse.

Now each piece was standing up, growing arms, and shuffling off to fetch more water. More and more—soon there was water everywhere! It was swirling around; the apprentice was swimming in it! What would happen?

The music composed by Dukas tells this story. It starts with quiet, mysterious-sounding music to introduce you to the sorcerer and his magic. When the apprentice casts his spell on the broom, the music turns into a kind of march that helps you imagine how a broom might walk! Then you hear the frightened apprentice whacking away with his ax. But the march goes faster

**Do It Yourself**

There is almost no way to share this portion of the book with your child without listening together to *The Sorcerer's Apprentice*. Many recordings are available in CD and digital recording formats. It's best to read the story here (maybe without the ending the first time around), listen to the music, and then talk through the story again. Once you have explored the music with your child, treat yourselves to the classic Disney animation, starring Mickey Mouse as the apprentice, from the 1941 film *Fantasia*.

and faster, louder and louder, as more brooms carry water, causing a swirling flood.

And then, all of a sudden, the music becomes slow, strong, powerful, and mysterious. The sorcerer has arrived home. When he sees the mess his apprentice has made, he uses his magic to put his house back in order. The apprentice has learned a lesson. One broom rests again in the corner, where it belongs.

## Move to the Music

A lot of music makes you want to move! Tap your feet, clap your hands, jump up and down, dance to the beat! People around the world love to dance. Sometimes they all follow the same steps, and sometimes they just move in whatever way they feel like moving. What about you? What kind of dancing do you like to do? Do you like to jump and move around, however the music makes you feel? Or do you like to follow special kinds of dance steps, like tap dancing or square dancing or ballet?

Tap dancers wear special shoes with flat pieces of metal, called taps, attached to the toes. They move quickly and swing their feet so that their shoes make *tap-tap-tapping* noises as they dance.

Square dancers take partners and begin by standing in a square. As the music starts, they listen to a person named a caller, who knows the steps and calls out what steps to do next. As the fiddler plays, the caller might say, "Swing your partner, 'round you go. Turn to your right and do-si-do."

Ballet is a dance to music that tells a story. Often the music is played by an orchestra, but no one sings or talks—the people on-stage tell the story by danc-ing. Some ballets tell stories you may

know. *The Sleeping Beauty* is a famous ballet, for example, based on the fairy tale.

Ballet dancers have to practice for years. They work hard, learn special steps, and exercise so they develop strong legs, arms, and bodies. Some ballet dancers wear special shoes called toe shoes so they can balance and dance on the tips of their toes. Sometimes they leap high into the air. Sometimes they spin around and around.

**Do It Yourself**

There are many good recordings of *The Nutcracker Suite*, but introducing it as a ballet performance with orchestral music is best of all. Wonderful recorded performances of *The Nutcracker* are available, including American Ballet Theatre's production with Mikhail Baryshnikov (Jodav Productions, 1977). Lovely books tell the story as well, such as *The Nutcracker Ballet* by Vladimir Vagin (Scholastic, 2002); *Nutcracker* illustrated by Maurice Sendak (Crown, 2012); and *The Nutcracker* illustrated by Susan Jeffers (HarperCollins, 2007).

## A Ballet About a Nutcracker

Around Christmastime, children around the world often enjoy a famous ballet called *The Nutcracker*. The music was written by the Russian composer Pyotr Ilyich Tchaikovsky [PEE-ter Ill-YICH chy-KAHV-skee], and it tells a story about a little girl who receives a Christmas gift of a toy nutcracker that comes to life. The nutcracker fights a battle against an army of mice and then he and the little girl travel to a magical land, where there are dancing flowers and a sugarplum fairy.

You can get to know this ballet by listening to the music, watching a recording of the ballet, or even, if you are lucky, attending a performance. Many pieces of music in *The Nutcracker*, especially in the second act, introduce different sets of characters—like Hot Chocolate, Candy Canes, Flowers, and a Sugar Plum Fairy. How would you dance, and what costumes would you create, for each of these episodes in the ballet?

## Jazz: America's Musical Gift to the World

People around the world enjoy making music. In fact, many different countries have songs and music they proudly call their own. The United States has special kinds of music that people first played right here, including the music called jazz. Jazz was invented by African Americans about one hundred years ago, and today it is played and enjoyed by people everywhere. Many say that jazz is America's most important gift to the world of music.

There's one big difference between jazz and most other music. If you sing a song you know—let's say "Row, Row, Row Your Boat"—you sing the same tune every time, and so does everyone else.

What if you decided you wanted to start with this song but make it different? Your words might come out something like this—and your rhythm and tune will change to match:

> Row, row, row-ba-doh-ba-doh,
> Row my little piddle-paddle boat.
> Row so merrily, be-bop-a-bearily,
> Down the ice-cream peanut-butter dreamy stream!

You could call that a jazz version of "Row, Row, Row Your Boat."

When people play jazz, they change the music every time. Jazz musicians like to experiment, to make up new sounds and rhythms as they go along and see how they sound. We can say that they **improvise,** which means that they make up the music as they play it and as they hear one another's instruments. And sometimes they make up silly words as well, like *"Row, row, row-ba-doh-ba-doh"* and *"be-bop-a-bearily."*

### Satchmo, a Great Jazz Musician

One of the first great jazz musicians was a man named Louis Armstrong. Some people called him by a nickname, "Satchmo," and others called him "Pops."

> **New Word**
>
> "Improvise" means to make up as you go along. Help your child understand the word "improvise" by improvising together, starting with a song she knows well and changing the melody, words, or rhythm.

This is a statue of Louis Armstrong.

**Talk and Think**

Here is a book based on a Louis Armstrong favorite: *What a Wonderful World*, written by Bob Thiele and George David Weiss, and illustrated by Ashley Bryan (Sundance, 1995). This delightful picture book turns a vintage Louis Armstrong ballad into a colorful puppet show. Reading this and listening to Armstrong's original version gives you many opportunities to talk about his music and improvisation.

When Louis was a boy, he lived in New Orleans, a city in Louisiana famous for its jazz music. He sang well, and he learned to play the cornet, a brass instrument like the trumpet. He became so good at playing jazz, even when he was young, that the other musicians in his band would stop playing and let him play a solo—all alone—so that his music came through loud and clear.

Louis Armstrong played and sang with many different jazz musicians and bands during his life. He became very famous and was loved by people all over the world. You can always recognize his warm and gravelly voice. He was one of those people who did things so well, everyone got to know him.

# A Few Favorite Songs

**PARENTS:** Here are some familiar songs that children like to sing. We encourage you to sing these and many other songs together. Children also enjoy listening to and singing along with recordings, such as the ones suggested on page 326.

## America the Beautiful

O beautiful for spacious skies,
For amber waves of grain,
For purple mountain majesties
Above the fruited plain!
America! America!
God shed his grace on thee
And crown thy good with brotherhood
From sea to shining sea!

## La Cucaracha (The Cockroach)

La cucaracha, la cucaracha,
Running up and down the house,
La cucaracha, la cucaracha,
Quiet as a little mouse.

He gets in trouble, a lot of trouble,
Snooping here and everywhere,
La cucaracha, la cucaracha,
Always keeps the cupboard bare.

## Blow the Man Down

Come all ye young fellows that follow the sea,
To me way, hey, blow the man down!
Now, pray, pay attention and listen to me,
Give me some time to blow the man down!

As I was a-walking down Paradise Street,
To me way, hey, blow the man down!
A pretty young damsel I chanced for to meet,
Give me some time to blow the man down!

She hailed me with her flipper, I took her in tow,
To me way, hey, blow the man down!
Yard-arm to yard-arm away we did go,
Give me some time to blow the man down!

## Billy Boy

Oh, where have you been,
Billy Boy, Billy Boy,
Oh, where have you been
Charming Billy?

I have been to seek a wife,
She's the joy of my life,
She's a young thing and cannot leave her mother.

Did she ask you to come in,
Billy Boy, Billy Boy,
Did she ask you to come in,
charming Billy?

Yes, she asked me to come in,
There's a dimple in her chin,
She's a young thing and cannot leave her mother.

Can she make a cherry pie,
Billy Boy, Billy Boy?
Can she make a cherry pie,
charming Billy?

She can make a cherry pie
Quick as a cat can wink her eye,
She's a young thing and cannot leave her mother.

## Down by the Riverside

Gonna lay down my sword and shield,
Down by the riverside,
Down by the riverside,
Down by the riverside,
Gonna lay down my sword and shield,
Down by the riverside,
Ain't gonna study war no more.
Ain't gonna study war no more, ain't gonna study war no more,
Ain't gonna study war no more.

Ain't gonna study war no more, ain't gonna study war no more,
Ain't gonna study war no more.


Gonna lay down my burden,
Down by the riverside,
Down by the riverside,
Down by the riverside,
Gonna lay down my burden,
Down by the riverside,
Ain't gonna study war no more.
Ain't gonna study war no more, ain't gonna study war no more,
Ain't gonna study war no more.

Ain't gonna study war no more, ain't gonna study war no more,
Ain't gonna study war no more.

## For He's a Jolly Good Fellow

For he's a jolly good fellow,
For he's a jolly good fellow,
For he's a jolly good fellow,
Which nobody can deny.
Which nobody can deny.
Which nobody can deny.
For he's a jolly good fellow,
For he's a jolly good fellow,
For he's a jolly good fellow,
Which nobody can deny.

## Down in the Valley

Down in the valley, the valley so low,
Hang your head over, hear the wind blow.
Hear the wind blow, dear, hear the wind
　　blow,
Hang your head over, hear the wind blow.

Roses love sunshine, violets love dew,
Angels in heaven know I love you.
Know I love you, dear, know I love you.
Angels in heaven know I love you.

Writing this letter, containing three lines,
Answer my question, "Will you be mine?
Will you be mine, dear, will you be mine?"
Answer my question, "Will you be mine?"

## Dry Bones

Ezekiel cried, "Them dry bones!"
Ezekiel cried, "Them dry bones!"
Ezekiel cried, "Them dry bones!"
Now hear the word of the Lord.

The foot bone connected to the leg bone,
The leg bone connected to the knee bone,
The knee bone connected to the thigh bone,
The thigh bone connected to the hip bone,
The hip bone connected to the back bone,
The back bone connected to the neck bone,
The neck bone connected to the jaw bone,
The jaw bone connected to the head bone,
Now hear the word of the Lord.

Them bones, them bones gonna walk around,
Them bones, them bones gonna walk around,
Them bones, them bones gonna walk around,
Now hear the word of the Lord.

Them bones, them bones, them dry bones,
Them bones, them bones, them dry bones,
Them bones, them bones, them dry bones,
Now hear the word of the Lord.

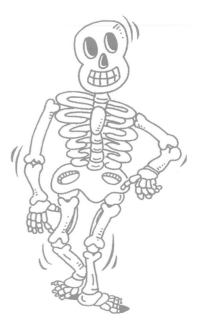

**Make a Connection**

Learn more about the skeleton in the "Science" chapter, on page 403.

## Frère Jacques/Brother John

[French]
Frère Jacques, Frère Jacques,
Dormez-vous, dormez-vous?
Sonnez les matines, sonnez les matines,
Din, dan, don. Din, dan, don.

[English]
Are you sleeping, are you sleeping
Brother John, Brother John?
Morning bells are ringing, morning bells are ringing,
Ding, dang, dong. Ding, dang, dong.

## Michael, Row the Boat Ashore

Michael, row the boat ashore, Hallelujah,
Michael, row the boat ashore, Hallelujah.

Sister, help to trim the sail, Hallelujah,
Sister, help to trim the sail, Hallelujah.

Jordan's River is chilly and cold, Hallelujah,
Chills the body but not the soul, Hallelujah.

The river is deep and the river is wide, Hallelujah,
Milk and honey on the other side, Hallelujah.

Michael, row the boat ashore, Hallelujah,
Michael, row the boat ashore, Hallelujah.

## On Top of Old Smokey

On top of Old Smokey,
All covered with snow,
I lost my true lover
For courting too slow.

Well, courting's a pleasure
And parting is grief,
But a false-hearted lover
Is worse than a thief.

On top of Old Smokey,
All covered with snow,
I lost my true lover
For courting too slow.

## She'll Be Comin' 'Round the Mountain

She'll be comin' 'round the mountain when she comes,
She'll be comin' 'round the mountain when she comes,
She'll be comin' 'round the mountain,
She'll be comin' 'round the mountain,
She'll be comin' 'round the mountain when she comes.

She'll be drivin' six white horses when she comes, [*etc.*]

Oh, we'll all go out to meet her when she comes, [*etc.*]

She'll be wearing pink pajamas when she comes, [*etc.*]

She'll be comin' 'round the mountain when she comes,
[*etc.*]

## Skip to My Lou

**chorus:**
Skip, skip, skip to my Lou,
Skip, skip, skip to my Lou,
Skip, skip, skip to my Lou,
Skip to my Lou, my darling!

Lost my partner, what'll I do?
Lost my partner, what'll I do?
Lost my partner, what'll I do?
Skip to my Lou, my darling!

[repeat chorus]

I'll find another one, prettier, too,
I'll find another one, prettier, too,
I'll find another one, prettier, too,
Skip to my Lou, my darling!

[repeat chorus]

Flies in the sugar bowl, shoo, fly, shoo,
Flies in the sugar bowl, shoo, fly, shoo,
Flies in the sugar bowl, shoo, fly, shoo,
Skip to my Lou, my darling!

Skip, skip, skip to my Lou,
Skip, skip, skip to my Lou,
Skip, skip, skip to my Lou,
Skip to my Lou, my darling!

## There's a Hole in the Bucket

There's a hole in the bucket, dear Liza, dear Liza.
There's a hole in the bucket, dear Liza, a hole.
Well, mend it, dear Henry, dear Henry, dear Henry.
Well, mend it, dear Henry, dear Henry, mend it.

With what shall I mend it, dear Liza, dear Liza?
With what shall I mend it, dear Liza, with what?
With a straw, dear Henry, dear Henry, dear Henry.
With a straw, dear Henry, dear Henry, with a
   straw.

But the straw is too long, dear Liza, dear Liza.
The straw is too long, dear Liza, too long.
Then cut it, dear Henry, dear Henry, dear Henry.
Then cut it, dear Henry, dear Henry, cut it.

With what shall I cut it, dear Liza, dear Liza?
With what shall I cut it, dear Liza, with what?
With an ax, dear Henry, dear Henry, dear Henry.
With an ax, dear Henry, dear Henry, with an ax.

But the ax is too dull, dear Liza, dear Liza.
The ax is too dull, dear Liza, too dull.
Then sharpen it, dear Henry, dear Henry, dear Henry.
Then sharpen it, dear Henry, dear Henry, sharpen it.

With what shall I sharpen it, dear Liza, dear Liza?
With what shall I sharpen it, dear Liza, with what?
With a stone, dear Henry, dear Henry, dear Henry.
With a stone, dear Henry, dear Henry, with a stone.

But the stone is too dry, dear Liza, dear Liza.

The stone is too dry, dear Liza, too dry.

Then wet it, dear Henry, dear Henry, dear Henry.

Then wet it, dear Henry, dear Henry, wet it.

With what shall I wet it, dear Liza, dear Liza?

With what shall I wet it, dear Liza, with what?

With water, dear Henry, dear Henry, dear Henry.

With water, dear Henry, dear Henry, with water.

In what shall I carry it, dear Liza, dear Liza?

In what shall I carry it, dear Liza, in what?

In a bucket, dear Henry, dear Henry, dear Henry.

In a bucket, dear Henry, dear Henry, in a bucket.

But there's a hole in the bucket, dear Liza, dear Liza.

There's a hole in the bucket, dear Liza, a hole.

Well, mend it, dear Henry, dear Henry, dear Henry.

Well, mend it, dear Henry, dear Henry, mend it!

## Take Me Out to the Ball Game

Take me out to the ball game,

Take me out with the crowd.

Buy me some peanuts and Cracker Jack,

I don't care if I never get back.

Let me root, root, root for the home team,

If they don't win it's a shame.

For it's one, two, three strikes, "You're out!"

At the old ball game.

## Suggested Resources

*RECORDINGS OF FAVORITE SONGS FOR CHILDREN*

Most of these are available either as compact discs or as MP3 files for download.

*Children's Favorites*, Vols. 1–4 (Walt Disney Records)

*Children's Songs: A Collection of Childhood Favorites* by Susie Tallman (Rock Me Baby Records)

*De Colores and Other Latin American Folk Songs* (Arcoiris Records)

*Family Folk Festival: A Multi-Cultural Sing Along* by various artists (Music for Little People)

*Kids' Pow-Wow Songs* by Black Lodge Singers (Canyon Records)

*Shake It to the One That You Love the Best: Play Songs and Lullabies from Black Musical Traditions* (Warren-Mattox Productions)

*Wee Sing: Sing Alongs* (Early Bird Recordings)


*MUSIC THAT TELLS STORIES*

Here are a few great picture books based on songs that tell stories.

*Abiyoyo* by Pete Seeger, illustrated by Michael Hays (Simon & Schuster, 2001). A lovely tale, available in a book-and-CD set for simultaneous listening and reading.

*The Fox Went Out on a Chilly Night: An Old Song* illustrated by Peter Spier (Dragonfly Books, 1994). A charming retelling of the folk song.

*This Land Is Your Land* by Woody Guthrie, illustrated by Kathy Jakobsen (Little, Brown, 2008). Illustrating the Woody Guthrie classic about the American landscape.


*BOOKS ABOUT MUSIC AND INSTRUMENTS*

*Ah, Music!* by Aliki (HarperCollins, 2005)

*Buzz and Ollie's High, Low Adventure; Buzz and Ollie's Loud, Soft Adventure;* and *Buzz and Ollie's Steady Beat Adventure* all by Donna Sloan Thorne and Marilyn Sloan Felts (Sloan Publishing, 2002)

*Max Found Two Sticks* by Brian Pinkney (Aladdin, 1997)

*My Family Plays Music* by Judy Cox (Holiday House, 2003)

*The Story of the Orchestra* by Robert Levine (Black Dog & Leventhal, 2000)

*Zin! Zin! Zin! A Violin* by Lloyd Moss (Aladdin, 2000)

### BOOKS ABOUT MOZART

*The Magic Flute: An Opera by Mozart* adapted by Kyra Teis (Star Bright Books, 2008)

*Moonlight on the Magic Flute* (Magic Tree House #41) by Mary Pope Osborne (Random House for Young Readers, 2010)

*Play, Mozart, Play!* by Peter Sis (Greenwillow, 2006)

*Wolfgang Amadeus Mozart: Getting to Know the World's Greatest Composers* by Mike Venezia (Children's Press, 1995)

### BOOKS ABOUT JAZZ

*Charlie Parker Played Be Bop* written and illustrated by Chris Raschka (Scholastic, 1997)

*Jazz Baby* by Lisa Wheeler (Houghton Mifflin Harcourt Books, 2007)

*The Jazz Fly* by Matthew Gollub (Tortuga Press, 2000)

*This Jazz Man* by Karen Ehrhardt (Houghton Mifflin Harcourt Books, 2006)

*When Louis Armstrong Taught Me Scat* by Muriel Harris Weinstein (Chronicle, 2008)

# V
# Mathematics

# Introduction

In this section we sometimes address your child and sometimes address you as parents, particularly in the directions for activities you can do with your children.

We encourage you to give the topics and activities in this section some special emphasis. In international evaluations of math performance by students in various countries, students in the United States have consistently performed near the bottom. One reason is that students in other countries begin to build a secure foundation in mathematics in the earliest years of their schooling; another is that they receive more consistent practice and more challenging work than do students in the United States.

In school, any successful program for teaching math to young children follows these three cardinal rules: (1) practice, (2) practice, and (3) practice. Not mindless repetition, of course, but thoughtful and varied practice, in which children are given opportunities to approach problems from a variety of angles and in which, as they proceed to learn new facts and operations, they consistently review and reinforce their earlier learning.

In school, first graders should practice math daily in order to ensure that they can effortlessly and automatically perform the basic operations upon which all problem solving and other sophisticated math applications depend. Some well-meaning people fear that practice in mathematics—for example, memorizing the addition and subtraction facts up to 12, or doing timed worksheets with twenty-five problems—leads to joyless, soul-killing drudgery. Nothing could be further from the truth. The destroyer of joy in learning mathematics is not practice but anxiety—the anxiety that comes from feeling that one is mathematically stupid or lacks any "special talent" for math.

We adults must be careful not to convey to our children any feelings that we "don't like math" or are "not good at math" or any other symptoms of what has been called "math anxiety." By engaging our children in the kinds of activities suggested in this section, we can let them know that math is important and interesting to us. Keep in mind, however, that the activities suggested here are supplemental ways for parents to reinforce their children's learning at home. They are not sufficient for teaching math in school, where children need more regular and structured opportunities for practice and review.

# Patterns and Classifications

**PARENTS:** Learning to see likeness, differences, and patterns is an essential part of mathematical and scientific thinking. A first grader should be able to sort objects according to some specific attributes, such as color, shape, and function; to define a set of items by what the items have in common; to tell which item does not belong to a set; and to recognize patterns and predict how a pattern will continue. To review these skills, see *What Your Kindergartner Needs to Know.* Your first grader should also learn to recognize likeness and difference in printed symbols. For example, ask your child to look at the following groups of squares and point to the one in each group that is different. Also, check your library for *Anno's Math Games* (Putnam, 1987).

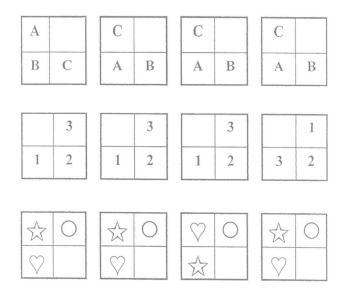

# Numbers and Number Sense

**PARENTS:** By now your first grader has probably had many experiences with numbers and counting. She knows her age and her address and can probably recite her telephone number. She can probably count to 30 or more, and she understands that each number stands for a specific quantity of items. (To review these concepts, see the section on "Numbers and Number Sense" in *What Your Kindergartner Needs to Know*.) Now your child is ready to learn that there are different ways of counting. By the end of first grade she should know how to count to 100 by ones, twos, fives, and tens, both forward and backward. She should also learn to write the words for the numbers from 1 to 12.

First graders should be learning to compare numbers to see which is greater and which is less and to have a sense of how big 100 is. They can begin to understand that a digit in the tens place of a number means something different from a digit in the ones place. In school, your child should also be introduced to number lines, tallies, and simple bar graphs and pictorial graphs.

## Some Things to Prepare in Advance

It helps to have real things for children to count. If you can gather and prepare these items in advance, you'll have a useful supply of materials to use for activities in this section and the "Computation" section.

- Keep a ready supply of countable things, such as dried beans, buttons, paper clips, or small pasta shapes like elbow macaroni.
- It's very handy to have a set of cards numbered from 0 to 100 for all sorts of games and counting activities. You can buy number cards at teacher supply stores and many toy stores, or you can make them out of index cards.

## Numbers from 1 to 10

Count out loud from 1 to 10. Afterward, practice writing the words for the numbers from one to ten.

| | | |
|---|---|---|
| 1 | one | ★ |
| 2 | two | ★★ |
| 3 | three | ★★★ |
| 4 | four | ★★★★ |
| 5 | five | ★★★★★ |
| 6 | six | ★★★★★★ |
| 7 | seven | ★★★★★★★ |
| 8 | eight | ★★★★★★★★ |
| 9 | nine | ★★★★★★★★★ |
| 10 | ten | ★★★★★★★★★★ |

### Zero

Zero is a special number. It tells how many you have when you don't have any. How many elephants do you have in your pocket?

0

## One More and One Less

In counting, the number that comes after another number is always 1 more. For example, 6 is 1 more than 5. If you had 5 star stickers and you got 1 more, you would have 6 star stickers.

In counting, the number that comes before another number is always 1 less. For example, 3 is 1 less than 4. If you had 4 pencils and you gave 1 away, you would have 3 pencils left.

To figure out what 1 less is, you can count backward. Learn to count backward from 10 to 0, like this:

10, 9, 8, 7, 6, 5, 4, 3, 2, 1, 0

## Number for Things in Order

Here are 10 fish. One fish is out of line. Which one? The seventh fish.

When you say "seventh," you are using a special kind of number called an ordinal number. Ordinal numbers name the number of something in an order. Practice saying and writing the first ten ordinal numbers in order. Except for first, second, and third, ordinal numbers end in "th."

Which one of the fish is facing the wrong way?

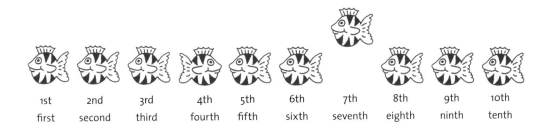

| 1st | 2nd | 3rd | 4th | 5th | 6th | 7th | 8th | 9th | 10th |
| first | second | third | fourth | fifth | sixth | seventh | eighth | ninth | tenth |

## Place Value

There are two digits in the number 10. A digit is any of the single numbers from 0 to 9. The two digits in 10 are a 1 and a 0.

In the number 10, we say that the first digit is in the tens place, and the second digit is in the ones place. The 1 in the tens place means 1 group of ten.

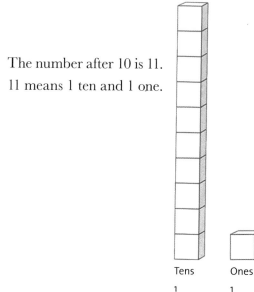

The number after 10 is 11.
11 means 1 ten and 1 one.

Tens    Ones
1         1

Tens    Ones
1         0

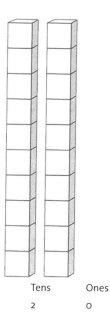

The next number is 12, which is 1 ten and 2 ones.
The numbers continue: 13, 14, 15, 16, 17, 18, 19.
19 means 1 ten and 9 ones.
After 19 the next number is 20.
20 means 2 tens and 0 ones.

Here are the words for the numbers from 11 to 20: eleven, twelve, thirteen, fourteen, fifteen, sixteen, seventeen, eighteen, nineteen, twenty.

Tens    Ones
2         0

## Place Value from 21 to 100

After 20, the numbers continue: 21, 22, 23, 24, 25, 26, 27, 28, 29, 30. 25 means 2 tens and 5 ones.

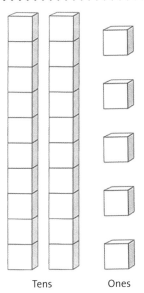

Tens          Ones

Let's count by tens: 10, 20, 30, 40, 50, 60, 70, 80, 90. The words for these numbers are: ten, twenty, thirty, forty, fifty, sixty, seventy, eighty, ninety.

30 means 3 tens and 0 ones. 40 means 4 tens and 0 ones. 67 means 6 tens and 7 ones.

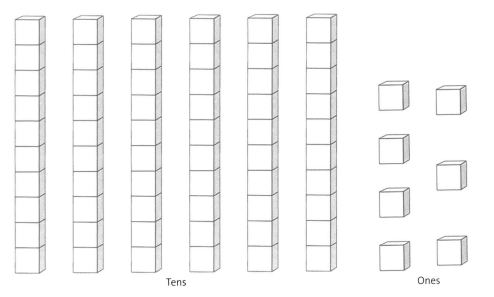

Tens          Ones

The numbers continue to 99, which is 9 tens and 9 ones. Do you know what comes after 99? The number after 99 is 100, which is written in words as one hundred.

## Counting to 100

Practice counting out loud from 1 to 100, so that soon you can do it easily.

Practice counting to 100 by tens: **10, 20, 30, 40, 50, 60, 70, 80, 90, 100**. Practice counting to 100 by fives: **5, 10, 15, 20, 25, 30, 35, 40,** and so on.

You should also practice counting by tens starting on different numbers, like this: **14, 24, 34, 44, 54, 64, 74, 84, 94**. Notice that when you count by tens, the ones place stays the same but the tens place gets one number larger each time.

Also practice counting backward from one ten to another. For example, try counting backward from 30 to 20, like this: **30, 29, 28, 27, 26, 25, 24, 23, 22, 21, 20**.

You should also be able to say the name of any number between 0 and 100. For example, when you see 78, you say "seventy-eight."

You should be able to read any number between 0 and 100 when it is spelled out. For example, eighty-three is 83.

## Twelve Is a Dozen

When you have 12 of something, you have a dozen. At the grocery store, eggs usually come in cartons of a dozen. You can use an empty egg carton to practice counting to twelve. You can place one button, dried bean, or coin into each compartment of the carton.

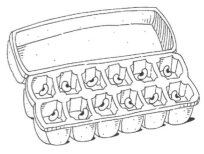

If you need half a dozen eggs to bake a cake, how many eggs do you need? (A half dozen is 6.)

## Greater Than and Less Than

Which number is greater, 5 or 4? 5 is greater than 4, because 5 is 1 more than 4. For example, 5 soccer balls are more than 4 soccer balls.

We say 5 is greater than 4, and we write that like this:

$$5 > 4$$

The sign > means "is greater than." When you count, 5 comes after 4. Numbers that are greater come after in counting.

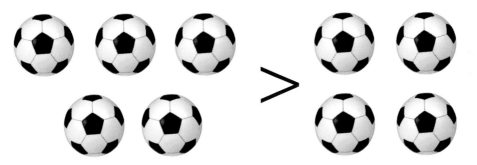

The number 3 is less than the number 4. For example, 3 nickels are less than 4 nickels.

We say 3 is less than 4, and we write it like this:

$$3 < 4$$

The sign < means "is less than." When you count, 3 comes before 4. Numbers that are less come before in counting.

Learn to compare numbers using the signs >, <, and =. Remember that =, the equals sign, means "is the same as." Notice that the small end of the signs < and > always points to the smaller number. What sign would you put between each pair of numbers here?

10 ___ 3    6 ___ 8    9 ___ 9

## Activity: Before and After

**PARENTS:** Show your child a book with numbered pages. Try to use a book with at least 96 pages. If your child is not familiar with reading numbers over 100, you may want to try to find a book that has only about 100 pages. Leaf through the book with your child and talk about how the pages are numbered in order.

Have your child open the book to any right-handed page. Ask her to predict the page number that comes right after that page. Then have her turn the page to check her prediction. Close the book, then open it again at random. Have her look at the number on a left-handed page, then ask her the number of the page just before. Have her turn back and check. Later you can ask your child to predict the page that comes before page 42, after page 13, and before page 60. Then try a more complicated task that asks her to count backward, such as predicting, in order, the pages that go from page 63 to page 56. Each time, have her say the numbers first and then check the book.

## Activity: Number Flash Cards Activities

**PARENTS:** You will need a deck of flash cards with the numbers from 0 to 100. You can make these from index cards or buy them at many toy stores and teacher supply stores. Here are some activities you can do quickly and repeat occasionally for practice:

- Hold up a card and have your child say the number on the card.
- Hold up two cards and ask which number is greater.
- Hold up two cards and ask your child to count forward or backward from one of the numbers to the other.
- Pick a card without showing it. Have your child guess the number by solving a number clue such as, "This number is 1 more than 63," or "This number is 1 less than 35," or "This number is between 59 and 61."
- After you use your 0 to 100 number cards, they'll probably be out of order. Before putting them away, ask your child to rearrange them in the correct order. This will provide an extra chance to practice counting from 0 to 100 in order.

## Using Graphs

The children in Ms. Williams's class took a vote on their favorite color. Different children chose red, blue, green, pink, and purple. The teacher counted their votes and put them on a special kind of chart called a graph.

Look at the graph and see if you can answer the questions on the next page:

| | | | | | | | | | | |
|---|---|---|---|---|---|---|---|---|---|---|
| **red** | | | | | | | | | | |
| **blue** | | | | | | | | | | |
| **green** | | | | | | | | | | |
| **pink** | | | | | | | | | | |
| **purple** | | | | | | | | | | |

- Which color was chosen as the favorite by the most children?
- Which color was chosen as the favorite by the fewest children?
- Which two colors were chosen as favorites by the same number of children?
- How many children chose each color?

The children in Ms. Johnson's class voted on their favorite flavor of ice cream: 7 children voted for chocolate, 5 children voted for vanilla, and 3 children voted for strawberry. Show how the children in Ms. Johnson's class voted by filling in a graph like the one below. Use a different color for each flavor of ice cream, such as brown for chocolate, yellow for vanilla, and pink for strawberry.

| chocolate | | | | | | | | | | |
|-----------|--|--|--|--|--|--|--|--|--|--|
| vanilla | | | | | | | | | | |
| strawberry | | | | | | | | | | |

## Fractions

A fraction is a part of something. ½ is a fraction. If something is divided into 2 equal parts, each part is ½. ½ is written in words as "one half."

Half of this circle is shaded.
Can you point to the shaded half?

⅓ is also a fraction. If something is divided into 3 equal parts, each part is ⅓. ⅓ is written in words as one third.

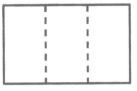

Each part is 1/3 of the rectangle.

If something is divided into 4 equal parts, each part is ¼. ¼ is written in words as one fourth. Sometimes people say "one quarter" instead of one fourth—they mean the same thing.

Each piece is 1/4 of the apple.

When you divide something into parts, the parts are equal only if they are the same size. For example, the parts of this rectangle are equal. But the parts of this square are not equal.

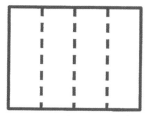

The rectangle has 4 parts. The parts are equal. Each part is 1/4.

The square has 3 parts. The parts are not equal.

Learn to recognize the fractions

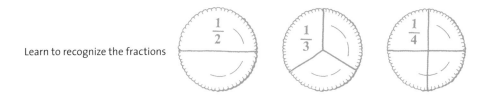

# Computation

**PARENTS:** From kindergarten, your child should understand that in a group of up to 10 objects there are ways to change the number of objects by adding to or taking away from them and that these changes can be shown in writing: for example, $2 + 2 = 4$, or $4 - 3 = 1$. In first grade, your child should learn more about how addition and subtraction work; with repeated and varied practice, he or she should know addition and subtraction facts to 12, as well as how to apply these memorized facts when solving problems that ask him or her to add or subtract two-digit numbers (without having to carry or borrow). Your child should also gain a firmer grasp of the connection between number sentences and the physical objects they represent.

## From Manipulatives to "Mental Math"

As children begin to learn to add and subtract, they may sometimes use countable objects, such as buttons, beans, or paper clips. Such objects, often called "manipulatives" in schools, can help children make the connection between numbers, which are symbols, and the actual items that are being added or subtracted. The goal in first grade, however, is for children to become more competent at working computations in their heads, without using countable objects. While children who are just learning their math facts should not be discouraged from using objects or counting on their fingers, they should, with repeated practice, make the transition to more "mental math."

You can help your child by playing the number games we suggest in this chapter, by using addition and subtraction flash cards (available at many toy stores and teacher supply stores), and, if you have access to a computer capable of running the software, by having your child play the computation games in such programs as Math Rabbit or Math Workshop.

## Learn a Fact a Day

You can use the charts on pages 348–49 to help your child learn one addition or subtraction fact a day. Pick one fact and, beginning in the morning, repeat it aloud together. For example, "9 minus 7 is 2." Say it over many times. Add a little fun by saying it in different voices (high, low, squeaky, growly), or even sing it! Repeat it often throughout the day. Later, use the charts for review and practice.

## Addition Facts from 0 to 12

| Sum of 0 | Sum of 1 | Sum of 2 | Sum of 3 | Sum of 4 |
|---|---|---|---|---|
| $0 + 0 = 0$ | $1 + 0 = 1$ | $2 + 0 = 2$ | $3 + 0 = 3$ | $4 + 0 = 4$ |
|  | $0 + 1 = 1$ | $1 + 1 = 2$ | $2 + 1 = 3$ | $3 + 1 = 4$ |
|  |  | $0 + 2 = 2$ | $1 + 2 = 3$ | $2 + 2 = 4$ |
|  |  |  | $0 + 3 = 3$ | $1 + 3 = 4$ |
|  |  |  |  | $0 + 4 = 4$ |

| Sum of 5 | Sum of 6 | Sum of 7 | Sum of 8 |
|---|---|---|---|
| $5 + 0 = 5$ | $6 + 0 = 6$ | $7 + 0 = 7$ | $8 + 0 = 8$ |
| $4 + 1 = 5$ | $5 + 1 = 6$ | $6 + 1 = 7$ | $7 + 1 = 8$ |
| $3 + 2 = 5$ | $4 + 2 = 6$ | $5 + 2 = 7$ | $6 + 2 = 8$ |
| $2 + 3 = 5$ | $3 + 3 = 6$ | $4 + 3 = 7$ | $5 + 3 = 8$ |
| $1 + 4 = 5$ | $2 + 4 = 6$ | $3 + 4 = 7$ | $4 + 4 = 8$ |
| $0 + 5 = 5$ | $1 + 5 = 6$ | $2 + 5 = 7$ | $3 + 5 = 8$ |
|  | $0 + 6 = 6$ | $1 + 6 = 7$ | $2 + 6 = 8$ |
|  |  | $0 + 7 = 7$ | $1 + 7 = 8$ |
|  |  |  | $0 + 8 = 8$ |

| Sum of 9 | Sum of 10 | Sum of 11 | Sum of 12 |
|---|---|---|---|
| $9 + 0 = 9$ | $10 + 0 = 10$ | $11 + 0 = 11$ | $12 + 0 = 12$ |
| $8 + 1 = 9$ | $9 + 1 = 10$ | $10 + 1 = 11$ | $11 + 1 = 12$ |
| $7 + 2 = 9$ | $8 + 2 = 10$ | $9 + 2 = 11$ | $10 + 2 = 12$ |
| $6 + 3 = 9$ | $7 + 3 = 10$ | $8 + 3 = 11$ | $9 + 3 = 12$ |
| $5 + 4 = 9$ | $6 + 4 = 10$ | $7 + 4 = 11$ | $8 + 4 = 12$ |
| $4 + 5 = 9$ | $5 + 5 = 10$ | $6 + 5 = 11$ | $7 + 5 = 12$ |
| $3 + 6 = 9$ | $4 + 6 = 10$ | $5 + 6 = 11$ | $6 + 6 = 12$ |
| $2 + 7 = 9$ | $3 + 7 = 10$ | $4 + 7 = 11$ | $5 + 7 = 12$ |
| $1 + 8 = 9$ | $2 + 8 = 10$ | $3 + 8 = 11$ | $4 + 8 = 12$ |
| $0 + 9 = 9$ | $1 + 9 = 10$ | $2 + 9 = 11$ | $3 + 9 = 12$ |
|  | $0 + 10 = 10$ | $1 + 10 = 11$ | $2 + 10 = 12$ |
|  |  | $0 + 11 = 11$ | $1 + 11 = 12$ |
|  |  |  | $0 + 12 = 12$ |

# Subtraction Facts from 0 to 12

**From 0**

$0 - 0 = 0$

**From 1**

$1 - 0 = 1$
$1 - 1 = 0$

**From 2**

$2 - 0 = 2$
$2 - 1 = 1$
$2 - 2 = 0$

**From 3**

$3 - 0 = 3$
$3 - 1 = 2$
$3 - 2 = 1$
$3 - 3 = 0$

**From 4**

$4 - 0 = 4$
$4 - 1 = 3$
$4 - 2 = 2$
$4 - 3 = 1$
$4 - 4 = 0$

**From 5**

$5 - 0 = 5$
$5 - 1 = 4$
$5 - 2 = 3$
$5 - 3 = 2$
$5 - 4 = 1$
$5 - 5 = 0$

**From 6**

$6 - 0 = 6$
$6 - 1 = 5$
$6 - 2 = 4$
$6 - 3 = 3$
$6 - 4 = 2$
$6 - 5 = 1$
$6 - 6 = 0$

**From 7**

$7 - 0 = 7$
$7 - 1 = 6$
$7 - 2 = 5$
$7 - 3 = 4$
$7 - 4 = 3$
$7 - 5 = 2$
$7 - 6 = 1$
$7 - 7 = 0$

**From 8**

$8 - 0 = 8$
$8 - 1 = 7$
$8 - 2 = 6$
$8 - 3 = 5$
$8 - 4 = 4$
$8 - 5 = 3$
$8 - 6 = 2$
$8 - 7 = 1$
$8 - 8 = 0$

**Make a Connection**

Do you remember the saying, "Practice makes perfect" from page 156? Practicing your math will help you perfect your math skills!

**From 9**

$9 - 0 = 9$
$9 - 1 = 8$
$9 - 2 = 7$
$9 - 3 = 6$
$9 - 4 = 5$
$9 - 5 = 4$
$9 - 6 = 3$
$9 - 7 = 2$
$9 - 8 = 1$
$9 - 9 = 0$

**From 10**

$10 - 0 = 10$
$10 - 1 = 9$
$10 - 2 = 8$
$10 - 3 = 7$
$10 - 4 = 6$
$10 - 5 = 5$
$10 - 6 = 4$
$10 - 7 = 3$
$10 - 8 = 2$
$10 - 9 = 1$
$10 - 10 = 0$

**From 11**

$11 - 0 = 11$
$11 - 1 = 10$
$11 - 2 = 9$
$11 - 3 = 8$
$11 - 4 = 7$
$11 - 5 = 6$
$11 - 6 = 5$
$11 - 7 = 4$
$11 - 8 = 3$
$11 - 9 = 2$
$11 - 10 = 1$
$11 - 11 = 0$

**From 12**

$12 - 0 = 12$
$12 - 1 = 11$
$12 - 2 = 10$
$12 - 3 = 9$
$12 - 4 = 8$
$12 - 5 = 7$
$12 - 6 = 6$
$12 - 7 = 5$
$12 - 8 = 4$
$12 - 9 = 3$
$12 - 10 = 2$
$12 - 11 = 1$
$12 - 12 = 0$

## Practice Your Addition

One way to practice addition is with things you can count. For example, if you have 3 keys, and you get 5 more keys, how many will you have?

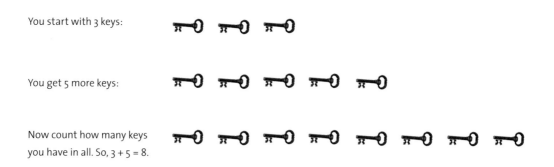

You start with 3 keys:

You get 5 more keys:

Now count how many keys you have in all. So, 3 + 5 = 8.

Another way to practice addition is to count forward. What does 5 + 2 equal? You want the number that is 2 more than 5. So count forward 2 numbers from 5, like this: 5 → 6 → 7. So, 5 + 2 = 7.

When you know how to add by counting forward, keep practicing your addition facts until you know them by heart, without counting. Practice writing and saying the addition facts a lot. It's important that you learn how to give the sums of addition facts quickly, without making mistakes.

## Addition Facts with the Same Sum

Learn to give all the addition facts that have the same sum. For example, if you were asked for all the addition facts with a sum of 6, you would write:

$6 + 0 = 6$
$5 + 1 = 6$
$4 + 2 = 6$
$3 + 3 = 6$
$2 + 4 = 6$
$1 + 5 = 6$
$0 + 6 = 6$

Try this: Can you write all the addition facts with a sum of 5?

## Things to Know About Addition

- When you add numbers together, the answer you get is called the "sum." The sum of $3 + 2$ is 5. The sum of $3 + 4$ is 7. What is the sum of $5 + 3$?
- When you add 0 to a number, you get the same number. That's because 0 means "nothing," so if you add 0, you're adding nothing. For example, $5 + 0$ adds up to 5. What is the sum of $8 + 0$? How much is $27 + 0$?
- It does not matter what order you add numbers in; the sum is still the same. $3 + 4 = 7$ and $4 + 3 = 7$. So, if you know that $2 + 6 = 8$, you also know what $6 + 2$ equals.
- You can write addition problems across or up and down. They both mean the same thing. For example:

$$5 + 3 = 8 \text{ is the same as } \begin{array}{r} 5 \\ +3 \\ \hline 8 \end{array}$$

## Activity: Dicey Addition

**PARENTS:** For this activity you will need number cards from 2 to 12, pencil and paper, and two six-sided dice.

Give your child a pencil and a sheet of paper. Ask her to place the number cards faceup in order. Now have her roll the dice, then add the two numbers that are rolled. She should say the numbers she has rolled aloud and then write them as an equation on her paper. For example, if she rolls a 6 and a 1, she writes (and reads aloud):

$$6 + 1 = 7$$

If she needs to, your child can count the dots on the dice to add the numbers. When she finds the correct sum, she turns the number card representing that sum facedown. When all the number cards from 2 to 12 have been turned facedown, the game is over. (You can also adapt this game to include two or more players.)

## Adding Three Numbers

To add three numbers, begin by adding the first two numbers. For example:

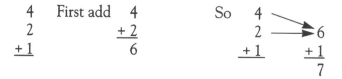

Can you solve this problem? Remember, begin by adding the first two numbers.

$$
\begin{array}{r}
5 \\
2 \\
+\ 3 \\
\hline
\end{array}
$$

## Subtraction: Taking Away Leaves the Difference

Subtraction means taking a number away. Pretend you have 5 toy robots. You take away 2 toy robots and give them to a friend. How many are left?

There were 5, but you took away 2. 5 take away 2 is 3. Or you can say, "5 minus 2 equals 3."

You can write this equation in two ways:

$$5 - 2 = 3 \quad \text{is the same as} \quad \begin{array}{r} 5 \\ -\ 2 \\ \hline 3 \end{array}$$

The number you have left after you subtract is called the difference. So the difference of 5 – 2 is 3. What is the difference of 7 – 4? The difference is 3.

You can practice subtraction by counting backward. What does 9 – 4 equal? You want the number that is 4 less than 9, so you can start at 9 and count backward 4 numbers, like this: 9 → 8 → 7 → 6 → 5. So 9 – 4 = 5.

Practice your subtraction facts until you know them without having to count backward. Practice writing and saying the subtraction facts up to 12 many times. (See the chart on page 349.) With practice, you will learn them so well that you don't have to stop and figure them out.

You know what happens when you add 0 to a number. What is 8 + 0? Yes, it's 8. What do you think happens when you subtract 0 from a number? When you subtract 0, you take away nothing, so you get the same number.

$$5 - 0 = 5 \qquad 12 - 0 = 12 \qquad 43 - 0 = 43$$

## Comparing Differences and Sums
· · · · · · · · · · · · · · · · · · · · · · · · · · · · · · · · · · · · · · · · · · · · · · · · · · · · · · · ·

You know these signs:

> greater than
< less than
= equals

You can use these signs to compare differences and sums. Here are some examples:

$$10 - 2 > 6 \qquad 6 - 4 < 5 - 1 \qquad 8 - 4 = 7 - 3$$

What sign belongs in the squares here?

$$5 + 3 \,\square\, 6 + 2 \qquad 9 - 7 \,\square\, 2 + 6 \qquad 10 - 3 \,\square\, 6 - 1$$

## Fact Families

A family is a group of related people. In math, a fact family is a group of related math facts.

A fact family brings together addition facts with their opposite subtraction facts. For example, here is a fact family:

$$5 + 2 = 7 \quad 7 - 2 = 5$$
$$2 + 5 = 7 \quad 7 - 5 = 2$$

Here is another fact family:

$$6 + 2 = 8 \quad 8 - 2 = 6$$
$$2 + 6 = 8 \quad 8 - 6 = 2$$

If you are given $4 + 2 = 6$, can you figure out all the facts in the fact family? Here they are:

$$4 + 2 = 6 \quad 6 - 2 = 4$$
$$2 + 4 = 6 \quad 6 - 4 = 2$$

Practice finding the facts in a fact family. For example, try to figure out the fact family for $3 + 2$. Try to figure out the fact family for $4 + 3$.

## Activity: Find the Mystery Number

**PARENTS:** You will need:

index cards
marker or crayon
number cards from 0 to 12
countable objects such as buttons, dried beans, or macaroni

Write a plus sign, a minus sign, an equals sign, and a question mark on individual index cards. If you do not have ready-made number cards, make cards for the numbers 0 to 12. Tell your child that you're going to ask him to solve some number problems.

Tell your child this number story. As you tell the story, use the cards to show what's happening. Say, "I have 5 buttons. I'll use this card with the number 5 to show how many buttons I have. Then I bought some more buttons. I'll use the plus sign to show that some buttons were added. This question mark shows that we don't know how many buttons were added. Now I have 9 buttons. I can show the equals sign and the sum of 9."

Ask your child to figure out the mystery number. This process is hard for many children, so be encouraging about his guesses, and help him as necessary to use the countable objects. Your child might need to set up 5 countable objects and then to add an object one at a time as he counts onward from 5 to find the mystery number.

When your child gets the correct answer, have him replace the question mark with the appropriate number card, then ask him to read the equation using the correct mathematical language, for example: "5 plus 4 equals 9."

Repeat the process with a subtraction story, such as: "I had 7 buttons in a box. Then I took away some of those buttons to sew on a jacket. Now I have 2 buttons left in the box. How many buttons did I take away?" Repeat the process using the cards to show the following:

$$7 - ? = 2$$

Have your child find the missing number, using countable objects as necessary, and again have him read the equation using the correct mathematical language. Continue with other addition and subtraction stories that you make up.

As your child becomes more confident with addition and subtraction, encourage him to try to figure out the missing number without using the countable objects.

## Activity: Addition and Subtraction Stories

**PARENTS:** Make up little stories that ask your child to add and subtract with numbers of 12 or less. Have on hand some countable objects (beans, buttons, macaroni, etc.) for your child to use as necessary, but encourage her to try to do these problems on paper or in her head.

For your addition and subtraction stories, you can use real-life or imaginary situations. For example:

- "Pretend you have a box of 10 crayons, and 2 of the crayons roll under the bed and you can't find them. How many crayons are left in the box?"
- "Once, a spaceship from another planet landed on Earth. Out of the ship came 3 space people. Then 5 more space people came out. How many space people came out of the ship in all?" After your child has solved that problem, you can continue the same story if you wish. For example: "That's right, there were 8 space people in all. But 4 of them got homesick and decided to go back to their own planet. How many stayed on Earth?"

## Activity: A Hundred Table

. . . . . . . . . . . . . . . . . . . . . . . . . . . . . . . . . . . . . . . . . . . . . . . . . . . . . . . . . . . .

**PARENTS:** Show your child the 1-to-100 number table on the facing page. Show how the table is laid out by counting with him from 1 to 21, having him point at the numbers as he counts. Then ask questions like these:

- "What's the largest number in the table?" (100)
- "What's the same about the number in the first box in each row?" (They all end in 1.)
- "What's the same about the number in the last box in each row?" (They all end in 0.)

The hundred table highlights number patterns that will help reinforce your child's understanding of place value and adding and subtracting with tens. This is a first step toward being able to compute with two-digit numbers. Here are some questions you can ask:

- "Look at the third row, with the numbers from 21 to 30. Look at the last number in the row: What's in the tens place?" (3 is in the tens place in the number 30.) "How is that different from all the other numbers in the row?" (All the other numbers have a 2 in the tens place.) "So, how many tens are in 30?" (3 tens are in 30.) "How many tens are in 25?" (2 tens are in 25.)
- "Find the number 53. Count to find 10 more than 53. What number do you get? Look at where 53 and 63 are on the table. What do you see?"
- "Let's look at the table again, but this time let's not count. What do you think 28 + 10 is? Now count to see if you were right."
- "What do you think will happen when you add 17 + 20? How can you figure it out using the number table?" (Look two rows down from 17 to find 37.)

| 1 | 2 | 3 | 4 | 5 | 6 | 7 | 8 | 9 | 10 |
|---|---|---|---|---|---|---|---|---|---|
| 11 | 12 | 13 | 14 | 15 | 16 | 17 | 18 | 19 | 20 |
| 21 | 22 | 23 | 24 | 25 | 26 | 27 | 28 | 29 | 30 |
| 31 | 32 | 33 | 34 | 35 | 36 | 37 | 38 | 39 | 40 |
| 41 | 42 | 43 | 44 | 45 | 46 | 47 | 48 | 49 | 50 |
| 51 | 52 | 53 | 54 | 55 | 56 | 57 | 58 | 59 | 60 |
| 61 | 62 | 63 | 64 | 65 | 66 | 67 | 68 | 69 | 70 |
| 71 | 72 | 73 | 74 | 75 | 76 | 77 | 78 | 79 | 80 |
| 81 | 82 | 83 | 84 | 85 | 86 | 87 | 88 | 89 | 90 |
| 91 | 92 | 93 | 94 | 95 | 96 | 97 | 98 | 99 | 100 |

Later you can use the same kind of questions with several cases of subtracting 10 from a number.

## Two-Digit Addition

You can use the addition facts you have learned so far to add numbers that have two digits. Let's look at this problem:

$$43$$
$$+ 25$$

First you add the 3 and the 5 in the ones place:

43
+ 25
 8

Then add the 4 and 2 in the tens place:

43
+ 25
68

So the sum is 68. Altogether you have 6 tens and 8 ones.

Sometimes one of the numbers you are adding has two digits, but the other has only one digit. For example, look at this problem:

$$22$$
$$+ \ 6$$

To solve that problem, you begin in the same way. First you add the numbers in the ones place. Then, since there are no tens to add to the 2 in the tens place, you just bring the 2 down into your answer.

*add the ones*

22
+ 6
 8

*bring down the 2 in the tens place*

22
+ 6
28

So the sum is 28, which is 2 tens and 8 ones. Do not forget to bring down the 2 tens into your answer!

## Two-Digit Subtraction

You can use the subtraction facts you have learned to do subtraction with two-digit numbers.

Find the difference:

$$
\begin{array}{r}
7\ 6 \\
-\ 3\ 4 \\
\hline
\end{array}
$$

First you subtract the numbers in the ones place:

$$
\begin{array}{r}
\overset{tens}{}\overset{ones}{} \\
7\ 6 \\
-\ 3\ 4 \\
\hline
2
\end{array}
$$

Then subtract the numbers in the tens place:

$$
\begin{array}{r}
\overset{tens}{}\overset{ones}{} \\
7\ 6 \\
-\ 3\ 4 \\
\hline
4\ 2
\end{array}
$$

So the difference is 42, which is 4 tens and 2 ones.

Let's look at another problem:

$$
\begin{array}{r}
57 \\
-\ 6 \\
\hline
\end{array}
$$

*subtract the ones*

$$
\begin{array}{r}
57 \\
-\ 6 \\
\hline
1
\end{array}
$$

*bring down the 5 in the tens place*

$$
\begin{array}{r}
57 \\
-\ 6 \\
\hline
51
\end{array}
$$

In a problem like that, don't forget to bring down the number in the tens place.

Practice doing many two-digit addition and subtraction problems, like these:

$$
\begin{array}{r}
34 \\
+\ 13 \\
\hline
\end{array}
\qquad
\begin{array}{r}
25 \\
-\ 12 \\
\hline
\end{array}
\qquad
\begin{array}{r}
52 \\
+\ 7 \\
\hline
\end{array}
\qquad
\begin{array}{r}
68 \\
-\ 5 \\
\hline
\end{array}
\qquad
\begin{array}{r}
75 \\
+\ 12 \\
\hline
\end{array}
\qquad
\begin{array}{r}
49 \\
-\ 27 \\
\hline
\end{array}
$$

# Money

**PARENTS:** Your first grader should already be familiar with the names of the coins and understand that each one has a particular value; if not, see the "Money" activities in *What Your Kindergartner Needs to Know*. Once your child is comfortable with different coin values, as well as with some basic addition (see previous section, "Computation"), you can do the following activity, which shows that different combinations of coins can equal the same amount of money.

## Activity: Coin Combinations

**PARENTS:** You will need:

    pencils and several sheets of plain paper
    pennies, nickels, dimes, and quarters

Before you start counting coins, make sure your child can name each one and tell you how many cents it is worth. A fun way to review the names of the coins is to make coin rubbings, by placing a coin under a sheet of paper and rubbing a pencil lightly over the coin until an impression shows up.

To get started, ask your child to show a combination of coins worth 11¢. Then ask her to show another coin combination worth the same amount. Offer help as needed. For example, your child might decide to show a dime and a penny, and eleven pennies. Then ask, "Can you think of any other ways to show 11¢? How about using two nickels? If you use just one nickel, what else do you need to make 11¢?"

Now repeat the above steps with a combination of coins of another amount up to 25¢.

To focus on the idea that different combinations of coins can be worth the same amount of money, ask questions like the following (have some real coins on hand for your child to use if she needs them to answer the questions):

- "What coin is worth the same as two nickels?"
- "If I give you two dimes and one nickel, what coin would you give me that is worth the same?"
- "If I have a dime and a nickel, and you have a dime and five pennies, does one of us have more money?"

When your child is comfortable with combinations up to 25¢, try combinations of coins from 26¢ to 35¢. Start with 26¢, and provide enough coins for your child to make as many possible combinations as you and she can think of.

# Geometry

## Flat and Solid Shapes

Math that has to do with shapes is called geometry. You probably know the names for many flat shapes. A shape with three sides is called a triangle. Here are two triangles. Count the sides on each.

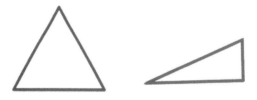

A rectangle has four sides.

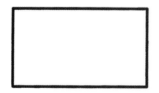

A square has four sides of equal length.

And this, of course, is a circle.

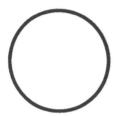

When two shapes are the same size and shape, we say they are **congru-ent.** Two of these triangles are congruent.

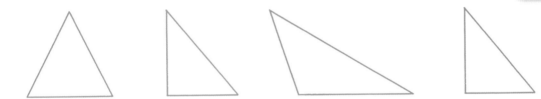

Here are six shapes. Two of them are congruent. Congruent means they are the same size and shape. But they may not be in the same position. Can you find the congruent shapes here?

Learn the names of these solid shapes, and look around your home or school for examples, such as a juice can (cylinder) or ball (sphere).

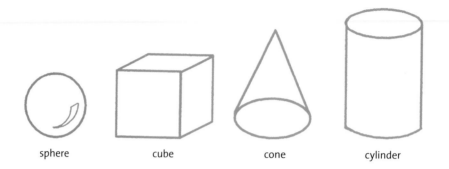

sphere          cube          cone          cylinder

**PARENTS:** Children often enjoy playing with a tangram, a seven-shape puzzle thought to have been created in China long ago. Check your library or bookstore for books like *Tangram* by Joost Elffers (Penguin, 1977), *The Fun with Tangrams Kit* or *Tangrams ABC Kit* by Susan Johnston (Dover Publications, 1979), and *Sam Loyd's Book of Tangrams* (Dover Publications, 2007).

## Activity: Simon Says

**PARENTS:** In first grade, your child should continue to refine her sense of spatial orientation and become more secure using terms of location such as "left," "right," "top," "middle," and "bottom," as well as terms of relative position such as "on," "under," "over," and "between." At home, you can adapt the old favorite game of Simon Says so that it helps your child practice direction words. To practice direction words, use commands that incorporate words like "over," "under," "left," "right," "behind," "between," and "around" as part of the game. For example, "Simon says put your left hand under your chin. Simon says walk around the kitchen table. Simon says hold your right knee between your hands."

# Measurement

**PARENTS:** By the end of first grade, children should become more familiar with a few standard measuring tools, as well as units such as inches and centimeters; cups, quarts, and gallons; pounds; and degrees Fahrenheit. To understand measurement, first graders need many opportunities to measure things.

First graders also need plenty of practice in measuring time. They need to work with terms and concepts such as before and after, and yesterday, today, and tomorrow. They should know the days of the week and the months of the year (see the "Literature" section of this book for the poem "Thirty Days Hath September"). By the end of first grade, your child should be able to read a clockface and tell time to the half hour. You can help her by regularly showing her a calendar and clock as you plan various tasks. Don't rely exclusively on digital clocks or watches; use a clock or watch with hands.

> **Make a Connection**
> See "Making Measurements" in the "Science" section of this book (pages 419–25) for activities involving length, volume, and temperature.

## Calendar Time

. . . . . . . . . . . . . . . . . . . . . . . . . . . . . . . . . . . . . . . . . . . . . . . . . . . . . . . . . . .

There are seven days in a week. Can you name them? (Sunday, Monday, Tuesday, Wednesday, Thursday, Friday, Saturday.) Of those seven days, five are called the weekdays and two days make up the weekend. Can you tell me which two days are the weekend days? (Saturday and Sunday.)

> **Make a Connection**
> When learning about calendars, review the poem "Thirty Days Hath September" on page 29.

There are twelve months in a year. Can you name them, starting with the first month? They are (1) January, (2) February, (3) March, (4) April, (5) May, (6) June, (7) July, (8) August, (9) September, (10) October, (11) November, and (12) December. Make sure you know the names of the months of the year, in order.

Do you remember ordinal numbers, the numbers that help you put things in order? For the last two months of the year, you can learn two new ordinal numbers, eleventh and twelfth. (Notice the funny spelling of "twelfth.") November is the eleventh month, and December is the twelfth month.

**PARENTS:** To strengthen your child's sense of calendar time, display the calendar for the current month and occasionally ask questions like the following:

- "What day is today?" (Ask for the day of the week as well as the month, date, and year.)
- "What day of the week was yesterday?"
- "What day of the week will tomorrow be?"
- "Can you show me where yesterday was on the calendar? Can you tell me what the date will be next Sunday?"

| Sun | Mon | Tue | Wed | Thu | Fri | Sat |
|-----|-----|-----|-----|-----|-----|-----|
| 1 | 2 | 3 | 4 | 5 | 6 | 7 |
| 8 | 9 | 10 | 11 | 12 | 13 | 14 |
| 15 | 16 | 17 | 18 | 19 | 20 | 21 |
| 22 | 23 | 24 | 25 | 26 | 27 | 28 |
| 29 | 30 | 31 | | | | |

# Activity: Telling Time

**PARENTS:** What follows is not so much a onetime activity as an explanation you can read aloud to your child, then refer to on many occasions. Most children need repeated practice and reinforcement before they master the skill of telling time. In school, your child should get plenty of practice in learning to tell time. If you want to supplement this, check your library or bookstore for books like *My First Book of Time* by Claire Llewellyn (Dorling Kindersley, 1992). Many teacher supply stores and some toy stores sell "hands-on" kits for learning to tell time.

### Get Ready

As you read aloud the following section to your child, it will be helpful to have a paper clockface to work with. You can make one from a paper plate, a sheet of colored paper, and a brad. To make clock hands, cut two narrow strips of paper from the sheet: One strip should be longer than the other. Then have your child help you turn the paper plate into a clockface by numbering around the rim from 1 to 12. Finally, use the brad to attach the ends of both strips to the center of the clockface. Your child can use this homemade clockface to show different times.

Ask your child to show the times on a homemade clockface as you read aloud the following:

Look at the clock. What time does the clock say it is?

When the long hand is on the 12 and the short hand is on the 8, then the time is eight o'clock. We can write that in two ways:

8:00 means the same as eight o'clock.

The long hand on a clock is also called the minute hand. The short hand is also called the hour hand. On this clock, the minute hand is on the 12 and the hour hand is on the 4. Can you tell me what time it is?

Look at this clock. Tell me where the minute hand is and where the hour hand is. Then can you tell me what time it is?

Yes, that clock shows ten o'clock. Can you show me ten o'clock on your paper clock?

Your clock could be showing 10:00 in the morning or 10:00 at night. If you want to tell someone to meet you at 10:00, how can you make sure he knows that you mean 10:00 in the morning and not 10:00 at night? One way is to say, "Meet me at 10:00 A.M." A time before noon, in the morning, is called A.M. Time after noon—whether afternoon or night—is called P.M. [Note: You may want to ask your child if he can recognize noon on a clock, and show him if he doesn't know how.]

Do you eat breakfast closer to 8:00 A.M. or 8:00 P.M.? Do you go to bed closer to 8:00 A.M. or 8:00 P.M.? Can you think of some things you normally do at about 10:00 A.M.? What are you normally doing at 10:00 P.M.?

Now let's look at this clock. What number is the minute hand on? And look at the hour hand—do you see how it's between 8 and 9? This clock is showing half past eight. Another way of saying half past eight is eight-thirty, which we can write like this:

$$8:30.$$

When we say eight-thirty, we mean that it's thirty minutes after eight o'clock. Eight-thirty is the same as saying "half past eight," because thirty minutes is half of an hour. A whole hour is sixty minutes. Sixty minutes is how long it takes for the minute hand to go around the clock once, starting at the 12 and coming back to the 12. While the minute hand makes one whole trip around the clock, the hour hand moves from one number to the next.

Can you tell what time it is on this clock?

Some clocks do not have hands. On a digital clock, the time appears in numbers. These two clocks are showing the same time in different ways. Can you tell me what time they are showing?

These two clocks are also showing the same time in different ways. Can you tell me what time they are showing?

# Suggested Resources

. . . . . . . . . . . . . . . . . . . . . . . . . . . . . . . . . . . . . . . . . . .

### NUMBERS AND NUMBER SENSE

*1, 2, 3 to the Zoo* by Eric Carle (Puffin, 1998)

*Animal Numbers* by Bert Kitchen (Lutterworth Press, 1992)

### COMPUTATION

*Math Fables: Lessons That Count* by Greg Tang (Scholastic Press, 2004)

*One Hundred Angry Ants* by Elinor J. Pinczes, illustrated by Bonnie MacKain (Houghton Mifflin, 1999)

*Safari Park* by Stuart J. Murphy (Harper Collins, 2002)

### MONEY

*The Coin Counting Book* by Rozanne Lanczak Williams (Charlesbridge Publishing, 2001)

*The Penny Pot* (MathStart, Level 3) by Stuart J. Murphy (HarperCollins, 1998)

### GEOMETRY

*The Shape of Things* by Dayle Ann Dodds, illustrated by Julie Lacome (Scott Foresman, 1996)

### MEASUREMENT

*Me Counting Time: From Seconds to Centuries* by Joan Sweeney, illustrated by Annette Cable (Dragonfly, 2001)

# VI
# Science

# Introduction

To gain knowledge about the world around them—to understand animals and their habitats, or human-body systems, or electricity—children need firsthand experience, with many opportunities to observe and experiment. In the words of *Benchmarks for Science Literacy* (a 2013 report from the American Association for the Advancement of Science): "For students in the early grades, the emphasis should overwhelmingly be on gaining experience with natural and social phenomena and on enjoying science." From the start, children should be "actively engaged in learning to view the world scientifically. That means encouraging them to ask questions about nature and to seek answers, collect things, count and measure things, make qualitative observations, organize collections and observations, discuss findings, etc. Getting into the spirit of science and liking science are what count most."

While experience counts for much, book learning is also important, for it helps bring coherence and order to a child's scientific knowledge. Only when topics are presented systematically and clearly can children make steady and secure progress in their scientific learning. The child's development of scientific knowledge and understanding is in some ways a very disorderly and complex process, different for each child. But a systematic approach to the exploration of science, one that combines experience with book learning, can help provide essential building blocks for deeper understanding at a later time. It can also provide the kind of knowledge that one is not likely to gain from observation: Consider, for example, how people long believed that the Earth stood still while the sun orbited around it, a misconception that "direct experience" presented as fact.

In this section, we introduce first graders to a variety of topics consistent with the early study of science in countries that have had outstanding results in teaching science at the elementary level. The text is meant to be read aloud to your child, and it offers questions for you and your child to discuss, as well as activities for you to do together.

# Living Things and Their Habitats

Do you recognize this big white furry animal? This is a polar bear. He lives near the North Pole. What's the weather like there? It's cold, cold, cold. Look at what's all around the polar bear in this picture: ice and snow.

Polar bears live where it's cold and icy all the time. If you went there, you would have to bundle up with a jacket and scarf and hat and mittens and boots. But polar bears stay warm in their own way. That thick white fur all over their bodies keeps polar bears warm, even at the cold North Pole.

Now, let's pretend that the polar bear goes on a trip to Hawaii, where palm trees grow and the sun shines brightly and the beaches are hot and sandy. Would that polar bear feel comfortable? When you feel hot, you can take off your jacket. But a polar bear can't take off his thick coat of fur! Polar bears would not be comfortable in a hot place. It just wouldn't feel like home.

That's because polar bears live in a habitat that is always cold. What is a habitat? A habitat is the place where an animal lives, eats, sleeps, makes its home, has babies, and shares things with other animals. A habitat is an animal's home. A habitat matches the animal, and the animal matches the habitat.

That polar bear doesn't match the hot, sunny beach, but he feels right at home at the cold, icy North Pole, which is the polar bear's habitat.

A fish that swims in the ocean would not do well in the forest, would it? That fish belongs in the ocean habitat.

Would a worm that crawls through the moist, rich soil of the forest be happy living in the desert? No, not at all. That worm belongs in the forest habitat.

Different animals live in different habitats. Let's explore a few habitats and some of the animals living in them.

## The Forest Habitat

Imagine you're taking a walk through a beautiful forest. Oak and maple trees stand tall around you. Their highest branches reach upward and form a leafy canopy, which makes it cool and shady for you as you walk along. You can feel the soft moss under your feet, and little purple flowers bloom nearby.

What's that *tap-tap-tapping* sound? It's a bird called a woodpecker. Woodpeckers peck into the trunks of old trees, looking for insects to eat. The woodpecker lives in this forest habitat.

A squirrel scampers up a tree. The squirrel also lives in this forest habitat. Squirrels build nests in the tree branches and eat acorns that grow on the oak trees.

You walk a little farther into the forest and—*pew!* What do you smell? It must be a skunk! When it gets scared, a skunk sends out a stinky spray to make larger animals stay away. Skunks burrow into holes in the ground or into rotten tree trunks. They eat berries and insects and eggs they steal from the nests of birds that also live in the forest habitat.

All these plants— the oak trees and the maple trees, the green moss and little woodland flowers—live in

the forest habitat. And all these animals—the woodpecker, the squirrel, the skunk, and many others—live in the forest habitat as well.

## What Do Animals Eat?

The woodpecker and the squirrel, lions and tigers, you and your family—every kind of animal needs food to eat. Some animals eat plants. Some animals eat other animals. And some animals eat both. There are special names for animals, depending on whether they eat plants, meat, or both.

Animals that eat only plants are called *herbivores* [HUR-buh-vores]. Many animals, including mice, cows, and horses, eat only plants. Even huge elephants eat only leaves, fruits, nuts, and grass—no meat. Some human beings choose to eat only plants and no meat.

Other animals would rather eat meat. Can you think of any? Dogs and cats, lions and tigers, sharks and snakes eat meat. They are called *carnivores* [CAR-nuh-vores]. A carnivore eats animal flesh, or meat.

**All Together**

Talk together about animals your child knows: dog, cat, bird, horse, squirrel. What does each animal like to eat? Then discuss each animal to determine whether it is an *herbivore*, a *carnivore*, or an *omnivore?* Say those words together each time. Finally, ask your child what she is!

What about you? Lots of people eat both plants and meat. They would be called *omnivores* [AHM-nuh-vores]. An omnivore eats both plants and animals. Bears are omnivores. They eat plants. They hunt for fruits and berries, and they eat animals, like fish. They also use their sharp claws to rip open logs and eat the insects they find inside.

## Walking Through the Forest Habitat

Let's go back to imagining you are walking through the forest. Pretend you can feel strands of sticky stuff on your face. You've walked into a spiderweb strung across your path. In the forest habitat, spiders weave webs, hoping to trap insects as they fly by. That's how many spiders get their food.

Every autumn, leaves fall from the trees and pile up on the forest floor. Snails, insects, and other animals crawl through the leaves and eat them. Then along comes a raccoon, which eats the snails. Raccoons eat snails and fruit and nuts and many other things. They are omnivores, and they aren't very picky eaters!

Spiders, insects, snails, raccoons—all these animals and many, many more live together in the forest. For home and food, they depend on the plants and other animals living in the forest habitat with them.

## The Underground Habitat

What if you brought a shovel with you on your walk through the forest? You could take it out and dig down under the leaves and mushrooms on the forest floor. What do you think you would see?

A shiny brown earthworm slithers deeper underground. It was squirming right under the leaves, but now it pokes its way under the soil. Push the soil away, and you might see a little white grub inching along. When you disturb it, it curls up into a ball. Soon it will grow into an insect. Maybe it will grow wings and fly up into the treetops.

The worm and the grub live together in the forest's underground habitat. Even some furry animals, like moles, live underground with them. Moles have broad paws and long claws just right for digging. They burrow underground, trying to find things to eat: things like roots and ants—and worms and grubs, like the ones we just discovered. Living underground as they do, moles don't use their eyes as much as they use their noses. They find their way around with a **keen** sense of smell.

Paws for digging and a strong sense of smell: Those are two of the ways that the mole is suited to its underground habitat.

### All Together

Go with your child to a place where he can dig in the dirt, whether that's your backyard, a nearby park, or a forest setting. Together, dig a little hole and then search through the dirt to find any creatures living in that underground habitat. Look for insects, worms, spiders, grubs.

### New Word

**Keen** means particularly strong.

## The Desert Habitat

Now let's think about the **desert** habitat. What can you tell me about the desert? It is very hot. It is very dry. There is lots of sunshine and not a lot of shade because there aren't big trees with lots of leaves. The desert habitat is very different from the forest habitat.

The forest is often cool. The desert is often hot.

The forest is moist. The desert is dry.

The forest is dark and shady. The desert is bright and sunny.

Sometimes it snows and rains in the forest, but it rarely snows or rains in the desert.

Since the desert is a very different habitat from the forest, the plants and animals living in the desert are different from those living in the forest.

Many lizards live in the hot desert. They like to live in a place that is hot and dry. Their bodies do well in the heat. They lie on warm rocks and bask in the blazing sunshine. Lizards belong in the desert habitat.

Cactus plants also live in the desert. They grow well in hot weather. They need a lot of sunshine, but they can grow for a long time without any rain at all. Cactus plants are well suited to the desert habitat.

**Talk and Think**

Look at pictures of a desert with your child and talk about how few plants and animals can be seen. The desert is really "deserted"—very few living things remain in it— and, in fact, those two words are related.

## Water Habitats

**Talk and Think**

Ask your child if she has ever heard the saying "like a fish out of water." What does that mean? How does a fish feel when it's out of water? Not very comfortable!

Since fish can't breathe out of water, people say this about someone in a very uncomfortable situation.

For example, a child who has never played soccer before is asked to join the team for an important game. "Everyone else on the team knows how to play," she might say. "I've never played soccer before. I'd feel like a fish out of water."

There are many animals that live in a water habitat. Can you name a few?

Fish live in water. There are fish that live in the ocean, fish that live in rivers, and fish that live in ponds, lakes, and streams. Fish eat other things that live in the water habitat. They eat smaller fish. They eat plants growing in or near the water. They eat insects they can catch in the water.

There are many ways that a fish is suited to its water habitat. Let's make a list.

First of all, fish are good swimmers. They don't have legs and feet. They don't walk. But they have fins and tails. Their bodies are made for swimming.

Also, fish can breathe underwater. Can you or I breathe underwa-

ter? We have to take a deep breath before going underwater and then we have to come back up for air. But fish have gills, which allow them to breathe in the water. The trouble is, they can't breathe out of water. A fish has to live in the water.

This bird hunts for fish in its water habitat.

Many other animals belong in a water habitat too. Some live all their lives underwater, like oysters and starfish. Some live part of their lives underwater and part on land, like frogs and salamanders. Some live on the land near the water, like herons and hermit crabs. All of these animals depend on other things in the water habitat. They depend on the water itself and on the plants and animals living in or near the water.

Not all water habitats are the same. The water habitat at ponds, lakes, and rivers is different from the ocean habitat. The difference is in the water itself.

When you play in the waves at the ocean and get some of that water in your mouth, you can tell that ocean water tastes very salty. Oceans are made of salt water.

This shark lives in salt water.

But when you play in a pond or lake or river, most of the time that water doesn't taste salty. We call that freshwater.

Salt water might not taste good to you, but many plants and animals depend on it to live. Clams, oysters, and jellyfish live in the salty ocean, along with plants such as seaweed. Whales, dolphins, sharks— *all* the animals that live in an ocean habitat—need salt water. If you put them into water without salt, they wouldn't survive. They belong to the saltwater habitat.

But the fish and other animals and plants living in a pond or river could not just move to the ocean either. They depend on freshwater to live. If you put a freshwater fish in salt water, it would not do well. It belongs to the freshwater habitat.

## The Food Chain

Every living thing needs food to survive. Plants make their own food. They do that by soaking up sunshine and air and taking water and nutrients from the soil in which they grow.

Animals can't make food from sunshine and water. Animals need to find food. They eat living things, which means they eat plants and other animals.

Some big animals eat plants. Other big animals eat little animals. When a big animal dies, it may be eaten by little animals. And when the little animals die, they become the nutrients in the soil that plants use to make food. All these connections make what we call a food **chain**.

Let's look at one example of a food chain. Imagine a green plant growing by the side of a river. A caterpillar comes along and chews on the leaves. Later the caterpillar grows into an insect and flies away. The insect is flying across the river when suddenly, *swoosh*, a fish leaps out of the water and swallows it. The fish splashes back into the water, feeling full and happy—but not for long. A big bear reaches into the river and grabs the fish in its paw. The bear eats the fish—a tasty supper.

Later that year the bear dies, and through the winter its body rots away. The rotting body turns to nutrients that soak into the soil by the side of the river. When spring comes, the nutrients help green plants grow. One of those green plants grows by the side of the river. A caterpillar comes along and chews on the leaves and . . .

Do you see? It's a cycle, starting over and going round and round again. It's a cycle of one creature feeding upon another, and then another— a cycle of life and death and life again.

Many animals eat plants, and these animals are sometimes eaten by other animals. Plants and animals die and rot, which returns nutrients to the soil, which helps more plants grow. It's all a part of the food chain that keeps nature alive.

A food chain

**New Word**
Talk with your child about the meaning of **chain**. He may know a chain from the lamp pull, or his bicycle, or a locked gate. Talk about how individual links connect, one to the other, and become a chain. That's why we call it a "food chain": because each plant or animal connects to the next in a web of nature.

## Taking Care of Earth's Habitats

The Earth is full of many different habitats—forest and desert, freshwater and salt water, and many others as well. Each habitat supports many different kinds of animals and plants. Most living things are so well suited to their habitat, they could not survive in another habitat. It might be too cold or too hot. They might not find the right amount of sunshine or food or water. They might not find what they need to make a home or nest.

Sometimes people do things that can mess up a habitat. People cut down forests to get trees for lumber. People put in pipes to bring water to the desert so that they can make more farms. People fill in ponds with dirt so that they can build houses. But what happens to the animals and plants when their forest or desert or pond habitat is destroyed? Sometimes they die.

## The Endangered Rain Forest Habitat

In one habitat, the world's rain forests, many animals and plants are in danger. That's because people are cutting down too many trees there.

Some rain forests grow in the hottest parts of the world. Rain forest trees grow very tall and spread out big leaves and branches. All sorts of vines and bushes grow in the hot shady places underneath the trees. There is always moisture in the air, and water constantly drips off the trees. It feels as if it is always raining, which is why these habitats are called rain forests.

Not many people live in the rain forests, but thousands of different plants and animals do. Special snakes, frogs, and birds, and other animals you might know, like orangutans and jaguars, live only in rain forests. People should take care not to hurt this precious habitat, or pretty soon the animals and plants will no longer have the habitat they need to survive.

Many different animals and plants are endangered, which means that there are not many left in the world, for example, jaguars are endangered. If we are not

careful, they will become extinct, which means there are none left. When an animal becomes extinct, every one of them has died and there will never be another one born. All we have are pictures. We can't even see them in zoos anymore.

## The Most Famous Extinct Animals: Dinosaurs

When an animal becomes extinct, every one of them on Earth has died. It's hard to imagine any animals you know becoming extinct, but you may already know about the most famous extinct animals: the dinosaurs.

Millions of years ago, dinosaurs lived on Earth. They lived on Earth when there were no people around to see them.

Some dinosaurs were huge. Brachiosaurus [BRACK-ee-uh-SAWR-us], for example, was as long as two school buses. It held its head up higher than the roof of a small house. Like many dinosaurs, the brachiosaurus was an herbivore. Do you remember what that means? It means that the brachiosaurus ate only . . . plants.

But not all dinosaurs were that big. Velociraptor [vuh-LOSS-uh-RAP-ter] was about as big as a dog can get and smaller than a pony. But this dinosaur was a carnivore, which means that velociraptors ate meat. They ate other dinosaurs!

Long, long ago, dinosaurs became extinct. No one knows exactly why, but they all died. So now we will never see living dinosaurs, but we can learn from their bones. Dinosaur bones have been found in the ground all around the world. Scientists study the bones and figure out a lot about what dinosaurs looked like, when they lived, how they moved, and what they ate.

Brachiosaurus

# Oceans and Undersea Life

There is a famous picture of our planet Earth taken by astronauts from outer space. When people see that picture, they say, "The Earth looks like a big blue marble!" Do you know what makes it look so blue? It's not the sky, because from outer space, the sky does not look blue. It's not the trees, because from outer space, the trees look brown and green. It's all the water that covers our planet. Take a look at a globe or a map of the world, and you will see how much water covers the Earth. Our planet is covered with more water than it is with land!

Where have you seen water covering the Earth? In lakes or rivers, maybe streams and ponds. Even in puddles! But the place where the most water of all can be found is in the oceans. Oceans are so big that if you were in a boat in the middle of one of them, you could not see a bit of land. Everywhere you looked—north, south, east, and west—all you would see is water.

**Talk and Think**

Look at a globe or map together and point out the big oceans, saying their names together: the Pacific Ocean, the Atlantic Ocean, the Indian Ocean, and the Arctic Ocean. Ask your child to put a finger in the middle of one of them and then imagine being on a boat there, where all she could see was water all around.

## Ocean Tides

All along the edge of an ocean, the place where the water meets the land is called the shore. Ponds, rivers, and lakes have shores, too. The ocean shore is sometimes a sandy beach, sometimes hard rocks, and sometimes a steep cliff.

At most of these ocean shores, something interesting happens over the course of a day. Sometimes the ocean water reaches high up, and sometimes the water drops way down. These changes at the ocean shore are called the "tides."

If you keep checking one place at the ocean beach for a few days, you begin to notice the pattern. Two times a day, every day, over and over, the level of the ocean water rises and then sinks. You can see it if you watch the water splashing against a dock. Sometimes the water's level reaches high up on the posts standing in the water, but a few hours later, the water's level does not reach as high at all.

And you can see it if you watch the waves splashing against a beach. At high tide, the edge of the ocean comes way up, covering the beach, so that all you see is a little stretch of sand. At low tide, the water level drops and the edge of the ocean moves farther away, leaving a big sandy beach for you to play on.

Low tide                                    High tide

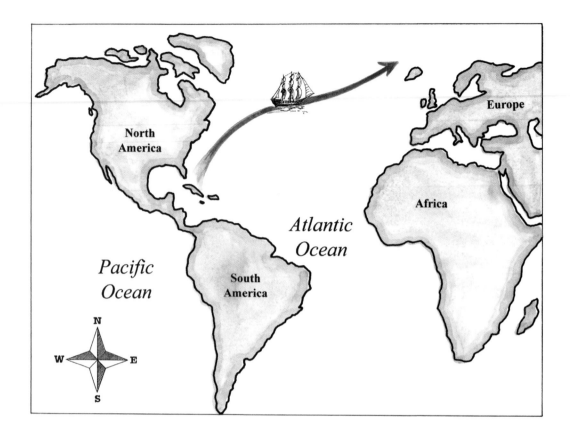

## Ocean Currents

The water in the ocean moves all the time. The wind blows across the ocean and pushes the water up into waves. The tides move the water up toward shore and back down again.

**Take a Look**
Use your finger to trace the Gulf Stream on the map.

In some parts of the ocean, water moves in great streams, almost like rivers flowing through the ocean. We call these moving streams "ocean currents." When ship captains sail the ocean, they pay close attention to currents, because a current can carry a ship along with it, just as a river carries a stick or a paper boat downstream.

When ship captains sail across the Atlantic Ocean, they pay special attention to a current called the Gulf Stream. The Gulf Stream runs from the Gulf of Mexico, up the coast of Florida, and then north up the coast of the United

States as far as North Carolina before it begins to cross the Atlantic Ocean. Long ago, before engines were invented, ships used sails to catch the wind to help them move through the water. Ships' captains often used the current of the Gulf Stream to help them go north and then east, from America to Europe.

## Underwater in the Ocean

From the land, the ocean looks like a big, flat sheet of water. But there are lots of things to see and learn about underwater. Let's take a look. Put on your scuba-diving gear. Is your mask on tight? Are the air tanks full? Okay, let's go underwater!

If you start walking into the ocean from the beach, at first the water will come up to your knees. As you continue walking out into the ocean, the water gets deeper. You keep walking, just as if you are walking on a floor that slants down, down, down. Now the water is even deeper. It comes up to your shoulders. Thank goodness you have your scuba gear on, because pretty soon you're all the way underwater!

The ocean floor has hills and valleys, just like the dry parts of the earth.

Even where the ocean is very deep, it has a bottom, called the ocean floor. Where the ocean is shallow, the ocean floor is close to the water's surface. Where the ocean is deep, the ocean floor drops way down.

Sometimes the ocean floor juts up out of the water, and that makes an island. And sometimes long, deep valleys cut through the ocean floor. The deepest valleys are called ocean trenches. You can think of the ocean floor as a landscape of mountains, valleys, and trenches, stretching out for thousands of miles underwater.

## Ocean Life

Many different animals live in the ocean. Some of them we can see, and some of them are so tiny we can't see them.

What ocean animals can you name? Many different kinds of fish live in the ocean. Sharks live in the ocean. There are porpoises, octopuses, jellyfish, starfish, and many other creatures that live in the ocean.

The ocean is home to some of the world's largest animals—whales. The blue whale, the biggest whale of all, can grow to ninety-eight feet long, head to tail. It's hard to imagine how big that is, but think about this: If thirty children as tall as you were to lie down in a line, head to toe, they might add up to the length of a blue whale.

How big is a blue whale? Compare it with an elephant.

A whale that big weighs about one hundred sixty-five tons. One ton equals two thousand pounds, so one whale weighs three hundred thirty thousand pounds! It would take a lot more than thirty children your size to add up to that much weight. It would take about six thousand children! That's a pretty big animal.

Amazingly enough, the ocean is full of tiny animals as well. Did you know that if you scoop up a handful of ocean water, you're holding a bunch of living creatures? These creatures are so tiny that you can't see them. It would seem as if you were holding just a handful of water, but really the water is full of little living things. All these teeny-tiny animals, along with many teeny-tiny plants, drift in the ocean's waters. They are called plankton.

Just as on the land, in the ocean there is a food chain linking the animals and plants that share habitats. Here is an amazing fact about the ocean food chain: Some whales eat only plankton. That means that some of the biggest animals in the ocean eat only the littlest plants and animals. When these whales are really hungry, they eat thousands of pounds of plankton every day.

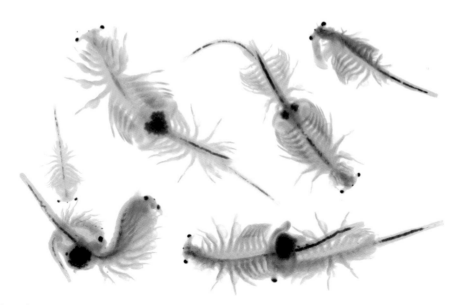

These funny animals are so tiny, you need a microscope to see them. They are one of many kinds of plankton that live in the ocean.

## Taking Care of the Ocean

People all over the world depend upon the oceans. Ships travel on the ocean, moving things from one continent to another. Fishermen catch food in the ocean for us to eat. Tuna fish comes from the ocean. So do shrimp. And many people around the world enjoy eating some kinds of seaweed.

The oceans help the world's people in other ways, too. With so much water covering so much of the planet Earth, the oceans help keep Earth healthy. That's why people have to be careful not to do things to hurt the ocean. We need to find ways to take care of the oceans.

People can hurt the ocean by putting the wrong things into it, like garbage and litter. When plastic toys or bottles or wrappers float on the ocean surface, some fish or birds think those things are food. They can get sick or die from eating plastic.

When oil from a tanker ship spills into the ocean, the oil spreads over the surface of the water and turns it black and dingy. Many of the animals that live in the ocean get sick or die. An oil spill even kills the tiny plankton. When a big accident like an oil spill happens in the ocean, lots of people work fast to clean it up, but it's a very hard job.

People can also hurt the ocean by taking too much from it. Let's say there is one kind of fish that everyone likes to eat. If lots of fishing boats go to the same place year after year to catch that one kind of fish, they might catch too many. If not enough fish are left behind to have babies, that kind of fish can become extinct. When one kind of fish disappears, it can disturb the entire habitat in that part of the ocean. Today, many states and countries have laws about fishing. These laws help take care of the ocean habitat.

This seabird is getting cleaned up after an oil spill.

# The Human Body

Have you ever thought about what happens inside your body when you breathe? When you eat? When you stand up? When you jump? When you run? Your body can do so many things! Different parts of your body work together to let you breathe, eat, stand up, jump, run, and lots more. A lot of the parts that help you do all those things are inside your body, invisible but very important. So let's find out about what's going on inside your body. Let's learn about some of the systems of your body.

# The Skeletal System

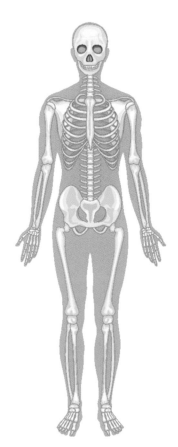

There are more than two hundred bones inside you.

Hold up a jacket by the collar. It just falls limp. Now put the jacket over a coat hanger. The hard coat hanger gives the soft jacket a shape like your shoulder.

Inside your body, there are hard things that give your body a shape. They are your bones— and your body has more than two hundred of them! They make up your *skeleton*. Your skeleton is the hard part inside your body. It looks something like the drawings you might see around Halloween time. You and all your friends and family—all human beings—have skeletons inside their bodies.

Squeeze one of your fingers: Do you feel the hard bone inside? Tap your head with your knuckles. You can hear a sound of one hard thing tapping on another. The sound you hear is the sound of your finger bones knocking against your skull, which is the bone that forms your head.

Bones are hard, but they can break. Sometimes, if a person falls too hard in the wrong direction, a bone can break. Doctors can help fix most broken bones. First they need to see where the bone is broken. They use a

> **Make a Connection**
> You can find the words to a song about the skeleton, "Dry Bones," on page 320 of this book.

This girl broke her arm. A cast will help her arm to heal.

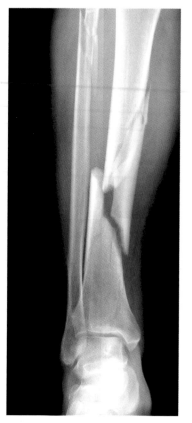

This is an X-ray of a broken leg bone.

special machine called an X-ray machine. An X-ray machine takes a picture through your skin and lets the doctor see the broken bone. Often the doctor will wrap something tight, like a cast, around the part of the body with the broken bone. That way, the pieces of bone stay straight and grow back together.

## The Muscular System

When you squeeze your arm, you can feel the solid bone inside. You feel something wrapping around it too: That is *muscle*.

Muscles wrap around bones and stretch from one bone to another. Hold one hand around your arm, between your wrist and your elbow. Make a tight fist with the arm that you're holding. Do you feel something tighten up inside? That's your muscle. See if you can do the same thing and feel your muscle in your leg and in your hand.

Thanks to your muscles, your body moves. You use your muscles to walk, run, jump, draw, stretch, and lift. You even use your muscles to talk, yawn, laugh, wink, and sing.

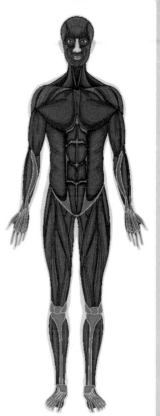

Your muscles help you move.

## The Circulatory System

Do you know how to feel your heartbeat? Put your right hand on your chest. Do you feel something going *thump-thump-thump* inside? That is your heart beating.

Here is an experiment. Run around fast until you are out of breath. Now feel your heartbeat again. It is beating harder and faster, isn't it? Your heart has been working hard while you were running.

Your heart is a muscle that keeps moving all the time, day and night. When your heart beats, it pumps blood. The blood flows through tubes that start at the heart, go all around inside your body, and then come back to your heart. By *beat-beat-beating*, your heart keeps the blood **circulating** to every part of your body. "Circulating" means going round and round. That's why

> **New Word**
> Help your child hear how the words "circle" and "circulate" sound alike. Then talk about how the blood circulates, or makes a circle starting at the heart, going through parts of the body, and coming back to the heart.

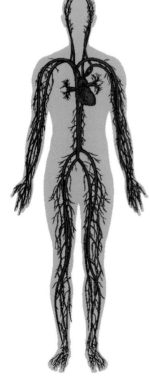

Your circulatory system moves your blood around your body.

your heart, your blood, and the tubes that carry your blood inside your body are all called the circulatory system.

## The Digestive System

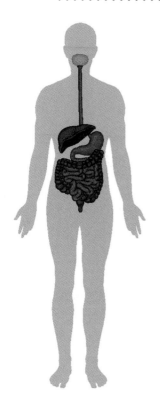

Your digestive system breaks your food down so your body can use it.

The food you eat helps your body grow and stay healthy and strong. You know what happens to your food—you put it into your mouth, eat it, and swallow it. But lots more happens after that, inside your body.

When you chew your food with your teeth, the food breaks down into little pieces. You can feel it getting softer. The inside of your mouth makes saliva, or spit, which also helps break down the food. When you swallow, the softened food goes down a tube and into your stomach. When you drink something and swallow, the liquid goes down the same tube to your stomach too.

That same work of turning the food soft and squishy keeps happening inside your body. Have you ever heard your stomach make some gurgling noises after you eat? That's the noise of your insides continuing the work of digesting your food.

Finally, the food has been broken down into very tiny bits. Some go into your blood and give you the energy you need to grow and think and do all the things you like to do. Some are extra bits of food your body cannot use. They come out of your body when you go to the bathroom.

# The Nervous System

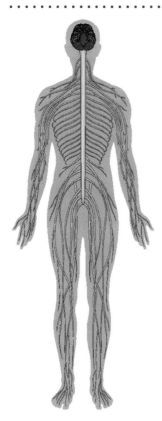

Your nervous system carries messages to and from your brain.

Remember what we call the bone in your head? That's your skull. And do you know what's inside your skull? It's a very important part of your body: your brain.

You use your brain to think, remember, talk, learn, and make decisions. Your brain is in charge: It's like the captain of a ship or the pilot of an airplane.

Your brain gets signals from the rest of your body and sends signals back, telling your body what to do. These signals are carried through the "nerves," which run throughout your body. The nerves look something like the branches of a tree, but they're *much* thinner.

When you feel an itch on the tip of your nose, nerves are sending a message from your nose to your brain. Then your brain sends a message along the nerves to your hand, saying, "Reach up and scratch my nose!" Now your nose feels better—and even that "feel better" message depends on nerves sending signals from your nose back to your brain.

sight

hearing

smell

taste          touch

**Make a Connection**

Your nerves carry messages from your five senses. Do you remember learning about your five senses (in the kindergarten book in this series)? Can you name them?

## Body Systems Working Well Together

So now you have learned about five different systems in your body. Your bones make up the skeletal system. Your muscles make up the muscular system. Your heart and the blood flowing through your body make up the circulatory system. Your mouth and stomach are important parts of the digestive system. And your brain and the nerves throughout your body make up your nervous system. When those parts work well together, you feel well.

What happens if something goes wrong? You start feeling sick. Maybe you catch a cold. Your nose gets stuffy, or you cough and sneeze a lot. Maybe you

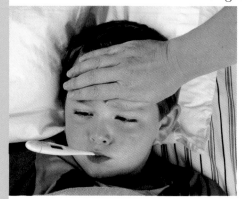

have a stomachache. You can't see the germs, but when they make you sick, your body knows it and works hard to fight them and get better. A lot of the time, when you get sick, your temperature rises and you feel hot all over. This is called a fever, and it is one of the ways your body tries to get rid of the germs making you sick.

Here is a story about a doctor who discovered an important way to help people stay well.

### Edward Jenner Discovers Vaccination

A long time ago—more than two hundred years ago—many people got sick and died from a disease called smallpox. People with smallpox would get terrible sores on their bodies, bigger and more painful than the sores children get with chicken pox today. Smallpox made people so sick some people died. But the people who got better never caught smallpox again—just as today, if you catch chicken pox once, you will never catch it again.

Doctors in those days started thinking. Maybe there was a way to deliberately make people catch a very mild case of smallpox. They might get a little sick, but they would never catch smallpox again. So doctors starting taking fluid from smallpox sores. They made a tiny cut on a well person's arm and put the fluid into the cut. Some people got sick, but many stayed well. Even when they were around people who were very sick with smallpox, they didn't catch it. Somehow that little bit of fluid had taught their bodies how to fight the disease. The question was, how could they make this idea work even better?

A boy named Edward Jenner was growing up in England at this time. When he was eight years old, he got the treatment for smallpox—and it worked. As he grew older, he became a doctor and put his mind to figuring out a treatment that worked for everyone.

One day Edward Jenner met a woman who worked at a dairy farm. She worked hard every day, milking the cows. When she heard how doctors were try-

ing to find a way to make sure no one would catch smallpox, she said she didn't need any help. "I shall never have smallpox," she told Edward Jenner, "for I have had cowpox."

Cowpox was a disease that cows got. It caused sores all over their bodies, just as smallpox caused sores on human bodies. When people got cowpox, they felt a little sick and got a few sores, but soon they got better. Edward Jenner started to think that maybe, by catching cowpox, a person could keep from catching smallpox.

Finally Jenner was ready to try an experiment. On May 14, 1796, he took fluid from a cowpox sore and put it into a cut on the arm of an eight-year-old boy named James Phipps. James got sick, but he soon got better. Now came the important and risky next step: On July 1, Jenner took fluid from a smallpox sore and put it into a cut on James's arm. For days and weeks, Jenner watched and waited. James Phipps stayed healthy. The cowpox protected him from the smallpox.

Jenner told other doctors about his discovery, but at first they didn't believe him. Jenner believed in his idea, though, and he believed so much, he even gave his own baby son cowpox germs to protect him against smallpox. Dr. Jenner called the procedure "vaccination," a word he made up from the Latin word for cow, which is *vacca*.

Today no one uses cowpox, but doctors give people vaccinations all the time. Vaccinations protect us from many serious diseases, such as polio, tuberculosis, and measles. Maybe you have been given a vaccination. If so, you have Edward Jenner to thank for inventing such a good way to keep people healthy.

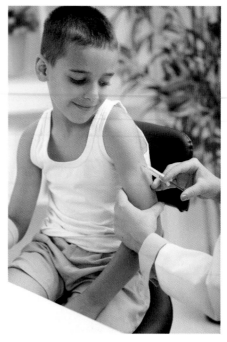

## Getting Sick and Staying Healthy

Vaccinations were an important discovery. They can keep us from getting very serious diseases. But they can't always keep us from getting everyday illnesses like colds, sore throats, or stomachaches.

Everybody gets sick now and then. Often it's germs that make your body sick. You can't see germs. They get into your body through your mouth or nose. Germs are the way that one sick person makes another person sick.

Many illnesses, like colds and flu, spread from one person to another. If a friend with a cold sneezes right in your face, his cold germs could get into your body. Then, in a few days, you might find that you have a cold like his. You caught his cold!

There are some things you can do to keep from spreading germs.

- Cover your face when you sneeze or cough.
- Use tissues when you blow your nose.
- Wash your hands after blowing your nose, after using the bathroom, and before every meal.

Your hands can pick up many germs without your even knowing it, so washing your hands often is a good rule to follow too.

As you already know, when you get sick, your body fights the germs, and sometimes when your body is working really hard to fight the germs, you get a fever. A lot of times when you are sick, just resting is a good idea. That way, your body can use all its energy to fight the germs.

Sometimes when you're sick, you go to a doctor. The doctor may use a thermometer to check your temperature. She may ask you to open your mouth wide and say, "A-a-a-a-ah," so that she can look inside your throat. She knows what a healthy throat should look like, and she is checking for signs that tell her what kind of illness you have. The doctor might use a stethoscope, which is a tool that helps her hear your heartbeat.

**All Together**
What does the inside of the throat look like? Use a mirror and a flashlight and take turns looking at each other's throat.

The doctor may decide that you need medicine to help you get better. Never take any medicine without permission, and only take the right amount at the right time, following your doctor's orders.

Sometimes the doctor may give you a shot. You may not like it, but be brave: The shot helps your body fight the disease. It might even be a vaccination to help keep you from getting sick with certain bad diseases. Vaccination shots might hurt a little, but they help you for a long time.

The best way to keep from having to take medicine is to do everything you can to stay healthy. Here is a short list of rules to follow:

- Wash your hands after using the bathroom and before every meal.
- Eat foods that are good for you.
- Get plenty of exercise.
- Take a regular bath or shower.
- Get a good night's sleep.

By following these rules, you are helping your body grow to be as strong and healthy as it can be.

All of these good health habits will help you fight germs, which is another way of saying they will help keep you healthy. Here is a story about a man who lived in France more than one hundred years ago. His work taught the world some important lessons about fighting germs.

## Louis Pasteur Invents Pasteurization

Take a look at the label on almost any carton of milk and you're likely to see the word "pasteurized" [PASS-chuh-rized]. It is a word that is made from the name of a man, Louis Pasteur [pass-TUR], whose discoveries helped the world become healthier.

Louis Pasteur was born in 1822 in a little town in France. As he grew up, he loved to paint. He loved to look at the world around him.

Louis Pasteur compared samples of different wines under his microscope. Do you know what he discovered?

He went to a university in Paris, and there he started looking at the world through a microscope. A microscope is an instrument that makes very little things look a lot bigger. Through a microscope, Louis Pasteur could see things that you cannot see by just looking with your eyes; he could look inside a drop of water and see lots of tiny living creatures swimming around. He called them "microbes" or "germs." Both words mean creatures so small we cannot see them, so small they can live in a drop of water—or inside our bodies.

One day a winemaker came into Pasteur's chemistry laboratory. "I have a problem with my wines, and I think a chemist might be able to solve it," he said. "Sometimes my wine tastes delicious, but sometimes it turns as sour as vinegar, and then I must throw it away." Louis Pasteur took samples of his wines, some good and some sour, and compared them under the microscope.

Inside the drops of sour wine, Pasteur saw some germs that he did not see in the good wine. Maybe these germs made the wine go sour, he thought. He experimented with different ways to kill the germs. He tried freezing the wine. He tried sending electricity through the wine. And he tried making the wine get really hot, which seemed to work best. So the winemaker started heating his wine before he put it into bottles, and every bottle of wine tasted good. Heating the wine killed the germs that made it go sour.

Soon farmers in dairies tried heating their cows' milk before they put it into bottles. It was a success! Heating the milk kept it from going sour so quickly. People named the process after the man who invented it. They called it pasteurization—heating a liquid to kill harmful germs in it. The milk you drink today has probably been pasteurized.

Louis Pasteur kept studying the germs he could look at under the microscope. He began to think that many times when people got sick, it was because bad germs got into their bodies, just as bad germs got into the wine or the milk. We have learned a lot more about what causes disease since Pasteur was alive, but we still agree with him that many illnesses are caused when tiny living things get inside our bodies. We can get better by fighting germs, and we can stay well by keeping germs away.

## Matter

. . . . . . . . . . . . . . . . . . . . . . . . . . . . . . . . . . . . . . . . . . . . . . . . . . . . . . . . . .

One day a sick little boy named Joseph Meister came into Pasteur's laboratory. His parents knew a dog had bitten him, and they were sure he had rabies. "We know we are taking a risk, letting you experiment on Joseph," they said, "but he will die of rabies soon unless you try your medicine." Joseph Meister was the first person to receive a rabies vaccine—and it worked. In just weeks he was well again.

Today we have many reasons to thank Louis Pasteur for his good ideas. Our milk and many other drinks are pasteurized and stay fresh. Our pets get rabies vaccines to keep them healthy. And we understand that, since germs can make us sick, we should do our best to stay clean and healthy and keep the germs away.

Close your eyes and imagine this:

Take a big bite of a juicy apple.

Take a drink of cool, clear water.

Take a deep breath and feel the air fill you up inside.

Now open your eyes and think about this riddle: What do these three things have in common: the apple, the water, and the air we breathe?

Did you say they are all going into your body? That's true. Anything else? They all make you healthy. There is one more important way that these three things are alike. They are all made of "matter."

## The World Is Made of Matter

Matter is the stuff that makes up all the things in the world. Your shoes, a flower, an egg, a dog, a rock, a tire, a book, a cloud, a goldfish, a jet plane, a pencil, a glass and the orange juice in it: Matter makes up all these things, and everything else as well. Matter even makes up your body.

Let's go back to the riddle and think about what is different about these three things: the apple, the water, and the air.

You can see and touch the matter in an apple. It's *solid*. Can you think of some other matter that's solid? How about a rock? A baseball? Your shoes?

You can see and touch the matter in the water too, but it's not solid. It's not hard, like a rock or an apple. It's *liquid*. Can you think of some other matter that's liquid? Such as juice? Or the saliva in your mouth?

Now, what about the air we breathe? Is it solid? No. Is it liquid? No. You can't see it. You can't reach out and touch it. But sometimes you can feel it, like when

When you blow on a dandelion, what happens? Your breath, air, is matter, and it pushes against the seeds. Sometimes they even fly off!

the wind blows. When you feel the wind blowing on your face, you are feeling the matter in the air. And think about this: When you blow up a balloon, what goes inside? Some stuff goes into the balloon and makes it grow bigger and bigger. That stuff is air, and air is matter. But air is not a solid and not a liquid. Air is a *gas*.

All matter, everything in the world, is made up of teeny-tiny bits called "atoms." Atoms are too small to see. How small? Think about this: Millions of atoms could fit on the period at the end of this sentence. That's how small!

The atoms in a solid are close together. That's what makes an apple feel hard.

The atoms in a liquid are farther apart. That's why you can stick your finger into the water, and that's why, when you pour water into a glass, it takes the shape of that glass.

The atoms in a gas are even farther apart. That's why it's hard to see and feel the air, even though it is made of matter.

## Changing States of Matter

Matter can be a solid, a liquid, or a gas. Scientists call those the three **states** of matter. Matter can change from one state to another. A solid can become a liquid. A liquid can become a gas. You already know this, because you have seen it happen all the time. You just didn't think about it quite this way.

> **New Word**
> Now, "states" here doesn't mean a place like Florida or California or Ohio. This kind of "state" means the way something is. Your mother might ask you, "What state is your room in right now?"

Water can be a solid, a liquid, or a gas. Can you point to and name each of them in this picture?

Here is a glass. Let's fill it with water. (You can do this for real, or you can look at these pictures.)

What state of matter is the water in? It's a liquid.

But let's say you take that glass of water and you put it in the freezer overnight. What is going to happen? The water will freeze into ice. It's still water, but now what state of matter is the water in? It's hard, isn't it? It's a solid.

How can we make that solid turn into a liquid? Or, to ask the question another way, how can we turn that solid ice back into liquid water?

We can let the ice melt. If we take the glass of ice out of the freezer and let it sit on the counter for a few hours, the solid will turn into a liquid.

Now if we take that liquid water, pour it into a pan, and heat it up on the stove, what happens? The water begins to boil. It bubbles and moves around. It also starts to rise up out of the pan as steam. It's still water, but now what state of matter is it in? The liquid water has turned to gas. (Be careful if you do this experiment in your own kitchen. Steam is very hot!)

If you boil the water for a long time, it will all turn to steam and the pan will be empty. Where has the water gone? It has been turned into a gas—steam—and has mixed with the air in the room. Now the water is part of the matter that makes up the air in the room.

## Measuring Matter

Now you know one important question to ask when you are studying things: Is this a solid, a liquid, or a gas?

Some other important questions have to do with numbers. How many of these things are there? Or how much of that stuff? How much does something weigh? How big is that thing we are studying? To find out the answers to all these kinds of questions, we need to take some measurements.

What is this boy measuring?

How many years old are you? How many inches tall are you? How many pounds do you weigh? The answers to all those questions come as numbers. They are all measurements.

## Why Measurements Matter

When you bake a cake, you use many measurements. You use a pan that is the right size, and you heat the oven to the right temperature. You also measure out each ingredient.

Here's a recipe for chocolate cake. But something is wrong with it.

| | |
|---|---|
| 1 sugar | 4 eggs |
| 1 butter | 4 chocolate |
| 1 milk | 3 baking powder |
| ½ salt | 2 flour |

Mix the sugar and margarine together in a large bowl until soft. Add all other ingredients; then put mixture in a pan 13 long and 9 wide. Bake at 350 for 45.

Do you see what's wrong with the recipe? Could you mix and bake this cake? You would begin by measuring out one—one what?—of sugar. One teaspoon? One cup? One *ton*?! The cake will taste very different depending on how much sugar you put in.

Is the pan 13 inches long and 9 inches wide, or 13 miles long and 9 miles wide? Inches and miles are both units for measuring length.

Do we bake it for 45 minutes or 45 days or 45 years? Minutes, days, and years are all units for measuring time.

Now do you see what's wrong with the recipe? Somebody forgot to write in the *units of measurement*. Measuring means counting, but you have to know *what* you're counting. To make sense, every measurement needs a number and a unit.

Let's look at the cake recipe as it should be, with numbers *and* units of measurement:

1 cup sugar

1 stick butter

1 cup milk

½ teaspoon salt

4 eggs

4 ounces chocolate

3 teaspoons baking

   powder

2 cups flour

Mix the sugar and butter together in a large bowl until soft. Add all other ingredients; then put the mixture in a pan 13 inches long and 9 inches wide. Bake at 350 degrees Fahrenheit for 45 minutes.

Now, that makes more sense. Sounds yummy too!

## How Long? How Tall? How Much?

**PARENTS:** Find a ruler to use while reading this section.

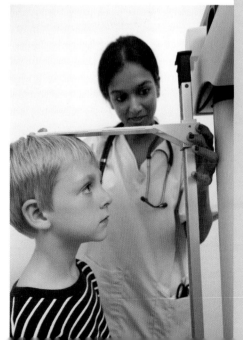

Do you know how tall you are? The answer to that question will come with a number and a word for a unit of length. It could be feet, or it could be inches, or it could be both feet and inches.

A handy way to measure things in your house (including you) is to use a ruler. Most rulers are twelve inches long. Twelve inches equal one foot, so you can also say that most rulers are a foot long.

You can see the big marks next to the numbers, 1, 2, 3, all the way up to 12. The distance between each mark on the ruler is one inch. The inches are all the same. There are little marks between the big ones. They measure parts of inches.

Some rulers also have centimeters marked on them. A centimeter is another unit used to measure length and height. It is even smaller than an inch.

Let's use the ruler to measure some things. Get a spoon from the kitchen, and put it right alongside the ruler. Make the end of the spoon match up with the end of the ruler. How many inches does it measure? That's how long the spoon is.

Now let's figure out how tall you are. Do you think we will measure in inches? That would take a lot of inches! Measuring in feet is a better idea.

Feet, inches, and centimeters measure length. But what if you're at the grocery store and you need to decide how much milk to buy? What units of measurement could you use? You wouldn't buy eight feet of milk, or eight inches of milk, or eight centimeters of milk. You are not measuring how long the milk is but *how much space it takes up*.

**Do It Yourself**

Help your child measure things around the house. What will you use as a unit of measure? Your hand? Your child's hand? A paper clip? A ruler? Find many things to measure using a few different units of measure.

We can use many different units to measure how much space something takes up. For example, when you shop for milk, you can buy a quart or a gallon. You could also buy four quarts, but it would be easier just to buy one gallon: That's because four quarts is the same amount as one gallon.

Every gallon jug holds the same amount of milk. Even if they have different shapes or different labels, all gallon containers hold the same amount—one gallon—and we all agree on how much one gallon is.

## How Much? Cups, Quarts, and Gallons

When you pick up a cup and hold it out, politely asking for a cup of milk, you know how much you are going to get. You'll get the amount that fits inside that cup. But when you follow the recipe for chocolate cake and it tells you to put in one cup of flour and one cup of milk, how do you know which cup to fill? A big cup or a little cup? The same cup for flour and milk, or different ones?

Here is the answer to those questions. As with gallons, we have all agreed on how much one cup is. One cup of flour fills up the same amount of space as one cup of milk. One cup is a unit of measurement we have all agreed on. When you follow a recipe that calls for one cup of flour and one cup of milk, you know how much of each to put in, because you and the person who wrote the recipe both agree on how much a cup is.

The other thing we have all agreed on is how many cups make a quart and how many quarts make a gallon. Let's figure that out. Here is an experiment to do outside, or in the bathtub, or someplace where it's fine to splash some water.

First, get your equipment together. Here is what you need:

- a 1-cup measuring cup
- a 1-quart container (such as an empty quart container for milk or a quart jar)
- a 1-gallon container (such as an empty gallon container for milk)
- a funnel (if you have one)

Find the line labeled "1 cup" on your measuring cup. Pour in water up to that line. That is a cup of water.

Now carefully pour the cup of water into the quart container. Do this again and again until the quart container is full.

How many times did you do that before the quart container was full? Four times. This shows you that four cups of water and one quart are the same. Four cups equal one quart.

Now let's do the same thing to find out how many quarts you need to fill the gallon container.

How many times did you have to pour a quart of water in to fill the gallon? Four times. So now you see that four quarts equal a gallon.

## How Hot? How Cold? Measuring Temperature

**PARENTS:** In this book, we introduce temperature only as measured in degrees Fahrenheit. Later books in this series will introduce your child to both degrees Fahrenheit and Celsius.

Before you get in the bathtub, do you stick your finger or toes into the water to see if it's too hot, too cold, or just right? That's your way of checking the temperature of the water in the tub. But fingers and toes aren't always a good way to measure temperature. Would you use your finger to make sure the oven was hot enough to bake a cake? Would you use your toes to find out how cold it was on a snowy day outside? For those sorts of things, we use a thermometer. Thermometers help us measure the temperature in units called degrees.

You might have seen a thermometer already in the doctor's office. Most times, when you visit the doctor, a nurse uses a thermometer to take your temperature—to measure the temperature inside your body. If you're healthy, your temperature will be about 98.6 degrees. If you're sick and have a fever, your temperature might be a little over 100 degrees. We use different kinds of thermometers to measure the temperatures of different things: your body, the oven, the air outside.

> **Make a Connection**
> Look at the picture on page 408. When we are sick, a thermometer is used to measure our body temperature. If it is too warm, we have a fever.

If your body temperature is 98.6 degrees, do you think the temperature of the air inside your home is higher or lower? Probably lower! Most people like to be in a building with a temperature of about 70 degrees. On a summer's day, when it is *really* hot, the temperature outside just *might* get up to 98.6 degrees or higher. We would not enjoy living in a house that stayed that hot.

On a winter's day, when it is *really* cold, we say the temperature has gone "below freezing." That's because water freezes when it gets colder than 32 degrees. When it gets *really, REALLY* cold, the temperature even goes "below zero." That's when the temperature outside drops from 32 degrees to 20, to 10, and even colder. If someone tells you it's 10 degrees below zero, then you know *that's cold*!

# Electricity: An Introduction to the Shocking Facts

Look around the room and see how many things you can turn on and off. Is there a light with a light switch? Is there a radio, or a television, or maybe a computer? Is there a toy that moves or makes noise when you turn it on?

All of these things use *electricity*. Electricity is the power that makes them work. Electricity makes them shine, beep, play music, show pictures, make noise, or move around.

## Static Electricity

Everything in the world, even your body, carries a little bit of electricity in it. Have you ever combed your hair and noticed the hairs on your head standing up as you pulled the comb away? That's electricity. Have you ever rubbed a balloon against your shirt, then pressed it against the wall and watched it stick? That's electricity too.

There's a special name for this force that attracts your hair toward a comb and a balloon toward the wall. It's called *static electricity*. Maybe you have walked across a room and touched a doorknob or somebody's hand and felt a little *zap*! That also happens because of static electricity. If it happens in a dark room, you might see a tiny flash of light. That zap of static electricity works the same way as a lightning bolt streaking through the sky in a thunderstorm. But the lightning bolt is *a lot* more powerful!

**Make a Connection**

Do you know about Ben Franklin's famous experiment with lightning and electricity? You can read about it on page 249 in this book.

## Turn It On, Turn It Off: Electricity

When you turn on a light, you are letting electricity flow through wires to the lightbulb. The electricity probably starts from a factory miles away, where big machines generate the electricity and send it through wires to your house and many others, and your school, and lots of other places in your neighborhood.

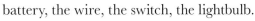

A big power company makes the electricity used in this home.

Look at the picture below to see a very simple model that will help you see what happens when you turn on a light. There are four parts in this model. Can you point to each of them? The battery, the wire, the switch, the lightbulb.

Let's talk about what each part does.

The battery is like a little electric power factory. It uses chemicals to make electricity. (But *never* try to open a battery! The chemicals inside could hurt you.)

The wire goes from one end of the battery to a switch, and then from the switch to the lightbulb, and then from the lightbulb back to the other end of the battery.

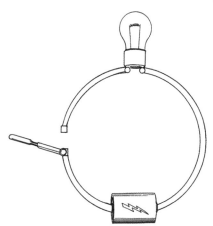

**New Word**

What is a circuit?
Think about the
word *circle*. Does
*circuit* sound a lot
like *circle*? How
might an electrical
circuit be like a
circle?

Electricity will flow through the wire only when the wire is connected to both ends of the battery—only when there is a complete **circuit** made from battery to lightbulb and back to battery again.

Let's follow the electricity on its path. The electricity from the battery flows through the wire, kind of like water flowing through a hose. When the electricity gets to the switch, what happens? It all depends on whether the switch is turned "off" or "on." If the switch is "on," then the electricity can continue along its path to the bulb. But if the switch is "off," then the path is broken and the electricity will not flow to the bulb.

Here's a way to imagine what is happening. Let's say you are walking along a path. You come to a river, but there's no bridge across the river, so you can't keep going.

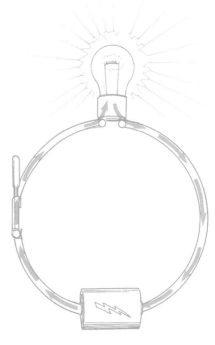

Now let's pretend you walk along that path and come to the river, and there *is* a bridge. Now there's no break in the path, and you can continue on your way.

That's what happens with electricity. As it travels along the wire, it comes to the switch. If the switch is turned "off," it's as if there's no bridge across the river. The electricity cannot continue along the path to the lightbulb.

But when the switch is turned "on," it's as if there is a bridge. The electricity can keep right on going through the turned-on switch to the bulb. And when electricity reaches the bulb, the light comes on.

Next time you flip a switch to turn on the light, you will know what is happening to make the light come on.

## What Conducts Electricity?

Our model used wires to help electricity flow from the battery to the lightbulb. Most electrical wires are made of copper covered in plastic. (But don't try to take the plastic off! It is wrapped around the wire so the electricity doesn't hurt you.)

Do you think we could substitute a piece of yarn or a piece of spaghetti? No, they wouldn't work as substitutes for electrical wires, because electricity flows through some materials but not through others.

Materials that allow electricity to flow through them are called *conductors*. They "conduct," or carry, electricity through them. Copper is a very good conductor of electricity, which is why it is the material used for electrical wires. Yarn and spaghetti are not good conductors.

Here is an experiment that you and a parent can do to find out what you have around the house that conducts electricity. Begin by collecting your equipment:

**PARENTS:** This experiment will require your time and assistance. The components of a simple tabletop electrical system like the one described below are often available at electronics and hobby shops. The image on the next page demonstrates how these materials may be configured.

- 2 D batteries
- a double battery holder
- a lightbulb
- a lightbulb holder
- 3 8-inch lengths of electrical wire
- 2 alligator clips
- various household items, such as a pencil, a shoelace, a metal spoon, a plastic utensil, a piece of paper, a safety pin, a crayon, a rubber band, a penny, a paper clip

Begin by connecting the batteries, the bulb, the wires, and the alligator clips as shown in the picture.

Now test your circuit. Clip the two alligator clips together. If you have built the circuit correctly, the lightbulb should light up. When the alligator clips touch, you are making a pathway going from the batteries, through the lightbulb, and back to the batteries again. Now pull the alligator clips apart. What happens? Why does the light go out?

You can use this system to test and see what things are good conductors of electricity. To test an item, clip on to one end of the item with an alligator clip, then clip on to the other end with the other alligator clip. Do not clip the alligator clips to yourself! Electrical safety is discussed below.

If the object you are testing is a good conductor, you will complete the circuit. The electricity will flow from the batteries, through the wires, through the object you are testing, to the bulb. If the object conducts electricity, the bulb will light up.

Here are some ideas of objects to try. Do they conduct electricity or not? Keep a list of what you learn.

| | Conducts | Does Not Conduct |
|---|---|---|
| stuffed animal | ☐ | ☐ |
| spoon | ☐ | ☐ |
| pencil | ☐ | ☐ |
| sock | ☐ | ☐ |
| paper clip | ☐ | ☐ |

## Stay Safe Around Electricity

. . . . . . . . . . . . . . . . . . . . . . . . . . . . . . . . . . . . . . . . . . . . . . . . . . . . .

We use electricity every day. It provides the power for cars, lights, machines, TVs, computers, and so much more. It is very useful—but it is also very powerful, and it can be dangerous. A little battery puts out a little bit of electricity, so you can use it safely for your experiments. But the electricity that comes through the wires in your house or school is *much* more powerful, so you need to remember some safety rules.

Inside the walls where you live or go to school, there are big wires that carry electricity. When you plug in a light or computer or other electrical appliance, you are completing a circuit and sending electricity through the wire.

You probably already know the rule "Don't stick your finger into the electrical outlet!" Now you know why that's important. If a person sticks a finger or something metal into the outlet, that person becomes a conductor and completes the electrical pathway. Your body is a pretty good conductor of electricity. The electrical current coming through the outlet would hurt *a lot* if it tried to use your body as a conductor.

Another rule you may have heard is: "Don't touch any electrical appliance when you are wet." Now you can understand why. Water is an excellent conductor of electricity. When your hands are wet or when your body is in a bathtub full of water, your wet body would be an especially good conductor. The electricity could flow right through you and give you an awful shock. It could even kill you.

Electricity is very useful, but it can be dangerous. Be careful, be safe, be smart. Let electricity help you, not hurt you.


## Thomas Edison

. . . . . . . . . . . . . . . . . . . . . . . . . . . . . . . . . . . . . . . . . . . . . . . . . . . . .

Do you like to listen to music? Do you turn on the lights after dark so you can see? Do you talk on the telephone? For all these things, we have a great inventor to thank. His name was Thomas Edison.

Edison was born in 1847, more than one hundred sixty years ago, at a time when people had none of these things we all use today. People had no radios, no CDs, no electric lights, no telephones. For music, people played instruments and sang together. People lit candles or lanterns to see in the dark. People wrote letters to tell their friends their news.

The one way people could send news to people far away was with a machine called the telegraph. To use the telegraph, you had to learn a special code. For every letter in the alphabet, there was a special combination of short or long sounds. The letter "S" was made with three short sounds: *dot-dot-dot*. The letter "O" was made with three long sounds: *dash-dash-dash*. These coded sounds traveled through electrical wires from one telegraph machine to another. Someone at the other end of the wires listened to the sounds coming through the telegraph, wrote them down, and turned them back into the letters of the alphabet so they could spell the words and understand the message.

Young Thomas Edison worked as a telegraph operator, but he thought all the time about how he could make the telegraph work better. Ever since he was young, he had loved to experiment with chemicals, batteries, and wires. He was fascinated by electricity. He began to invent new machines. He figured out how to send lots of messages all at the same time through the same telegraph wires. He made such good inventions that he decided to build a science laboratory in Menlo Park, New Jersey, where he and other inventors could make new things using electricity.

Thomas Edison

One day Edison invited his friends into his lab to see a new invention. It looked like a big metal drum with a handle. He turned the handle, and as he did so he said, "Mary had a little lamb." He adjusted the machine, then turned the handle again. The machine made a noise, then it played back the words "Mary had a little lamb"! Thomas Edison had invented a way to use electricity to record sound. Today we have iPods and CDs, and we are surrounded by recorded music and talking. But it was a strange, new, and wonderful thing when Edison was alive. People were so amazed at what Thomas Edison had invented, they began calling him "the Wizard of Menlo Park."

Next, Edison put his mind to the problem of making light with electricity. For hundreds of years, people had been using candles or lamps that burned oil. Candles and lamps made light, but they were not very safe or clean.

Thomas Edison asked a glassblower to make him a round bulb with a long neck. Inside the bulb he placed a thin wire. He connected the wire to a source of electricity. The wire glowed—but then it burned out, very fast. It did not work as an electric light. For months everything he tried would not work, but Edison didn't give up. He kept on trying until he found the right choice of wires. He sent electricity through a specific wire in a bulb, and the electricity lit up the wire— and it didn't burn out! Thomas Edison had invented the lightbulb.

Thomas Edison didn't stop there. His mind jumped to another project. He thought, "If I can record sound, perhaps I can record pictures too." He invented a machine that shone light through pictures and projected the pictures onto a wall. He figured out how to change the pictures very fast, and it looked as if the pictures on the wall were moving. Moving pictures—that was what people first called movies. The very first movie was really short, and it showed a man sneezing. Not very exciting for us today, but for people in that time it was just amazing. They watched that man sneeze over and over.

Sound recordings, electric lights, and the motion picture: These are considered Thomas Edison's most important inventions. But they are only three of the more than *one thousand* things he invented! What a genius!

But as Edison himself said, "Genius is one percent inspiration and ninety-nine percent perspiration." In other words, good ideas, or inspiration, is important, but working hard, or perspiration, is even more important.

# Astronomy: Our Solar System

Let's pretend you are an astronaut. Pull on your space suit, climb into the space-ship, strap into your seat, and 5 . . . 4 . . . 3 . . . 2 . . . 1—*blast off!*

Now you are flying way, way up, high above Earth. You keep going up and up, far into space.

Now you can look back and see where you started on planet Earth. And this is what our planet looks like: Earth looks like a big round ball in the air. How do we know? Because an astronaut used a camera to take this picture from way up in space!

## Our Sun and Our Solar System

Let's come back down to Earth for a minute and think how wonderful it feels on a sunny day. You can feel the warmth of the sun on your cheeks. Sunlight makes everything bright and colorful.

It's hard to look straight at the sun on a bright, sunny day. But early in the morning or at the end of the day, there are times when you can look at the sun. What does it look like?

The **sun** may look like a big round ball in the air, something like the photograph of Earth taken by an astronaut. But there is a big difference between the sun and the Earth. Earth is a planet, but the sun is a star, like many of the stars that you see shining in the sky on a clear night. What makes the sun different from those other stars? The big difference is that the sun is closer to us than any other star.

The sun is Earth's star, and, even though you can't feel it, the Earth is going

around the sun all the time. It takes one year for the Earth to circle around the sun in its **orbit**.

Earth is not the only planet going around the sun. There are seven others.

Earth, those seven other planets, and the sun make up our solar system. You would have to travel far, far out in space in order to see the whole solar system, with the sun in the middle and all the planets going around it. Each planet circles around the sun in its own orbit.

## A Journey Through the Solar System

Let's take an imaginary rocket-ship journey. We'll start near the sun, at the center of our solar system, and move out from there. This really is an imaginary ride, because the sun is a huge ball of superhot burning gases. It's so hot, you could never fly close to it. Your rocket would melt long before it could land. But we will pretend you start at the sun and fly out to each planet orbiting it.

As you fly away from the sun, what's the first planet you see? It's the planet Mercury. Mercury is a small planet, and it's the closest planet to the sun.

Keep flying, and next you come to Venus, the second planet from the sun.

After that, you see the third planet from the sun—and it looks very familiar! It's Earth, your home planet. Earth is ninety-three million miles from the sun. That sounds far, but five more planets are even farther away. Let's keep going!

As you move out from the sun, you see Mercury, Venus, Earth, Mars, Jupiter, Saturn, Uranus, and Neptune.

Mars

The fourth planet from the sun is Mars. Some people nickname Mars "the red planet" because, when you are lucky enough to see it in the nighttime sky, it seems to have an orangey-red color.

Next comes Jupiter, the fifth planet from the sun. Jupiter is the largest planet in our solar system.

The sixth planet out is Saturn. There's something unusual about this planet. It is surrounded with beautiful rings.

The next two planets, Uranus and Neptune, like Jupiter and Saturn, are very large compared with Earth. They are far, far, far away from Earth. How far? More than a billion miles away—a distance so huge it's hard to imagine.

Saturn

## The Moon

We have talked about the planets, and we have talked about the sun, and we have even talked a little bit about the stars. But there is one great big thing you can see in the sky at night that we haven't talked about. What are we missing? It's the moon.

You already know a lot about the moon. It's round, sort of like Earth. It's big—bigger than anything else we see in the sky. That's because it's the closest to us. The moon that you see in the sky goes around the Earth. It orbits the Earth, just as the Earth and the other planets orbit the sun.

But the moon doesn't always look round, does it? Have you noticed that it seems to change shape? Sometimes it's a full moon, with a big round face. Sometimes it's a half-moon, shaped like a big slice of watermelon. Sometimes it's only a thin crescent. And some nights we don't see the moon at all. When this happens, we call it a "new moon." All these different shapes are called the phases of the moon.

The moon only *seems* to change shape. Really, it's always a big round ball.

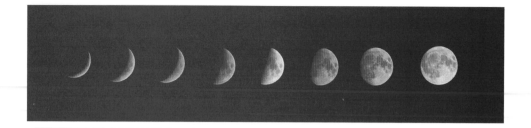

Sometimes we see one whole side of the moon, and sometimes we see only part of it. We see the part that is lit by the sun. In fact, the only reason we see the moon at all is because the sun lights it. When the moon seems to shine, it's really reflecting light from the sun.

Sometimes when the moon is bright and big in the sky, it almost looks as if it has a face. People even call that face "the man in the moon," but the fact is, there are no people on the moon. There are no animals or plants either. The moon may look lovely, but it's not a friendly place to visit.

An astronaut puts the American flag on the moon.

Astronauts have traveled from Earth and visited the moon. They had to wear special space suits to walk on the moon, so they could breathe. They had to go back into their spaceship for food and water. They didn't stay on the moon for very long. They returned to Earth in their spaceship.

So far, astronauts have visited the moon, but no one has landed on another planet. Not yet, at least. Who knows what may happen by the time you grow up? Maybe astronauts will make a trip to Mars. Maybe you will be one of them!

## Constellations: Connect-the-Dot Stars

For thousands of years, people have looked up in wonder at the stars. And long ago, people used their imaginations and found pictures among the stars, like big connect-the-dots drawings. They imagined they saw a bear, a flying horse, a dragon, and a man shooting an arrow. We still enjoy finding those connect-the-dot pictures today. They are called the constellations.

Here's a constellation you can look for: the Big Dipper. It got that name because it looks like a pan with a long handle, the kind you would use to dip water out of a bucket. On a clear night, ask an adult to help you look north. In that direction, look for four stars that you can connect in your imagination to form a pan. Then look for three more bright stars that seem to connect to one corner of the pan and form a handle. There are a lot of other stars in the sky near these, but if you just concentrate on the brightest ones, you can see the Big Dipper.

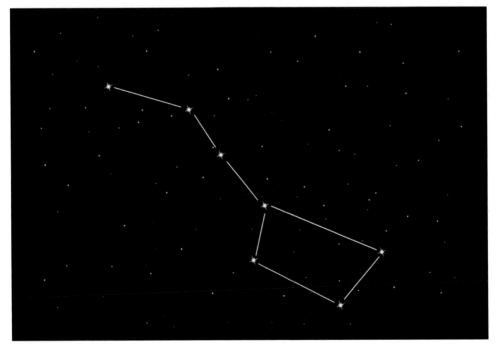

The Big Dipper

## Our Big, Round, Moving Planet

Photographs taken from outer space show that the Earth is a big, round ball. But from here on Earth, it doesn't seem round, does it? The Earth is so large, you can't see how its surface curves.

But if you could stand on a shore and watch a boat sail straight out into the ocean, where there's nothing but water as far as the eye can see, you would get a sense of how the Earth is round. You would see the boat sailing toward the horizon, which is what we call the line where the sky meets the sea. Then the boat would seem to disappear over the horizon. Finally you would see just the very top of the boat, and then even that would go out of sight below the horizon. The boat didn't go away. It just went around the globe to a part you cannot see.

As it sails away, a boat seems to sink below the horizon.

Try this: Stand up and be as still as you can. It doesn't feel as if the ground beneath your feet is moving, does it? But in fact the Earth is spinning around all the time. It spins like a top. And that's not all. As the Earth spins around like a top, it is also circling through space in an orbit around the sun. Whoa, we're really moving here!

Hundreds of years ago, people believed that the sun went around the Earth. It's easy to see why people thought so, because the sun does seem to travel slowly across the sky, from morning to night. But a man named Nicolaus Copernicus [nick-uh-LAY-us kup-ERN-ick-us] showed people that they had it backward.

The sun doesn't move around the Earth, said Copernicus. People may talk about the sun rising in the morning and setting in the evening, but it's the Earth that does the moving, like a top. Earth spins around once every day, or once every twenty-four hours.

That's what makes day and night.

The earth spins like a top.

**Do It Yourself**

You can help your child visualize night and day with a bright desk lamp, a globe, and a chunk of clay. Put half the clay on the globe where you live and the other half on a point of land around the world. In a dark room, shine the light directly on the globe to show that when your part of the world is in daylight, the other is in darkness, and vice versa. Spin the globe to show how daytime turns to night and back again.

# Our Planet Earth

You already know a lot of things about our home planet, called Earth. You know that it is shaped like a big, round ball. You know that its surface is covered with land (the continents) and water (the oceans).

Now imagine a line around the Earth, just like a big belt around its middle. That imaginary line is called the **equator**. The sun always shines strongly at the equator, so the land and oceans near the equator stay warm all year round. The rain forest habitats we read about before (see page 390) are all near the equator, for example.

Now imagine putting one finger at the very top and another finger at the very bottom of the Earth. These two places are called Earth's poles. The *North Pole* is on top. The *South Pole* is on the bottom. The sun never shines as directly at the poles as it does at the equator, so the land and oceans near the poles stay cold all year round. In fact, there's a lot of snow and ice at the poles all year long.

If you look at a globe, you might think that when people visit the South Pole, they stand upside down. But in fact, standing at the South Pole feels just like standing in your own neighborhood—feet down, head up, only much, much colder!

## Inside the Earth

Have you ever started digging a hole and wondered how far you could go? What would it be like to dig and dig and keep digging down into the Earth?

Scientists have used special equipment to drill deep down into the Earth, through many layers of dirt and rock and other things. That is one of the ways that they have learned about what's inside this planet of ours.

The outermost layer is called the "crust." That's the surface of the Earth, the part we live and walk on. Mountains and valleys, riverbeds and deserts, ocean floors and continents make up the Earth's crust. The crust is a thin outer coating, sort of like the skin of a peach or an apple, compared to what is inside.

Beneath the crust lies a thick layer of hot, melted rock called the "mantle." The deeper the mantle, the hotter it gets. In the middle is Earth's core, made of red-hot liquid and a ball of solid metal.

No one has ever traveled through the Earth's mantle to the core. No one would want to! It gets as hot as 7,000 degrees down there—so hot that the rocks are melted. Then how do we know what it's like? Sometimes holes open in the Earth's crust. When these holes open, hot gas and liquid can escape from deep down in the Earth. They give us clues about what it is like deep down in the mantle of the Earth.

At some of those places, boiling-hot steam shoots high up into the air.

can see the layers of the earth in this image. From the inside out, you the inner core, outer core, mantle, and crust.

That is called a "geyser." The most famous geyser in the United States is named "Old Faithful." It is in Yellowstone National Park in the state of Wyoming. Very regularly, about once an hour, Old Faithful shoots out more than ten thousand gallons of water—boiling hot, so it's steam. It shoots one hundred fifty feet up or higher, far above the tops of the trees that stand around it.

At other places, red-hot melted rock bursts out through the holes in Earth's crust. That is called a "volcano." Volcanoes give us an idea of what it's like beneath the Earth's crust. We know that the melted rock comes from deep down inside the Earth's mantle layer. When a volcano erupts, hot melted rock called lava spurts out through the top of a mountain. The lava can travel in fiery streams down the mountainside, burning everything in its path.

Sometimes a volcano can erupt, then remain quiet for many years, and then erupt again. In 1980, Mount St. Helens erupted in the state of Washington. People knew that the mountain was a volcano, but it hadn't erupted for more than

one hundred years. When a volcano erupts, the people who live near it have to move away. When they come back, everything has been burned by the red-hot lava.

## Earth and Its Rocks

It's hard to imagine that rocks could get so hot that they would melt. They seem so hard and solid.

The next time you have a chance, pick up a handful of rocks and look at them. You'll notice how different rocks can be. Some seem all one color, while others are streaked or speckled. Some are dark, some are light, and some you can almost see through, like looking through a foggy glass. Some are smooth, while others are rough and jagged.

Earth's surface contains many different rocks, and each one has a name:

granite, limestone, sandstone, marble, and many more. Scientists group rocks according to how they were formed. There are three kinds of rocks:

- igneous [IG-nee-us]
- sedimentary [sed-ih-MEN-tuh-ree]
- metamorphic [met-uh-MORE-fik]

**Make a Connection**
Look at the picture of the Sphinx on page 173. The Great Sphinx is made from sandstone.

**All Together**
Say the three words that name types of rock together so your child becomes familiar with them. She does not need to memorize them or the names of the rocks in each category, however.

Let's see what those three words mean.

Igneous means "made by fire." Granite is one of the most common igneous rocks. It is made underground, where it's very hot. Some igneous rocks come from volcanoes. Volcanoes have been erupting on Earth for millions of years. Whenever lava flows out, it cools and hardens into rock. Pumice is an igneous rock that's full of little holes. Even though pumice is a rock, it floats in water!

Sedimentary means "made by settling down." Sometimes—often underwater in the ocean or a riverbed—lots of little rocks settle down on top of one another. Over thousands and thousands of years, they

Marble

Sandstone

press down until they form one big rock. Sandstone is a sedimentary rock. You can see and feel the grains of sand that settled down together to form sandstone.

Metamorphic means "made through change." Deep inside the Earth, powerful forces and superhot heat are squeezing and cooking and changing the material down there. For example, these forces can change limestone, which is a sedimentary rock. Deep in the Earth, limestone gets heated and squeezed and changed into another kind of rock, called marble. Marble is a metamorphic rock: It was made through change. Marble is often used for walls and stairs and columns in big buildings. Artists like to make sculptures out of marble too. Marble has beautiful streaks of color, formed over a long time through changes that happened to it deep underground.

**What About You?**

Take a nature hike together and collect rocks. Bring them home and sort them by color. Ask your child to choose her favorite. Look closely together and see the different colors and patterns visible in the rocks you find.

## Earth's Minerals

An uncut diamond (center) looks very different from what you find in jewelry.

Just as it takes different ingredients to bake a cake, it also takes different ingredients for the Earth to make rocks. These ingredients are called "minerals." There are many different minerals on Earth. Some of them you already know, and some of them you may never have heard of.

Gold and silver are minerals. You might think of gold as belonging in a ring or a necklace, or you might think of silver as belonging in a coin or a fork or spoon. But all the gold and silver in the world started out as bits of mineral in the ground.

Just like gold and silver, diamonds can be seen in fancy jewelry, but all the diamonds in the world are minerals that came from the Earth. When people first find diamonds in the Earth, they don't look that pretty. It takes a lot of work to make them sparkle. People use diamonds in many important ways, not only

**Make a Connection**

Your child is learning to name the shape "diamond" as he learns geometry (page 364). Talk together about why that shape was named after the mineral. Do they have that shape when they come out of the ground? Do they have that shape after people have worked on them to make them sparkle?

in jewelry. Diamonds are harder than any other rock or mineral, so people use diamonds to cut other rocks!

Quartz is a mineral. Quartz is much more common than gold or silver or diamonds. In many places, you can find quartz lying on the ground. Quartz comes in many forms, such as white quartz, rose quartz, amethyst, and tiger's eye. Sometimes you can find a big piece of quartz. Sometimes you find little tiny pieces of quartz, like grains of sand.

People use minerals in many ways. We *mine* minerals, which means we dig them out of the ground in order to be able to use them. For example, we mine the mineral called halite, then use it to make salt for our food. We mine the mineral iron ore, then use it to make steel, which goes into cars, refrigerators, and bicycles. We mine the mineral copper, then use it to make cooking pots, electrical wiring, and pennies.

**Make a Connection**

Ask your child to remember what it was about the mineral copper that made it the best choice for the wires that bring electricity to your house. Does she remember the word for it? Copper is an excellent conductor (page 427).

Quartz

## Suggested Resources

*LIVING THINGS AND THEIR ENVIRONMENTS*

*Afternoon on the Amazon* (Magic Tree House, No. 6) by Mary Pope Osborne and Sal Murdocca (Random House Books for Young Readers, 1995)

*Animal Homes* (An Usborne Lift-the-Flap Book) by Debbie Martin (Usborne Publishing Ltd., 2004)

*Desert Giant: The World of the Saguaro Cactus* (Tree Tales) by Barbara Bash (Sierra Club Books for Children, 2002)

*The Great Kapok Tree: A Tale of the Amazon Rainforest* by Lynne Cherry (Voyager Books, 2000)

*Here Is the African Savanna* (Web of Life) by Madeleine Dunphy (Web of Life Children's Books, 2006)

*I See a Kookaburra!: Discovering Animal Habitats Around the World* by Steve Jenkins and Robin Page (Houghton Mifflin, 2005)

*Life in a Pond* (Pebble Plus: Living in a Biome) by Carol K. Lindeen (Capstone Press, 2003)

*DINOSAURS*

*My Visit to the Dinosaurs* (1985) and *Digging Up Dinosaurs* (1988) by Aliki (Harper Collins)

*OCEANS AND UNDERSEA LIFE*

*Sea Monsters: A Nonfiction Companion to Dark Day in the Deep Sea* by Mary Pope Osborne, Natalie Pope Boyce, and Sal Murdocca (Random House Books for Young Readers, 2008)

*Starfish* (Let's-Read-and-Find-Out-Science) by Edith Thacher Hurd, illustrated by Robin Brickman (HarperTrophy, 2000)

*THE HUMAN BODY*

*The Busy Body Book* by Lizzy Rockwell (Random House Children's Books, 2008)

*Eating Well* (Looking After Me) by Liz Gogerly and Mike Gordon (Crabtree Publishing Company, 2009)

*Germs Make Me Sick!* by Melvin Berger, illustrated by Marylin Hafner (Scott Foresman, 1995)

*The Magic School Bus Inside the Human Body* by Joanna Cole and Bruce Degen (Scholastic Press, 1990)

*Me and My Amazing Body* written and illustrated by Joan Sweeney (Dragonfly Books, 2000)

*Stay Fit* (Snap Books: Healthy Me) by Sara R. Hunt (Capstone Press, 2011)

### MATTER

*What Is the World Made Of? All About Solids, Liquids, and Gases* (Let's-Read-and-Find-Out Science, Stage 2) by Kathleen Weidner Zoehfeld (HarperTrophy, 1998)

### INTRODUCTION TO ELECTRICITY

*Switch On, Switch Off* by Melvin Berger (HarperTrophy, 2001)

### ASTRONOMY

*Astronomy* (DK Eyewitness Books) by Kristin Lippincott (DK Children, 2008)

*Midnight on the Moon* (Magic Tree House, No. 8) by Mary Pope Osborne and Sal Murdocca (Random House Books for Young Readers, 1996)

*Our Solar System* by Seymour Simon (Collins, 2007)

### INSIDE THE EARTH

*Let's Go Rock Collecting* (Let's-Read-and-Find-Out Science 2) by Roma Gans and Holly Keller (HarperCollins, 1997)

*The Pebble in My Pocket: A History of Our Earth* by Meredith Hooper, illustrations by Chris Coady (Viking Juvenile, 1996)

*Rocks in His Head* by Carol Otis Hurst and James Stevenson (HarperCollins, 2001)

*Volcanoes: Mountains That Blow Their Tops* by Nicholas Nirgiotis (Grosset & Dunlap, 1996)

# Illustration and Photo Credits

# Text Credits and Sources

## POEMS

"Hope," from *Collected Poems* by Langston Hughes. Copyright © 1994 by the Estate of Langston Hughes. Reprinted by permission of Alfred Knopf, Inc.

"I Know All the Sounds That the Animals Make," from *Something Big Has Been Here* by Jack Prelutsky. Copyright © 1990 by Jack Prelutsky. Used by permission from Greenwillow Books, a division of William Morrow and Company, Inc.

"The Pasture," by Robert Frost, from *Complete Poems of Robert Frost* (Holt, Rinehart, and Winston © 1949).

"Rope Rhyme," by Eloise Greenfield, from *Honey, I Love and Other Poems* by Eloise Greenfield. Text copyright © 1978 by Eloise Greenfield. Selection reprinted by permission of HarperCollins Publishers.

"Sing a Song of People," from *The Life I Live* by Lois Lenski. Used by permission from the Lois Lenski Covey Foundation.

"Washington," by Nancy Byrd Turner from *The Picture Book of Poetry*, edited by Marjorie Barrows (New York: Rand McNally & Co., 1932).

## STORIES

"All Stories Are Anansi's," a retelling created by the Core Knowledge Foundation from multiple sources.

"The Boy at the Dike," adapted from "The Leak in the Dike," in *Everyday Classics Third Reader* by Franklin Baker and Ashley Thorndike (Macmillan, 1920); and *Child Life in Many Lands: A Third Reader* by Etta and Mary Frances Blaisdell (Macmillan, 1908). Concluding stanza of poetry adapted from the narrative poem by Phoebe Cary (1824–1871), from "The Leak in the Dike."

"Brer Rabbit Gets Brer Fox's Dinner," a retelling created by the Core Knowledge Foundation from multiple sources.

"The Crowded, Noisy House," a retelling created by the Core Knowledge Foundation from multiple sources.

"The Frog Prince," by Wanda Gag, from *Tales from Grimm* by Jacob and Wilhelm Grimm. Copyright © 1936 by Wanda Gag. Used by permission of the Wanda Gag Estate.

"Hansel and Gretel," adapted from *Household Stories from the Collection of the Brothers Grimm*, translated by Lucy Crane (1886).

"In Which Tigger Comes to the Forest and Has Breakfast," by A. A. Milne, illustrations by E. H. Shepard, from *The House at Pooh Corner* by A. A. Milne, illustrations by E. H. Shepard. Copyright © 1928 by E. P. Dutton, renewed © 1956 by A. A. Milne. Used by permission of Dutton Children's Books, a division of Penguin Books USA, Inc.

"Issun Boshi: One-Inch Boy," retelling created by the Core Knowledge Foundation from multiple sources.

"Jack and the Beanstalk," adapted and condensed from *English Fairy Tales* by Joseph Jacobs (Putnam's, 1892).

"The Knee-High Man," from *The Knee-High Man and Other Tales* by Julius Lester. Copyright © 1972 by Julius Lester. Used by permission of Dial Books for Young Readers, a division of Penguin Books USA, Inc.

"The Little Half-Chick (Medio Pollito)," a retelling created by E. D. Hirsch, Jr., and the Core Knowledge Foundation from multiple sources.

"Mozart the Wonder Boy," from *Mozart* by Ann Rachlin. Copyright © 1992 by Aladdin Books Ltd. Text copyright © Ann Rachlin/Fun with Music, reprinted by arrangement with Barron's Educational Stories, Inc., Hauppauge, New York.

"The Pied Piper of Hamelin," a new retelling freely incorporating and adapting lines from the famous poem by Robert Browning, and also from versions in *The Merrill Fourth Reader* by Franklin Dyer and Mary Brady (Merrill, 1916); *The Progressive Road to Reading: Book Two* by Georgine Burchill et al. (Silver, Burdett and Co., n.d.); and *Child Life in Tale and Fable: A Second Reader* by Etta and Mary Frances Blaisdell (Macmillan, 1909).

"Pinocchio," retelling based on episodes from C. Collodi, *The Adventures of Pinocchio*.

"The Princess and the Pea," an original retelling based on the story by Hans Christian Andersen, versions in *Story Hour Readers Revised: Book Two* by Ida Coe and Alice Dillon (American Book Company, 1923), and *Everyday Classics Third Reader* by Franklin Baker and Ashley Thorndike (Macmillan, 1917).

"Puss-in-Boots," adapted from "The Master Cat or Puss in Boots," in *The Blue Fairy Book*, edited by Andrew Lang (Longmans, Green, and Co., 1889), and "Puss in Boots" in *Fables and Folk Stories*, retold by Horace E. Scudder (Houghton Mifflin, 1890).

"Rapunzel," a retelling created by the Core Knowledge Foundation, adapted from *Household Stories from the Collection of the Brothers Grimm*, translated by Lucy Crane (1886).

"Rumpelstiltskin," adapted from *Household Stories from the Collection of the Brothers Grimm*, translated by Lucy Crane (1886), and *Third Year Language Reader* by Franklin Baker et al. (Macmillan, 1919).

*The Tale of Peter Rabbit*, by Beatrix Potter. Copyright © Frederick Warne & Co. Used with permission from Frederick Warne & Co.

"Tom Thumb," adapted from *Household Stories from the Collection of the Brothers Grimm*, translated by Lucy Crane (1886), and *Fables and Folk Stories*, retold by Horace Scudder (Houghton Mifflin, 1890).

"Why the Owl Has Big Eyes," retelling by Lindley Shutz, based on multiple sources.

## SONGS

. . . . . . . . . . . . . . . . . . . . . . . . . . . . . . . . . . . . . . . . . . . . . . . . . . . . . . . . . . . .

"She'll Be Comin' 'Round the Mountain," from *The American Songbag* by Carl Sandburg (New York: Harcourt, Brace & Company, 1927).

# Index

# About the Editors

E. D. HIRSCH, Jr., is the founder and chairman of the Core Knowledge Foundation and professor emeritus of education and humanities at the University of Virginia. He is the author of several acclaimed books on education issues, including the bestseller *Cultural Literacy*. With his subsequent books *The Schools We Need: and Why We Don't Have Them*, *The Knowledge Deficit*, and *The Making of Americans*, Dr. Hirsch solidified his reputation as one of the most influential education reformers of our time. He and his wife, Polly, live in Charlottesville, Virginia, where they raised their three children.

JOHN HOLDREN is senior vice president of content and curriculum at K12 Inc., America's largest provider of online education for grades K–12. He lives with his wife and two daughters in Greenwood, Virginia.